THE **BIG** BOOK OF
WOK

NICOLA GRAIMES

THE **BIG** BOOK OF
WOK

365 FAST, FRESH, AND
DELICIOUS RECIPES

DUNCAN BAIRD PUBLISHERS
LONDON

The Big Book of Wok
Nicola Graimes

First published in the United Kingdom and Ireland in 2006 by
Duncan Baird Publishers Ltd
Sixth Floor, Castle House
75–76 Wells Street, London W1T 3QH

Conceived, created and designed by Duncan Baird Publishers

Managing Editor: Grace Cheetham
Editor: Cécile Landau
Managing Designer: Manisha Patel
Designer: Sailesh Patel
Studio photography: William Lingwood
Food stylist: Marie-Ange LaPierre
Prop stylist: Helen Trent

Library of Congress Cataloging-in-Publication Data is available

Distributed in the United States and Canada by
Sterling Publishing Co., Inc.
387 Park Avenue South, New York, NY 10016-8810

ISBN-10: 1-84483-326-7
ISBN-13: 9-781844-833269

10 9 8 7 6 5 4 3 2 1

Typeset in Univers and Din
Color reproduction by Scanhouse, Malaysia
Printed in China by Imago

Publisher's Note: While every care has been taken in compiling the recipes
in this book, Duncan Baird Publishers, or any other persons who have been
involved in working on this publication, cannot accept responsibility for any
errors or omissions, inadvertent or not, that may be found in the recipes or text,
nor for any problems that may arise as a result of preparing one of these recipes.

All recipes serve 4.

Contents

INTRODUCTION

The wok has been an essential piece of equipment in Asian homes for centuries. Yet, despite this ancient lineage, the wok fits perfectly into today's Western-style kitchens and with contemporary styles of cooking.

The great beauty of the wok lies in its simple basic design, which has remained largely unchanged since its conception. While in the Western kitchen its role is often restricted to stir-frying, it is far more versatile: It also makes the ideal tool for steaming, blanching, braising, deep-frying, and even smoking food.

A wok, particularly when it is used for stir-frying or steaming, is the key to meals that are not only quick and easy to prepare, but also have the bonus of being healthy. This is largely because the shape of a wok lends itself so well to stir-frying, in which the food cooks rapidly in the minimum amount of oil, helping to keep fat levels down and to retain essential nutrients.

The recipes in this book reflect the true versatility of the wok. They present a huge variety of mouthwatering ways of preparing meat, poultry, fish, vegetables, and rice and noodles, as well as soups, dim sum, and other appetizers. Inspired by the traditions of some of the world's great cuisines, most notably those of Asian countries such as China, Japan, Thailand, India, Vietnam, and Indonesia, they offer even the most inexperienced cook the route to serving up a feast.

CHOOSING A WOK

Although all woks are basically of the same design, there are a few things to consider when buying one, such as size, manufacturing material, and shape.

If you only intend to buy one wok, choose one that will lend itself to a wide range of cooking methods and which is not too small—preferably about 12–14 inches in diameter. Remember that it is better to have a large wok with a small amount of food in it than vice versa, especially when stir-frying.

A wok will usually have one of two types of handle: a single, long handle or two short, rounded handles on either side. The style you opt for is largely a matter of personal preference, although a single, long handle is generally better for stir-frying, as it distances you from the dangers of any spitting fat, makes it easier for you to toss around the ingredients being cooked, and lets you pick up the wok with one hand. Two-handled models, however, do tend to be more stable, which can be an important attribute when deep-frying or steaming.

Originally, woks were made from cast iron, which retains heat well but makes for a very heavy pan that is difficult to lift. The best modern woks are made from lightweight carbon steel, which is a good heat conductor and is nonstick when seasoned properly (see below). Stainless steel and aluminum woks are lighter still, but tend to scorch and blacken. Nonstick woks may seem like a good idea and are becoming increasingly popular, but bear in mind that they need special care to prevent scratching. Electric woks are convenient, but choose the highest wattage possible, since some models do not heat up sufficiently for successful wok cooking.

Shape is another important consideration. Woks come with either a rounded base or a flat base. A round-based wok is ideal for use on a gas range, as its shape allows the heat to spread evenly over the surface for rapid cooking, but you will need a wok stand (see page 10) to hold the wok stable while cooking. Flat-based woks are best for electric ranges, since they allow better direct contact with the heat source and they are independently stable. Whatever shape you opt for, make sure your wok has deep sides, making stir-frying and deep-frying easier and to prevent spillage.

SEASONING A WOK

Your new wok, with the exception of nonstick ones, will need cleaning and seasoning before use. Manufacturers often coat a wok in a protective layer of mineral oil that will need to be removed. To do this, scrub the wok well with hot, soapy water, a kitchen cleanser, or baking soda, then dry thoroughly over low heat. Now season the wok by pouring in 2 tablespoons of cooking oil and rubbing it all over the inner surface using crumpled paper towels. Next, place the wok over low heat for 10–15 minutes, then wipe the inside again with more paper towels, held with tongs to avoid burning your fingers. Repeat the oiling, heating, and wiping process until the paper towels come away clean. By regularly seasoning your wok in this way, a thin, oily coating will build up on the surface, making it nonstick and preventing rusting. Your wok will also become darker and, with continued use, will begin to impart a highly desirable, "smoky" flavor to food cooked in it.

LOOKING AFTER YOUR WOK

Once your wok has been seasoned, it should ideally never be cleaned using a detergent; hot water and a cloth or bamboo brush should be all that are necessary to remove any stuck-on food. After using, let the wok cool, then wash it in hot water and dry by placing over low heat for a minute or two. You can then wipe the inside of the wok with a little cooking oil. If your wok does rust, or if you find it very difficult to remove burned-on food, you may need to use some detergent, but you will then have to re-season the wok before you can cook in it again.

COOK'S TOOLS

Specialist tools are not essential when cooking with a wok, but certain implements do make the process that much easier.

Wok stand: This metal ring is useful if you have a round-based wok, since it makes it more stable on the stovetop, especially when deep-frying or steaming.

Wok lid: Not all woks come with a lid, but one is useful and can be bought separately. A light, domed lid is essential for steaming (if you are not using a bamboo steamer) and also prevents sauces, soups, and curries from drying out.

Rack: This metal or wooden trivet can be used when steaming food to raise it above the water line. A rack is also useful when using a wok to smoke foods or for placing cooked food on to keep warm while something else is being cooked.

Wok stirrer, scoop, or paddle: This is indispensable for turning and tossing food when stir-frying. A spade-like implement, it has a slightly curved tip that matches the curve of the inside of the wok, making turning food much easier.

Bamboo steamer: These are available in a wide range of different sizes. The food is placed in the steamer, which is then placed on top of a wok of simmering water. A number of bamboo steamers can be stacked up on top of each other in order to steam a variety of different foods at the same time. Bamboo steamers come supplied with a lid to prevent the steam from escaping.

Chopsticks: Long, wooden chopsticks are very useful for turning deep-fried foods.

Skimmer or ladle: A mesh ladle or metal slotted spoon is useful for lifting and draining food that has been stir-fried or deep-fried. Non-perforated ladles are good for adding liquid to a wok.

Bamboo brush: This stiff, short brush is useful for cleaning a wok without scratching it or scrubbing off the seasoned surface.

Cleaver: This large, flat-bladed, all-purpose knife is perfect for cutting up lots of ingredients quickly and can then be used to scoop up the food and carry it to the wok. The side of a cleaver can also be used to crush garlic or to flatten meat and poultry.

COOKING TECHNIQUES

The wok is an extremely versatile piece of kitchen equipment that lends itself to a multitude of different cooking techniques.

Stir-frying: The secret to successful stir-frying lies in the preparation. Before you begin cooking, any solid food should be cut into uniform, bite-sized pieces and all liquids and flavorings should be measured out and, in many cases, mixed together, ready to add to the wok.

Meat and poultry should be cut into long, thin strips across the grain or into bite-sized cubes, as these will cook quickly without drying out. Slicing is usually easier if the meat or poultry is placed in a freezer for about 30 minutes beforehand. Trim off any fat, as the fast cooking time means it will not cook through properly. Often meat and poultry are marinated before cooking to add extra flavor, but remember to drain off the marinade before stir-frying them.

Certain oils are better than others for stir-frying. You should choose an oil that has a mild flavor and a high smoking-point, such as sunflower, vegetable, peanut, or safflower.

When stir-frying, first heat your wok over high heat until it starts to "smoke," then, when it is really hot, add the oil and swirl it around to coat the inside of the wok. Flavorings, such as garlic and ginger, can then be added, but will only need stir-frying for a few seconds to prevent them from burning. Add the ingredients that will take longest to cook next and toss them around constantly using a stirrer, scoop, or paddle. Keep moving the food from the center of the wok to the sides until it is cooked. You may sometimes need to add a little water or reduce the heat slightly if the stir-fry becomes dry or is scorching, but stir-fried food should never be allowed to become greasy or watery, as this means the ingredients are being stewed rather than seared.

Meat and poultry are generally cooked first—in batches, if necessary, to prevent overcrowding in the wok. The meat should be allowed to sit in the wok briefly until lightly browned, and only then be stirred. This prevents it from sticking. After cooking, remove the meat from the wok and set on one side while you cook the remaining ingredients. The meat can then be returned to the wok, usually just prior to any liquid ingredients, such as soy sauce or a marinade.

Only thick, firm fillets of fish are suitable for stir-frying. They should be cut into large, even-sized pieces or, where appropriate, can be left whole. Like meat, fish should be left to brown lightly before moving or turning, and even then great care should be taken to avoid breaking up the fish.

Vegetables will also need to be cut into uniform-sized pieces. Broccoli, for example, should be cut into small florets, with the stems cut into thin sticks or slices. The stem and leafy parts of vegetables such as bok choy should be separated, with the stem being thinly sliced and the leaves left whole or torn. Long vegetables, like beans, asparagus, and scallions, are often cut on the diagonal, which not only looks appealing but also allows quicker cooking. Remember that hard vegetables, such as broccoli and carrots, require a longer cooking time than leafy vegetables, such as bok choy and spinach, which cook very quickly and so will only need to be added toward the end of the cooking time. Note that once liquid has been added, covering the wok with a lid can prevent any sauce that is formed from evaporating, as well as speeding up the final stages of cooking.

Steaming: Steaming is a healthy, gentle method of cooking that helps to retain a food's nutrients. It is particularly good for cooking delicate fish, as well as vegetables and dim sum. There are two main methods of steaming using a wok. This first is to place a plate of the food on a wooden or metal rack, which is balanced inside the wok, over about 2 inches of simmering water. The second method is to place the food in a bamboo steamer (see page 10), lined with parchment paper, then place this in a wok about one-third full of simmering water, so that the steamer is perched on the sloping sides of the wok, above the simmering water. The bottom of the steamer should never touch the water. Remember to keep an eye on the water level in the wok while steaming, as it may need replenishing from time to time. Bamboo steamers can be stacked on top of one another to allow several different dishes or types of food to cook at the same time, but you may need to swap the position of the steamers around midway through cooking so that all the food cooks evenly.

Deep-frying: Woks are also suitable for deep-frying and their shape means that you need less oil than in a conventional pan or fryer. If done correctly, deep-fried food should be crisp and golden, never greasy or soggy. The type of oil used is crucial—peanut and vegetable oils are ideal, because of their mild flavor and high smoking-point. The correct temperature of the oil is also crucial to achieving a cooked center and a crisp, not burned, exterior. A thermometer is a useful tool, but if you don't have one, try the bread test. Heat the oil until it gives off a haze and almost begins to smoke, then drop in a day-old cube of bread; if it bubbles all over and browns in about 25–35 seconds, then the oil is hot enough for successful deep-frying.

Before you begin, make sure the wok is stable on the burner. To prevent any splattering, make sure the food is dry before placing it in the hot oil: If food has been marinated, drain it first before frying. Or, if it has been dipped in batter, let any excess drip off first. Deep-fry the food in batches to avoid it sticking together and the temperature of the oil dropping, then remove, using a mesh strainer, slotted spoon, or spatula, and drain on paper towels. You may have to keep one batch of food hot while cooking the remainder and you may have to reheat the oil between batches.

Braising: "Red" braising is a technique used in Chinese cooking and involves stewing particularly tough cuts of meat and certain vegetables in a mixture of soy sauce, sugar, and water, plus any flavorings, such as ginger and dried spices. The food takes on a reddish-brown tinge during cooking, as well as absorbing the flavor of the spices and aromatics. The braising sauce can be saved and used again for another recipe, which increases the intensity of its flavor.

Meat and poultry are often browned before braising, then put in a stock and cooked slowly until tender.

Smoking: Smoking foods, such as meat, poultry, and fish, in a wok is a simple process and gives them a wonderful aromatic flavor. First line the wok and lid with foil to protect them, then put a smoking mixture, such as rice, tea, sugar, and spices, into the bottom of the wok. It is best to marinate food to be smoked. Then put it on an oiled rack over the smoking mixture and cover it with a lid. Heat the wok until the mixture reaches smoking-point, then leave over low heat until the food has cooked through. Make sure you open a window to keep the kitchen well ventilated.

rempeh paste

1 tsp vegetable oil
6 Asian red shallots, chopped
1 tsp turmeric
3 candlenuts or blanched almonds
1 tsp ground coriander

4 hot, red Thai chilies, chopped
3 hot green chilies, chopped
2 pandanus leaves or a
   few drops vanilla extract
salt

1 Put all the ingredients in a food processor or blender and process to form a coarse paste.

jungle curry paste

1 tbsp shrimp paste
10 medium-sized, mildly hot, red chilies,
   seeded and chopped
6 shallots or 4 Asian red shallots
4 cloves garlic, chopped
2 stalks lemongrass,
   peeled and chopped

½-inch piece coriander root,
   peeled and chopped
2-inch piece galangal,
   peeled and chopped
½ tsp salt
½ tsp freshly ground black pepper
1 tsp kaffir lime zest

1 Wrap the shrimp paste in foil, then place under a hot broiler for 1 minute. Turn over and broil for 1 minute on the other side. Leave until cool enough to handle, then unwrap the cooked shrimp paste and put it in a food processor or blender with the rest of the ingredients. Process to form a coarse paste.

laksa paste

2 cloves garlic, sliced
1-inch piece fresh ginger,
   peeled and chopped
2 candlenuts or 3 blanched almonds
2 hot red chilies, seeded and chopped
3 shallots, chopped

1 tbsp tamarind paste
2 tbsp peanut oil
2 tsp ground coriander
1 stalk lemongrass,
   peeled and chopped
1 tsp turmeric

1 Put all the ingredients in a food processor or blender and process to form a coarse paste.

rogan josh paste

2 tsp coriander seeds, crushed
1 tsp mustard seeds, crushed
2 tsp cumin seeds, crushed
2 mildly hot, long, red chilies, seeded
   and chopped
2-inch piece fresh ginger,
   peeled and chopped
3 cloves garlic, chopped

2 whole cloves, crushed
1 tsp black peppercorns, crushed
1 small cinnamon stick, crushed
2 tsp paprika
1 tsp salt
1 tsp peanut oil
6 tbsp water

1 Put the coriander, mustard, and cumin seeds in a dry wok and heat gently until they smell aromatic. Let cool a little, then put with the rest of the ingredients in a food processor or blender and process to form a coarse paste.

massaman curry paste

1 tsp cumin seeds
1 tsp coriander seeds
4 cardamom pods, split
2 whole cloves
6 small, hot red chilies, seeded and
   chopped
2 cloves garlic, chopped

1 tsp ground cinnamon
1-inch piece fresh ginger, peeled and
   chopped
3 shallots, chopped
1 stalk lemongrass, peeled and chopped
1 tbsp sunflower oil
juice of 1 lime

1   Put the cumin, coriander, and cardamom seeds in a dry wok and heat gently until they
     smell aromatic. Let cool a little, then transfer to a food processor or blender with the rest
     of the ingredients. Process to form a coarse paste.

thai green curry paste

6 hot green chilies, seeded and chopped
2 stalks lemongrass, peeled and
   chopped
2 shallots, peeled and chopped
grated zest of 1 kaffir lime and juice of 2
3 cloves garlic, chopped
1 tsp ground coriander
1 tsp ground cumin

1-inch piece fresh ginger, peeled and
   chopped
large handful of cilantro leaves,
   roughly chopped
handful of coriander roots,
   roughly chopped
1 tbsp sunflower oil
1 tsp salt

1   Place all the ingredients in a food processor or blender and process to form a
     coarse paste.

thai red curry paste

½ tsp dried shrimp paste
6 hot red chilies, seeded and chopped
2 stalks lemongrass, peeled and
   chopped
3 shallots, peeled and chopped
grated zest of 1 kaffir lime and juice of 2
3 cloves garlic, chopped
1 tsp ground coriander

1 tsp ground cumin
1-inch piece fresh ginger, peeled and
   chopped
1 tbsp sunflower oil
1 tsp salt
1 tsp tamarind paste
½ tsp freshly ground black pepper

1   Wrap the shrimp paste in foil and place under a hot broiler for 1 minute. Turn over and
     broil on the other side for another minute. Leave until cool enough to handle, then unwrap
     the foil and place the cooked shrimp paste in a food processor or blender with the rest of
     the ingredients. Process to form a coarse paste.

CHAPTER 1
APPETIZERS & SOUPS

Fragrant and nourishing, soups play a major role in Asian cuisine. Each country has its own, almost signature, soup, ranging from the light, lemongrass-infused, chilied broths of Thailand to Malaysia's creamy, coconut-rich laksas and Japan's hearty, noodle-based ramens. You are likely to find that some of the soups in this chapter, such as Tom Yam Kung and Miso and Tofu Broth, are better served as a light snack or appetizer, while others, such as Tahini Broth with Marinated Tuna, Chili Coconut and Shrimp Soup, and Pork and Soba Noodle Ramen, make a satisfying one-dish meal.

Similarly, the selection of appetizers will sit happily on menus for a whole host of different occasions. Many make good, quick-to-serve snacks, while others are perfect, palate-tingling openers to a dinner party. For classic dim sum, look no further than the recipes for Pork Wonton, Shrimp and Ginger Dumplings, and Yum Cha Salmon Buns. For a taste of Japan, sample the golden Seafood and Vegetable Tempura or the wasabi-infused Salmon and Lime Cakes. Or, try Vietnamese Shrimp Rolls or the ever-popular Thai Crab Cakes with Sweet Chili Dip. This chapter will introduce you to the sheer excitement and variety of Asian food—and all you need is a wok.

001 shrimp & ginger dumplings with cucumber dip

PREPARATION TIME: *25 minutes* **COOKING TIME:** *40 minutes*

8 oz raw tiger shrimp, peeled
2 scallions, chopped
2-inch piece fresh ginger, peeled
   and minced
2 tbsp light soy sauce
20 wonton wrappers

CUCUMBER DIP:
½ English cucumber, seeded and diced
2-inch piece fresh ginger, peeled
   and minced
1 tsp palm sugar or light brown sugar
1 small, hot red chili, minced
2 tbsp fish sauce
juice of 1 lime
2 tbsp light soy sauce

1. Put the shrimp, scallions, ginger, and soy sauce in a food processor or blender and process to form a coarse paste.
2. Take one wonton wrapper, keeping the others covered with a damp cloth, and place a heaped teaspoon of the shrimp mixture in the center. Brush the edges with a little water, then fold the wrapper over the filling to form a triangle. Pick up the filled wonton, tap the bottom to flatten it, then pinch the edges together to seal. Cover with a damp cloth. Repeat with the remaining wonton wrappers and filling.
3. Place the filled wontons in a large bamboo steamer that is lined with parchment paper. Cover and steam over a wok of simmering water for about 8 minutes, adding extra water if needed to avoid boiling dry.
4. Meanwhile, mix together all the ingredients for the cucumber dip in a bowl. Serve the hot dumplings with the dip.

002 tofu patties with sweet chili dip

PREPARATION TIME: *25 minutes* **COOKING TIME:** *20 minutes*

1 stalk lemongrass, peeled
   and minced
2 cloves garlic, chopped
2 shallots, chopped
3 scallions, chopped
2 hot red chilies, seeded and chopped
2-inch piece fresh ginger, peeled
   and minced
¼ cup cilantro leaves
9 oz firm tofu, chopped
1 tbsp lime juice
1 tsp sugar
3 tbsp all-purpose flour

1 medium egg, lightly beaten
salt and freshly ground black pepper
vegetable oil for frying

SWEET CHILI DIP:
3 tbsp mirin
3 tbsp rice vinegar
2 scallions, finely sliced
1 tbsp sugar
2 hot red chilies, seeded
   and minced
handful of cilantro leaves,
   minced

1. Mix together all the ingredients for the sweet chili dip in a small bowl and set aside.
2. Put the lemongrass, garlic, shallots, scallions, chilies, ginger, and cilantro in a food processor or blender and process to form a coarse paste. Add the tofu, lime juice, and sugar, and process to mix in. Next, add the flour, egg, and seasoning, and process again until the mixture forms a stiff paste. Cover and set aside in a cool place for 30 minutes.
3. Divide the tofu mixture into eight, then, with floured hands, shape each piece into a patty.
4. Heat 3 tablespoons of oil in a wok and fry the patties, in batches of three to four, until golden, 2–3 minutes on each side. Add more oil if necessary. Drain on paper towels before serving with the chili dip.

003 vegetable spring rolls

PREPARATION TIME: *20 minutes* **COOKING TIME:** *20 minutes*

1 tbsp sunflower oil,
   plus extra for deep-frying
1 tsp toasted sesame oil
2 carrots, cut into thin strips
6 oz fine green beans,
   sliced and blanched
3 scallions, finely sliced
2-inch piece fresh ginger,
   peeled and finely grated
2 cloves garlic, minced
handful of beansprouts

1 tbsp dark soy sauce
2 oz dried rice noodles, cooked and cut
   into 1-inch lengths
salt and freshly ground black pepper
16 small egg-roll wrappers
1 egg white, lightly beaten

SWEET PLUM DIP:
6 tbsp plum sauce
2 tbsp light soy sauce

1   Heat the oils in a wok until hot. Add the carrots, green beans, and scallions and stir-fry for
    2 minutes. Add the ginger, garlic, beansprouts, and soy sauce and stir-fry until the liquid
    evaporates, about 1 minute. Transfer the vegetables to a bowl and set aside to cool. Stir the
    prepared noodles into the cooled vegetables. Season to taste with salt and pepper.
2   Lay an egg-roll wrapper on a work surface, keeping the others covered with a damp cloth
    until ready to use. Place a heaped teaspoon of the vegetable and noodle mixture just in from
    the corner of the wrapper nearest to you, then fold the corner over the filling toward the center.
    Fold in the two sides of the wrapper to enclose the filling, then continue to roll. Brush the far
    edge with a little egg white and fold over to seal. Repeat with the remaining wrappers and
    filling to make 16 rolls.
3   Heat enough oil to deep-fry the spring rolls in a wok. When the oil is hot enough to brown a
    cube of day-old bread in 35 seconds, fry four or five spring rolls in the oil until golden and crisp.
    Drain on paper towels and keep warm. Repeat with the remaining spring rolls, frying in batches
    of four or five at a time.
4   Mix together the ingredients for the dip in a small bowl and serve with the warm spring rolls.

004 potato & vegetable pakoras

PREPARATION TIME: *20 minutes* **COOKING TIME:** *25 minutes*

1 extra large egg white
2 cups all-purpose flour
1 tsp mustard seeds
1 tsp turmeric
1 tsp ground cumin
1 hot green chili, seeded
   and minced
1 tsp salt

1 cup water
2 potatoes, peeled and thinly sliced
   into rounds
6 broccoli raab florets
1 zucchini, cut into ½-inch-thick slices
1 red bell pepper, thickly sliced
vegetable oil for deep-frying
mango chutney for serving

1   Beat the egg white until it forms stiff peaks. Mix the flour with the mustard seeds, turmeric,
    cumin, chili, and salt in a large bowl. Gradually whisk in the water, followed by 2 tablespoons
    of the egg white, until thoroughly mixed. Carefully fold in the remaining egg white. Set the
    batter on one side.
2   Pat the vegetables dry. Pour enough oil into a wok to deep-fry the vegetables, then heat it
    until it is hot enough to brown a cube of day-old bread in 40 seconds.
3   Dip the potato slices in the batter to coat them and fry in small batches in the hot oil for
    5 minutes. Drain on paper towels and keep warm. Next, fry the broccoli florets, then the
    zucchini and red pepper slices, draining and keeping the cooked vegetables warm while
    preparing the remainder. Serve with mango chutney.

005 yum cha salmon buns

PREPARATION TIME: *25 minutes, plus 2 hours rising time* **COOKING TIME:** *30–45 minutes*

15 oz canned salmon, bones and
   skin removed
2-inch piece fresh ginger, peeled
   and minced
6 scallions, finely chopped
2 tbsp light soy sauce
salt and freshly ground black pepper

DOUGH:
1 cup warm water
2 tbsp sugar
1 tsp active dry yeast
2½ cups all-purpose flour
1 tsp salt
1 tbsp sunflower oil
1½ tsp baking powder

1   Prepare the dough by putting the warm water in a bowl and sprinkling the sugar and yeast over. Stir until the sugar dissolves, then cover the bowl and leave until frothy, about 10 minutes. Sift the flour and salt into a large bowl and make a well in the center. Pour the yeast mixture into the well and gradually mix in the flour to form a ball of soft dough. Turn out onto a lightly floured surface and knead until smooth and elastic, about 10 minutes, adding a little more flour if the dough is very sticky.

2   Wipe the inside of a large bowl with the oil, add the dough, and turn it to coat with the oil. Cover the bowl with plastic wrap and leave in a warm place until the dough has doubled in size, about 2 hours. Turn out onto a lightly floured surface. Flatten the dough into a round and sprinkle with the baking powder. Fold over and knead for 5 minutes. Divide into 12 balls.

3   Mix together the salmon, ginger, scallions, and soy sauce, and season to taste with salt and pepper.

4   Take a dough ball and flatten it into a round about ¼ inch thick. Put a large tablespoon of the salmon mixture in the center, pull up the edges over the filling, and press together to seal. Place the bun on a lightly floured surface. Repeat with the remaining dough balls and filling.

5   Place the buns in a large bamboo steamer that has been lined with parchment paper. Cover and steam over a wok of simmering water for about 15 minutes, adding more water if necessary to avoid boiling dry.

006 vietnamese shrimp rolls

PREPARATION TIME: *20 minutes* **COOKING TIME:** *4 minutes*

1 tbsp sunflower oil
6 scallions, cut into thin strips
1 yellow bell pepper, cut into thin strips
2-inch piece fresh ginger,
  peeled and minced
3 kaffir lime leaves, shredded
12 oz raw tiger shrimp, peeled
2 tbsp sweet chili sauce
2 tbsp light soy sauce

juice of 2 limes
1 tbsp sugar
2 handfuls of beansprouts
12 medium rice-paper wrappers
1 small English cucumber, seeded
  and cut into thin strips
a handful of cilantro leaves
  for garnish

1 Heat a wok until hot. Add the oil, then the scallions, yellow pepper, ginger, and lime leaves, and stir-fry them for 1 minute. Toss in the shrimp with the sweet chili sauce, soy sauce, lime juice, and sugar, and stir-fry for 2 minutes longer. Add the beansprouts and toss through until wilted. Remove from the heat.

2 Fill a heatproof bowl with just-boiled water. Put 2 rice-paper wrappers on top of one another and soak in the water until they are pliable and opaque, about 20 seconds. Carefully remove, using a slotted spatula, drain for a second, and place flat on a plate.

3 Pat dry a few strips of cucumber and arrange down the center of the double-layered wrapper, followed by 2 teaspoons of the shrimp mixture. Fold over one end to make a base, then roll the wrapper around the filling, leaving the top open. Repeat with the remaining wrappers and shrimp mixture.

4 Serve the rolls sprinkled with cilantro leaves.

007 spicy chickpea fritters

PREPARATION TIME: *20 minutes* **COOKING TIME:** *15 minutes*

2 cups chickpea flour, sifted
½ tsp ground cumin
½ tsp ground coriander
⅓ tsp medium-hot chili powder
1 tsp salt
½ tsp baking soda
1¾ cups water

sunflower oil for deep-frying

YOGURT DIP:
6–8 tbsp plain yogurt
½ small English cucumber, peeled
  and diced
sprinkling of cayenne pepper

1 Put the flour, spices, salt, and baking soda in a large bowl. Gradually pour in the water, whisking well to make a smooth batter. Let the batter stand for 10 minutes.

2 Heat 3 tablespoons of oil in a wok until it is hot enough to brown a cube of day-old bread in 35 seconds. Carefully drop in 2 ladlefuls of the batter and cook until puffed up and golden, about 2 minutes. Remove with a slotted spoon, drain on paper towels, and keep warm. Repeat with the remaining batter, cooking two fritters at a time and adding more oil when necessary.

3 Mix together the ingredients for the yogurt dip and serve with the warm fritters.

008 seafood & vegetable tempura

PREPARATION TIME: *15 minutes* **COOKING TIME:** *25 minutes*

12 raw large shrimp, peeled
1 red bell pepper, cut into strips
12 asparagus tips
1 egg yolk
1 cup ice water

1 cup all-purpose flour,
   plus extra for dusting
pinch of salt
sunflower oil for deep-frying

1. Dry the shrimp, red pepper, and asparagus tips thoroughly with paper towels.
2. Prepare the batter just before cooking: Place the egg yolk in a large mixing bowl, then pour in the ice water and use a chopstick to mix briefly. Add the flour and salt and stir lightly with the chopstick until barely mixed; the batter should be thin and lumpy.
3. Heat oil for deep-frying in a wok until it is hot enough to brown a cube of day-old bread in 35 seconds.
4. Dip the shrimp and vegetables into the extra flour to dust them lightly. Starting with the asparagus tips, dip a batch of four, one at a time, into the batter to coat them, then slip into the hot oil and deep-fry until golden, about 2 minutes. Drain on paper towels and keep warm. Repeat with the remaining asparagus. Then dip the strips of red pepper into the batter and deep-fry in two batches until lightly golden, about 2 minutes per batch. Set aside with the asparagus to keep warm. Finally, coat the shrimp in the batter and deep-fry in three batches until golden, 2–3 minutes per batch. Remove from the oil using a slotted spoon, drain on paper towels, and serve immediately with the warm asparagus and pepper tempura and a small bowl of Sweet Chili Dip (see page 18).

009 corn fritters

PREPARATION TIME: *15 minutes* **COOKING TIME:** *20 minutes*

2 cups fresh or canned corn kernels
5 scallions, minced
1-inch piece fresh ginger,
   peeled and finely grated
2 cloves garlic, crushed

1 tsp light soy sauce
1 egg, lightly beaten
3 tbsp all-purpose flour
salt and freshly ground black pepper
sunflower oil for frying

1. Crush the corn lightly using the back of a large spoon, or a pestle and mortar, and place in a large bowl. Mix in the scallions, ginger, garlic, soy sauce, beaten egg, and flour to form a batter. Season to taste with salt and pepper and set aside in a cool place for 1 hour.
2. Heat enough oil to cover the bottom of a wok and drop 3 large tablespoonfuls of the corn batter into the hot oil. Fry until golden, 2–3 minutes on each side. Drain on paper towels and keep warm while frying the remaining batches of fritters, adding more oil to the wok when necessary. Serve with a bowl of Sweet Chili Dip (see page 18).

010 rice-paper rolls with caramelized pork

PREPARATION TIME: *20 minutes, plus 1 hour marinating* **COOKING TIME:** *10 minutes*

2 tbsp light soy sauce
1 tbsp palm sugar or
    light brown sugar
2 tsp fish sauce
1¼ lb lean pork tenderloin,
    cut into thin strips
1–2 tbsp sunflower oil
20 medium rice-paper wrappers

about ¼ cup hoisin sauce, plus extra
    for serving
2½ oz rice noodles, cooked
fine strips of scallion, mild red chili, and
    English cucumber
a handful of cilantro leaves
    for garnish

1. Mix together the soy sauce, sugar, and fish sauce in a large shallow dish. Stir in the pork so that it is well coated, then let marinate for 1 hour, spooning the marinade over the meat from time to time. Drain, reserving the marinade.
2. Heat a wok until hot. Pour in half the oil and swirl it around the wok, then stir-fry half of the pork for 3–4 minutes. Remove the meat from the wok with a slotted spoon and drain on paper towels. Heat the remaining oil in the wok, add the rest of the meat, and stir-fry for 3–4 minutes. Return the first batch of meat to the wok with the reserved marinade and cook over high heat until caramelized.
3. Fill a heatproof bowl with just-boiled water. Put 2 rice-paper wrappers on top of one another and soak in the water until they are pliable and opaque, about 20 seconds. Carefully remove, using a slotted spatula, drain for a second, and place flat on a plate.
4. Spread a teaspoonful of hoisin sauce over the double-layered wrapper, then top with a small bundle of noodles, a few strips of the caramelized pork, and a few strips each of cucumber, red chili, and scallion. Roll the wrapper around the filling, folding in the edges to enclose it. Repeat using the remaining wrappers and filling ingredients.
5. Slice the prepared rolls in half diagonally and serve, sprinkled with cilantro leaves and with a bowl of extra hoisin sauce for dipping.

011   crab spring rolls with chili dip

PREPARATION TIME: *25 minutes*   **COOKING TIME:** *20 minutes*

1 tbsp toasted sesame oil

3 scallions, chopped

1 clove garlic, crushed

2-inch piece fresh ginger,
    peeled and minced

1 hot red chili, seeded and minced

large handful of minced
    napa cabbage

1 yellow bell pepper, minced

6 oz canned crab meat in brine,
    well drained

2 tbsp light soy sauce

salt and freshly ground pepper

16 small egg-roll wrappers

1 egg white, lightly beaten

sunflower oil for deep-frying

CHILI DIP:

juice of 1 small lemon

2 tbsp chili sauce

1½ tbsp light brown sugar

1. Heat a wok until hot. Add the sesame oil and swirl it around the wok, then toss in the scallions, garlic, ginger, chili, napa cabbage, and yellow pepper, and stir-fry for 1 minute. Next, add the crab and soy sauce, and stir-fry for 30 seconds. Season to taste with salt and pepper and transfer to a bowl. Set aside to cool.

2. Lay one egg-roll wrapper on a flat work surface, keeping the others covered with a damp cloth. Put a heaped teaspoon of the crab mixture just in from the corner that is nearest to you, then fold the corner over the filling toward the center. Fold in the two sides of the wrapper to enclose the filling, then continue to roll. Brush the far edge with a little egg white and fold over to seal. Repeat with the remaining wrappers and filling.

3. Heat enough sunflower oil in a wok to deep-fry the spring rolls. When the oil is hot enough to brown a cube of day-old bread in 35 seconds, add three or four spring rolls and fry until golden and crisp. Drain on paper towels and keep warm. Repeat with the remaining spring rolls, cooking in batches of three or four.

4. Mix together the ingredients for the chili dip and serve immediately with the warm spring rolls.

012   salmon & lime cakes

PREPARATION TIME: *25 minutes*   **COOKING TIME:** *20 minutes*

12 oz potatoes, boiled and cooled

1 tsp sansho pepper

1 tsp wasabi

12 oz canned salmon, bones and
    skin removed

finely grated zest and juice of 1 lime

2 tbsp butter, melted

1 egg, lightly beaten

salt

flour for dusting

sunflower oil for frying

1. Press the potatoes through a ricer into a large bowl. Stir in the sansho pepper and wasabi. Break up the salmon into large pieces with a fork and stir it into the potato mixture. Add the lime zest and juice, melted butter, and beaten egg, and mix well. Season with salt.

2. Using floured hands, divide the mixture into 12 and shape each portion into a round cake about ¾ inch thick. Dust it in flour.

3. Heat 3 tablespoons of oil in a wok. Fry the salmon cakes, in batches of three or four, until golden, about 3 minutes each side. Drain on paper towels and keep warm while cooking the remaining cakes. If necessary, add more oil to the wok before frying the next batch.

013 thai crab cakes

PREPARATION TIME: *20 minutes, plus 30 minutes chilling* **COOKING TIME:** *15 minutes*

9 oz fresh or canned white crab meat
(about 2 cups)
9 oz firm white fish fillet, skinned
2 cloves garlic, chopped
1 medium-sized, mildly hot, red chili,
seeded and chopped
2 stalks lemongrass, peeled
and minced

2-inch piece fresh ginger, peeled
and finely grated
large handful of cilantro leaves,
minced
1 egg white
salt and freshly ground black pepper
sunflower oil for frying
cilantro leaves for garnish

1   Put the crab meat, fish, garlic, chili, lemongrass, ginger, minced cilantro, and egg white in a
food processor or blender. Season to taste with salt and pepper and process to form a coarse
paste. Cover and chill for 30 minutes.
2   Heat 3 tablespoons of the oil in a large wok. Place 3–4 separate heaped tablespoons of the
crab mixture into the oil and fry until golden, 3–4 minutes on each side. Drain on paper towels
and keep warm. Repeat, cooking three or four cakes at a time and adding more oil to the wok if
necessary. Garnish with cilantro leaves and serve with Sweet Chili Dip (see page 18).

014 vegetable gyoza

PREPARATION TIME: *45 minutes* **COOKING TIME:** *25 minutes*

1 carrot, peeled and finely grated
2½ cups minced napa cabbage
¼ cup minced water chestnuts
4 scallions, minced
2 cloves garlic, crushed
2-inch piece fresh ginger,
peeled and minced
1 tsp cornstarch
2 tsp toasted sesame oil
1 tbsp hoisin sauce

2 tsp Chinese rice wine
or dry sherry
25 round gyoza or Shanghai dumpling
wrappers or wonton wrappers
3 tbsp sunflower oil
⅔ cup vegetable stock
Chinese black vinegar
or soy sauce for serving

1   Place the carrot, napa cabbage, and water chestnuts in the center of a clean cloth, wrap up
tightly, and squeeze to extract any water, then place in a large bowl. Add the scallions, garlic,
ginger, cornstarch, sesame oil, hoisin sauce, and wine, and mix well.
2   Place a teaspoon of the mixture in the center of a gyoza wrapper, keeping the rest of the
wrappers covered with a damp cloth. Brush the edge of the wrapper with a little water, then
fold over the filling to form a half moon shape. Tap the bottom of the gyoza to make a flat
surface and pinch the edges together to seal them. Repeat with the remaining mixture until all
the wrappers are filled.
3   Heat one-third of the oil in a wok over medium-high heat. Swirl the oil around the wok, then
cook one-third of the gyoza (flat-side down) until their bases are golden, about 2 minutes.
Carefully pour in one-third of the stock, reduce the heat, cover, and simmer until the liquid has
evaporated, 3–4 minutes. Repeat with the remaining gyoza, oil, and stock, keeping each batch
warm until ready to serve.
4   Serve with Chinese black vinegar or soy sauce for dipping.

015 golden purses

PREPARATION TIME: *15 minutes* **COOKING TIME:** *25 minutes*

1 tbsp sunflower oil, plus extra for deep-frying	2 cups ground chicken
2 cloves garlic, minced	2 tsp light soy sauce
5 scallions, minced	2 tsp Chinese rice wine or dry sherry
2-inch piece fresh ginger, peeled and minced	salt and freshly ground black pepper
	20 wonton wrappers

1   Heat a wok until hot. Add 1 tablespoon of oil, then the garlic, scallions, ginger, and ground chicken and stir-fry until cooked through, about 4 minutes.

2   Pour in the soy sauce and wine and cook, stirring, until all the liquid has evaporated, about 1 minute longer. Season to taste with salt and pepper.

3   Place one wonton wrapper on a flat surface, keeping the others covered with a damp cloth. Put a tablespoon of the chicken filling in the center of the wrapper. Brush the wrapper with a little water, then gather the sides up around the filling and pinch together to make a moneybag or coin purse shape, enclosing the filling. Set on one side, covered with a damp cloth. Repeat with the remaining wrappers and filling.

4   Heat enough oil in a wok to deep-fry the purses. When the oil is hot enough to brown a cube of day-old bread in 35 seconds, add three or four purses and cook until golden, 1–2 minutes. Drain on paper towels and keep warm. Repeat with the remaining purses. Serve immediately.

016 indonesian hot & spicy shrimp

PREPARATION TIME: *15 minutes, plus marinating* **COOKING TIME:** *10 minutes*

4 tbsp kecap manis
  (Indonesian soy sauce)
½ tsp cayenne pepper
1 tsp salt

20 raw tiger shrimp, peeled
all-purpose flour for dusting
peanut oil for deep-frying

1 Mix together the kecap manis, cayenne pepper, and salt in a shallow bowl. Dip the shrimp
   into the marinade and let marinate for 30 minutes.
2 Heat enough oil in a wok to deep-fry the shrimp. When the oil is hot enough to brown a cube of
   day-old bread in 35 seconds, remove the shrimp from the marinade, dip into the flour, and
   deep-fry, in batches, until golden, about 2 minutes per batch. Drain on paper towels and serve .

017 pork wonton

PREPARATION TIME: *25 minutes* **COOKING TIME:** *20–40 minutes*

9 oz lean pork tenderloin,
  roughly chopped
1 carrot, finely grated
2 cloves garlic, crushed
2 scallions, minced
1 tbsp all-purpose flour

3-inch piece fresh ginger,
  peeled and minced
1 tbsp light soy sauce
2 tsp Chinese rice wine or dry sherry
2 tsp toasted sesame oil
24 wonton wrappers

1 Put all the ingredients, except the wonton wrappers, in a food processor or blender and
   process to form a coarse paste.
2 Take one wonton wrapper, keeping the others covered with a damp tea towel, and place a
   heaped tablespoon of the pork mixture in the center. Brush the edges with a little water, then
   gather the sides up to enclose the filling and pinch together to seal. Cover with a damp cloth.
   Repeat with the remaining wonton wrappers and filling.
3 Place the wonton in a large bamboo steamer that is lined with parchment paper. Cover and
   steam over a wok of simmering water for about 10 minutes, adding more water if necessary
   to avoid boiling dry. Serve immediately.

018 rice & vegetable fritters

PREPARATION TIME: *30 minutes* **COOKING TIME:** *20 minutes*

1 cup brown rice, cooked
  and cooled
4 scallions, minced
1 red bell pepper diced
1 hot red chili, seeded
  and minced
2 cloves garlic, crushed

2-inch piece fresh ginger,
  peeled and finely grated
1 egg, lightly beaten
4 tbsp heavy cream
4 tbsp all-purpose flour
salt and freshly ground black pepper
vegetable oil for frying

1 Mix the rice with the scallions, red pepper, chili, garlic, ginger, egg, cream, and flour in a mixing
   bowl. Season well with salt and pepper.
2 Heat enough oil to coat the bottom of a wok. Place 2–3 separate heaped tablespoons of the
   rice mixture into the hot oil and flatten each slightly with the back of a spoon. Cook until
   golden, about 3 minutes on each side, then drain on paper towels and keep warm. Repeat with
   the remaining rice mixture, adding extra oil to the wok when necessary. Serve hot.

019 tahini broth with marinated tuna

PREPARATION TIME: *15 minutes, plus 1 hour marinating* **COOKING TIME:** *25 minutes*

4 tuna fillets, about 4 oz each
6 cups vegetable stock
2 tbsp light soy sauce
2 cloves garlic, crushed
½ tsp dried chili flakes
2-inch piece fresh ginger,
   peeled and thinly sliced
2 heaped tbsp tahini
2½ cups cooked udon noodles

2 scallions, thinly sliced
1 carrot, cut into thin strips

MARINADE:
1 clove garlic, crushed
3 tbsp dark soy sauce
2 tbsp sweet chili sauce
1½ tbsp toasted sesame oil

1. Mix together all the ingredients for the marinade in a shallow dish. Add the tuna and spoon the marinade over until well coated. Let marinate for at least 1 hour.
2. Put the stock, soy sauce, garlic, chili flakes, and ginger in a wok and bring to a boil. Reduce the heat and simmer for 10 minutes, then stir in the tahini.
3. Meanwhile, preheat the broiler and line the broiler pan with foil. Broil the tuna fillets, about 4 inches from the heat, for 1½–2 minutes on each side, occasionally spooning over a little of the marinade.
4. Divide the cooked noodles among four shallow serving bowls and ladle in the broth. Place a piece of tuna in each bowl, then sprinkle with the scallions and carrot, and serve.

020 tom yam kung

PREPARATION TIME: *10 minutes* **COOKING TIME:** *12 minutes*

5 cups vegetable stock
2 stalks lemongrass,
   peeled and crushed
2 hot Thai chilies, seeded and minced
4 kaffir lime leaves
2 cloves garlic, finely sliced
4 scallions, finely sliced
   diagonally

juice of 1 lime
1 carrot, cut into fine strips
6 oz Japanese tofu, sliced
salt
2 large handfuls of cilantro leaves,
   roughly chopped

1. Put the stock in a wok with the lemongrass, half of the chili, the kaffir lime leaves, garlic, and 2 scallions. Bring to a boil, then reduce the heat and simmer for 10 minutes. Strain the stock, discarding the solids.
2. Return the stock to the wok and stir in the remaining chili and scallions, the lime juice, carrot, and tofu. Season to taste with salt and heat through for 2 minutes. Serve immediately, sprinkled with the chopped cilantro.

021 indonesian-style vegetable soup
PREPARATION TIME: *20 minutes* **COOKING TIME:** *23 minutes*

1 tbsp sunflower oil
1 large onion, chopped
2 cloves garlic, chopped
2-inch piece fresh ginger,
   peeled and minced
1 long, mildly hot, red chili,
   thinly sliced
1 tsp turmeric
5 cups vegetable stock
1 cup coconut milk

1 tsp palm sugar or light brown sugar
1 large carrot, cut into thin strips
5 leaves napa cabbage, sliced
2 handfuls of fine green beans,
   trimmed and halved
6 ears baby corn, halved lengthwise
2 tbsp light soy sauce
juice of 2 limes
salt and and freshly ground pepper

1 Heat the oil in a wok and stir-fry the onion for 4 minutes. Add the garlic, ginger, chili, and turmeric, and stir-fry for 30 seconds.
2 Pour in the stock and coconut milk. Bring to a boil, then reduce the heat until bubbling very gently. Stir in the sugar and, when dissolved, add the carrot, napa cabbage, green beans, and baby corn.
3 Simmer the soup until the vegetables are cooked, about 15 minutes, then stir in the soy sauce and lime juice. Season to taste with salt and pepper, and serve.

022 malaysian laksa
PREPARATION TIME: *20 minutes* **COOKING TIME:** *16 minutes*

1 tbsp peanut oil
1 lb skinless, boneless chicken breast,
   cut into bite-sized pieces
1 recipe quantity Laksa Paste
   (see page 14)
2½ cups chicken stock
1¾ cups coconut milk
3 kaffir lime leaves
2 small heads bok choy, halved lengthwise

9 oz raw tiger shrimp, peeled
salt
6 oz rice noodles, cooked
handful of beansprouts
2 onions, chopped and fried until crisp
large handful of cilantro leaves,
   roughly chopped
1 mildly hot, long, red chili, seeded
   and sliced

1 Heat a wok until hot. Add the oil, then the chicken and stir-fry until it is cooked, 3–4 minutes. Remove from the wok using a slotted spoon and drain on paper towels.
2 Add the laksa paste to the wok and stir until it smells aromatic, about 1 minute. Pour in the stock and coconut milk and add the lime leaves. Bring to a boil, then reduce the heat and simmer for 7 minutes.
3 Add the bok choy, shrimp, and cooked chicken, and cook for 3 minutes longer. Season with salt to taste.
4 Divide the cooked noodles among four bowls and ladle the soup over the top. Sprinkle with the beansprouts, crisp onions, chopped cilantro, and chili, and serve.

023 coconut & sweet potato noodle soup

PREPARATION TIME: *20 minutes* **COOKING TIME:** *25 minutes*

2 tbsp sunflower oil
2 large onions, chopped
2 cloves garlic, chopped
12 cremini mushrooms, sliced
3 medium-sized sweet potatoes,
    peeled and diced
1 recipe quantity Thai Red Curry Paste
    (see page 15)
5 cups vegetable stock
1 cup coconut milk

2 tbsp light soy sauce
salt and freshly ground
    black pepper
handful of cilantro leaves,
    roughly chopped
6 oz rice noodles, cooked

1   Heat 1 tablespoon of the oil in a wok and stir-fry half the chopped onions until crisp and golden.
    Remove from the wok and set on one side.
2   Heat the remaining oil in the wok. Add the rest of the chopped onion and stir-fry for 4 minutes.
    Add the garlic, mushrooms, and sweet potatoes, and stir-fry for 2 minutes longer. Stir in the
    curry paste and cook for 3 minutes.
3   Pour in the vegetable stock and bring to a boil. Reduce the heat and simmer for 10 minutes. Stir
    in the coconut milk and soy sauce, and cook for 5 more minutes. Season to taste with salt and
    pepper, then stir in the cilantro.
4   Divide the noodles among four bowls and ladle the soup over the top. Sprinkle with the
    crisp-fried onions and serve.

024 thai shrimp, basil & noodle soup

PREPARATION TIME: *20 minutes*   **COOKING TIME:** *10 minutes*

12 oz raw tiger shrimp
5 cups fish stock
2 tbsp light soy sauce
2 stalks lemongrass, peeled and
   lightly crushed
3 kaffir lime leaves
1-inch piece galangal, peeled and
   thinly sliced

1 tbsp fish sauce
1 hot red chili, minced
1 tsp palm sugar or light brown sugar
juice of 1 lime
salt and freshly ground black pepper
2 bundles dried rice vermicelli, cooked
handful of Thai basil leaves, torn

1   Peel the shrimp and put the shells and heads in a wok; set the shrimp aside. Heat until the
    shells and heads are colored. Add the stock and bring to a boil, then reduce the heat and
    simmer for 3 minutes. Strain the stock.
2   Pour the strained stock back into the wok. Add the soy sauce, lemongrass, lime leaves,
    galangal, fish sauce, and chili, and simmer over low heat for 5 minutes. Stir in the sugar
    and lime juice. Season to taste with salt and pepper, then add the shrimp to the broth and
    cook until pink, about 2 minutes.
3   Divide the noodles among four bowls, ladle in the hot broth and shrimp, sprinkle the basil
    leaves over the top, and serve.

025 spicy vegetable & rice soup

PREPARATION TIME: *15 minutes*   **COOKING TIME:** *20 minutes*

1 tbsp peanut oil
1 large onion, chopped
2 cloves garlic, minced
3-inch piece fresh ginger,
   peeled and minced
4 cardamom pods, split
2 bay leaves
4 tsp garam masala
2 tsp ground cumin
2 tsp ground coriander
2 tsp turmeric

1 large carrot, diced
6 cremini mushrooms, sliced
5 cups vegetable stock
1 cup coconut milk
8 oz fresh spinach, tough stems removed
   and leaves shredded
½ cup frozen petit pois (petite
   green peas)
1 cup brown rice, cooked and cooled
salt and freshly ground black pepper

1   Heat the oil in a wok and stir-fry the onion for 4 minutes. Add the the garlic, ginger, cardamom,
    bay leaves, and ground spices, and stir-fry for 1 minute longer. Add the carrot and mushrooms,
    and stir-fry for 2 more minutes.
2   Add the stock and coconut milk and bring to a boil, then reduce the heat and simmer for
    10 minutes.
3   Add the spinach, peas, and rice, and simmer until the vegetables are cooked and the rice is
    heated through, about 2 minutes longer. Season to taste with salt and pepper, and serve.

026 indian spiced vegetable & chickpea soup

PREPARATION TIME: *20 minutes* **COOKING TIME:** *30 minutes*

3 tbsp sunflower oil
2 large onions, finely sliced
6 cardamom pods, split
   and seeds removed
2 tsp cumin seeds
2 tsp ground coriander
1-inch piece fresh ginger,
   peeled and grated
2 hot red chilies, seeded
   and finely sliced
4 large cloves garlic, crushed
2 bay leaves

1 medium-sized butternut squash,
   peeled and cut into cubes
6 cups vegetable stock
juice of 1 lemon
1 cup canned chickpeas,
   drained and rinsed
salt and freshly ground black pepper
4 tbsp plain yogurt
handful of cilantro leaves,
   roughly chopped

1 Heat half the oil in a wok until hot. Add half the onions and stir-fry until crisp and golden, about 6 minutes. Remove from the wok, drain on paper towels, and set aside.

2 Add the remaining oil to the wok and stir-fry the remaining onion for 4 minutes. Add the cardamom seeds, cumin, coriander, ginger, chilies, garlic, and bay leaves, and cook for 1 minute longer, stirring.

3 Add the squash and stock to the wok. Bring to a boil, then reduce the heat and simmer, covered, until the squash is tender, 10–12 minutes. Remove the bay leaves, then purée in a blender or food processor.

4 Return to the wok, add the lemon juice and the chickpeas, and simmer for 3–5 minutes. Season to taste with salt and pepper.

5 Divide the hot soup among four serving bowls. Top each with a spoonful of yogurt and a sprinkling of the crisp-fried onions and cilantro, then serve.

027 pork balls in fragrant thai broth

PREPARATION TIME: *25 minutes* **COOKING TIME:** 30 minutes

6 cups chicken stock
3 kaffir lime leaves
2 stalks lemongrass,
   peeled and crushed
1 tbsp fish sauce
½ tsp sugar
juice of 1 lime
1-inch piece fresh ginger,
   peeled and cut into 6 slices

1 recipe quantity Pork Balls
   (see page 117), prepared
   but left uncooked
1 mildly hot, long, red chili, seeded
   and minced
8 oz fresh spinach, tough stems removed
   and shredded
salt and freshly ground black pepper
handful of cilantro leaves,
   roughly chopped

1 Put the stock, lime leaves, lemongrass, fish sauce, sugar, lime juice, and ginger in a wok. Bring to a boil, then reduce the heat and simmer for 10 minutes. Strain the broth, discard the solids, and return the broth to the wok.

2 Place the prepared pork balls in the broth with the chili and simmer, covered, for 6 minutes. Add the spinach, cover again, and simmer for 2 minutes longer. Season to taste with salt and pepper and serve, garnished with the chopped cilantro.

028 noodle soup with tofu

PREPARATION TIME: *20 minutes, plus 1 hour marinating time* **COOKING TIME:** *20 minutes*

9 oz firm tofu, sliced
1 tbsp sunflower oil,
    plus extra for greasing
4 shallots, sliced
6 ears baby corn, halved lengthwise
2-inch piece fresh ginger,
    peeled and grated
3 kaffir lime leaves
1 hot red chili, seeded and
    minced
5 cups vegetable stock
1 cup coconut milk
1 tbsp palm sugar or
    light brown sugar

3 tbsp light soy sauce
juice of 1 lime
8 oz fresh spinach, tough stems removed
    and shredded
salt and freshly ground black pepper
6 oz cellophane noodles, cooked
handful of Thai basil leaves, torn

MARINADE:
3 tbsp light soy sauce
2 tbsp sweet chili sauce
1 tsp toasted sesame oil

1   Mix together the ingredients for the marinade. Add the tofu and turn it to coat well. Let
    marinate for at least 1 hour, turning occasionally.
2   Preheat the oven to 350°F. Grease a baking sheet and arrange the tofu on it. Roast in the oven
    until golden and slightly crisp, about 20 minutes, turning over halfway through cooking.
3   Meanwhile, heat the oil in a wok until hot. Add the shallots and stir fry for 2 minutes. Add
    the baby corn and stir-fry for another 2 minutes, then add the ginger, lime leaves, and chili
    and stir-fry for 1 minute longer. Pour in the stock and coconut milk. Bring to a boil, then reduce
    the heat and simmer for 10 minutes. Stir in the sugar, soy sauce, lime juice, and spinach, and
    simmer for 2 more minutes. Season to taste with salt and pepper.
4   Divide the noodles among four serving bowls. Ladle in the soup, top each serving with
    the tofu and basil leaves, and serve.

029 fish poached in ginger broth

PREPARATION TIME: *15 minutes* **COOKING TIME:** *10 minutes*

5 cups fish stock
1-inch piece fresh ginger,
    peeled and cut into fine strips
2 tbsp light soy sauce
2 tbsp Shaoxing wine or medium sherry
½ tsp Chinese five-spice
4 scallions, white and green parts
    separated and thinly sliced

2 small heads bok choy, sliced
1¼ lb firm white fish fillet,
    cut into large chunks
salt and freshly ground black pepper
2 bundles dried rice vermicelli, cooked
1 carrot, cut into thin strips

1   Mix together the fish stock, ginger, soy sauce, wine, five-spice, and white part of the scallions
    in a wok. Bring to a boil, then reduce the heat and simmer for 2 minutes.
2   Add the bok choy and fish, and simmer until cooked through, 4–5 minutes. Season to taste with
    salt and pepper.
3   Divide the cooked noodles among four bowls and ladle the fish and broth over the top. Sprinkle
    with the carrot strips and the green part of the scallions, and serve.

030 asian pea broth with pork wonton

PREPARATION TIME: *10 minutes, plus preparing wonton* **COOKING TIME:** *12 minutes*

1 tbsp sunflower oil

2 tsp butter

3 medium-sized leeks, sliced

3 cloves garlic, minced

2-inch piece fresh ginger,
  peeled and minced

4 tbsp Chinese rice wine
  or dry sherry

6 cups vegetable stock

3 tbsp light soy sauce

2 cups frozen petit pois (petite green peas)

salt and freshly ground black pepper

½ recipe quantity Pork Wonton, freshly
  steamed (see page 27)

handful of Chinese chives, chopped

1   Heat the oil and butter in a wok and stir-fry the leeks for 2 minutes. Add the garlic and ginger, and stir-fry for another 2 minutes. Pour in the wine and continue cooking until most of it has evaporated.

2   Add the stock and bring to a boil, then reduce the heat and simmer for 5 minutes. Add the soy sauce and peas and cook for 2–3 minutes longer.

3   Season the soup to taste with salt and pepper and pour into four warm serving bowls. Divide the pork wontons among the four bowls. Garnish with the chives and serve.

031 chili coconut & shrimp soup

PREPARATION TIME: *15 minutes* **COOKING TIME:** *22 minutes*

1 tbsp sunflower oil

3 shallots, minced

2 stalks lemongrass,
  peeled and bruised

1 red bell pepper, cut into long strips

large handful of fine green beans,
  trimmed and thinly sliced

3 cloves garlic, crushed

3 heaped tbsp Laksa Paste
  (see page 14)

5 cups vegetable stock

3-inch piece fresh ginger,
  peeled and minced

1¾ cups coconut milk

3 kaffir lime leaves

juice of 1 lime

12 oz raw large or medium shrimp,
  peeled

handful of cilantro leaves,
  roughly chopped

1 Heat the oil in a wok, add the shallots and lemongrass, and stir-fry for 2 minutes. Add the red pepper, green beans, and garlic, and stir-fry for 1 minute longer. Stir in the laksa paste and cook for 2 more minutes.

2 Stir in the stock and bring to a boil. Reduce the heat, add the ginger, coconut milk, and lime leaves, and stir. Simmer over low heat until thickened, 12–15 minutes.

3 Stir in the lime juice and shrimp, and simmer until the shrimp turn pink, about 2 minutes. Serve immediately, sprinkled with the chopped cilantro.

032 vegetable ramen

PREPARATION TIME: *20 minutes* **COOKING TIME:** *5 minutes*

1 tbsp sunflower oil

1 tsp toasted sesame oil

2 medium-sized leeks, shredded

2 zucchini, thinly sliced diagonally

8 button mushrooms, sliced

0 oz spinach, tough stems removed
  and shredded

handful of beansprouts

6 cups vegetable stock

3 tbsp light soy sauce

2-inch piece fresh ginger,
  peeled and grated

6 oz ramen noodles,
  cooked

2 eggs, hard-cooked and halved

2 scallions, minced

½ tsp dried chili flakes

1 Heat the oils in a wok until hot. Add the leeks, zucchini, and mushrooms, and stir-fry for 2 minutes. Add the spinach and beansprouts, and stir-fry for 1 minute longer.

2 Pour the stock into the wok and add the soy sauce and ginger. Bring to a boil.

3 Divide the cooked noodles among four serving bowls. Ladle in the hot broth and vegetables. Top each serving with half of a hard-cooked egg and a sprinkling of scallions and chili flakes, then serve immediately.

033 pork & soba noodle ramen

PREPARATION TIME: *20 minutes, plus 1 hour marinating* **COOKING TIME:** *15 minutes*

10 oz lean pork tenderloin
1 tbsp sunflower oil
6 cups chicken stock
½-inch piece fresh ginger, peeled
   and sliced into matchsticks
2 tbsp miso paste
4 tbsp sake or dry sherry
4 tbsp dark soy sauce
2 carrots, thinly sliced
4 small heads bok choy, sliced
   lengthwise

3 scallions, minced
large handful of beansprouts
6 oz soba noodles, cooked
½ tsp dried chili flakes
large handful of cilantro leaves,
   roughly chopped

MARINADE:
1 tbsp hoisin sauce
2 tbsp light soy sauce
1 tbsp sake or dry sherry

1 Mix together the ingredients for the marinade and add the pork tenderloin. Let marinate for 1 hour, then drain.
2 Heat the oil in a wok, add the pork, and brown on all sides, about 6 minutes. Remove from the wok and set on one side.
3 Heat the stock in the wok and stir in the ginger, miso paste, sake or sherry, and soy sauce. Bring to a boil and cook for 5 minutes.
4 Reduce the heat, add the carrots, bok choy, and scallions, and simmer for 2 minutes. Add the beansprouts and cook for 1 more minute.
5 Thinly slice the cooked pork. Divide the noodles among four bowls and ladle in the vegetables and broth. Arrange the pork slices on top, sprinkle with the chili flakes and cilantro, and serve.

034 chinese seafood & corn soup

PREPARATION TIME: *15 minutes* **COOKING TIME:** *13 minutes*

1 lb firm white fish fillet, such as haddock
   or cod, cut into thick slices
1 egg white, lightly beaten
2 tsp sunflower oil
3 shallots, chopped
2 tbsp Chinese rice wine or dry sherry
2-inch piece fresh ginger,
   peeled and grated
6 cups fish or chicken stock
1 tbsp light soy sauce

1½ tbsp cornstarch
1 cup canned whole kernel corn,
   drained and rinsed
4 small squid, cleaned and cut
   into rings
salt and freshly ground black pepper
2 scallions, green part only,
   thinly sliced

1 Dip the white fish slices into the egg white and set on one side.
2 Heat the oil in a wok and stir-fry the shallots for 2 minutes. Pour in the wine and continue cooking until it has almost evaporated. Add the ginger, stock, and soy sauce. Mix the cornstarch into a little water and stir into the soup.
3 Bring to a boil, stirring, then reduce the heat and simmer until thickened, about 5 minutes. Add the corn and white fish, and simmer for 3 minutes, then gently stir in the squid and cook for 2 minutes longer.
4 Season to taste with salt and pepper, then serve immediately with the sliced scallion greens sprinkled over the top.

035 vietnamese chicken noodle soup

PREPARATION TIME: *15 minutes*   **COOKING TIME:** *37 minutes*

2 skinless, boneless chicken breast
   halves, about 5 oz each
6 cups chicken stock
2 stalks lemongrass,
   peeled and crushed
2 star anise
1 tbsp coriander seeds
2-inch piece fresh ginger,
   peeled and thinly sliced
2 tbsp fish sauce
1 tsp palm sugar or
   light brown sugar

juice of 1 lime
salt and freshly ground black pepper
6 oz cellophane noodles, cooked
4 scallions, finely sliced
3–4 shallots, chopped and
   fried until crisp and golden
1 hot red chili, seeded and
   finely sliced
handful of beansprouts
handful of cilantro leaves,
   roughly chopped

1   In a covered wok, poach the chicken in half of the stock until cooked, 15–20 minutes. Remove
    the chicken using a slotted spoon and set aside.
2   Pour the remaining stock into the wok and add the lemongrass, star anise, coriander seeds, and
    ginger. Bring to a boil, then reduce the heat and simmer for 15 minutes.
3   Strain the broth, discarding the spices. Return the broth to the wok and stir in the fish sauce,
    sugar, and lime juice. Season to taste with salt and pepper and heat to just below boiling point.
4   Slice the chicken breasts. Divide the noodles among four bowls and top with slices of chicken,
    scallions, crisp shallots, chili, and beansprouts. Ladle in the hot broth, then sprinkle with the
    cilantro and serve.

036 miso & tofu broth

PREPARATION TIME: *10 minutes, plus 10–15 minutes soaking time*   **COOKING TIME:** *6 minutes*

3 tbsp dried wakame seaweed
5 cups hot water
4–6 tbsp miso paste, according to taste
8 asparagus spears, sliced diagonally
1-inch piece fresh ginger, peeled and
   sliced into thin strips

2 tbsp tamari
6 oz Japanese tofu, sliced
3 scallions, white and green parts
   separated and sliced diagonally
¼ tsp ground sansho pepper

1   Soak the wakame in a large bowl of hot water until softened, 10–15 minutes. Drain and
    cut into small pieces.
2   Put the hot water and miso paste in a wok and stir until the miso has dissolved. Add the
    wakame, asparagus, ginger, tamari, tofu, and white part of the scalliions. Stir in the sansho
    pepper and heat until the liquid is just beginning to bubble up. Reduce the heat and simmer
    for 3 minutes.
3   Pour the miso soup into four serving bowls. Sprinkle with the green part of the scallions and
    serve immediately.

037 vietnamese beef & lemongrass broth

PREPARATION TIME: *20 minutes* **COOKING TIME:** *25 minutes*

2 tbsp peanut oil
1¼ lb lean beef tenderloin,
   thinly sliced
6 cups beef stock
2 tbsp fish sauce
2 star anise
3 hot Thai chilies, seeded and halved
2-inch piece fresh ginger,
   peeled and sliced
2 stalks lemongrass,
   peeled and crushed
4 cloves garlic, sliced

3 kaffir lime leaves
4 small heads bok choy, halved
   lengthwise
2 handfuls of beansprouts
juice of 2 limes
1 tsp palm sugar or
   light brown sugar
1 tbsp light soy sauce
4 scallions, finely sliced
handful of cilantro leaves,
   roughly chopped

1   Heat the oil in a wok until hot. Add half of the beef and stir-fry for 1 minute. Remove from the wok and set aside. Stir-fry the remaining beef for 1 minute and add to the first batch. Pour off any oil left in the wok, then wipe the wok with paper towel.

2   Put the stock, fish sauce, star anise, chilies, ginger, lemongrass, garlic, and lime leaves in the wok. Bring to a boil, then reduce the heat and simmer for 15 minutes. Strain, discarding the spices and flavorings, and return the broth to the wok.

3   Add the slices of beef and simmer for 4 minutes, then add the bok choy and beansprouts. Simmer for 2 minutes longer. Stir in the lime juice, sugar, soy sauce, scallions, and cilantro, and serve immediately.

038 chinese mushroom broth

PREPARATION TIME: *10 minutes, plus 20 minutes soaking time* **COOKING TIME:** *18 minutes*

1½ oz dried sliced Chinese mushrooms
   (about ¾ cup)
1 tbsp sunflower oil
2 tsp butter
4 shallots, thinly sliced
3 scallions, white and green parts
   separated and minced
16 cremini mushrooms, thinly sliced

2 cloves garlic, chopped
1-inch piece fresh ginger,
   peeled and thinly sliced
5 cups vegetable stock
½ tsp sugar
3 tbsp light soy sauce
freshly ground black pepper

1   Soak the dried mushrooms in hot water for 20 minutes. Drain, reserving the soaking liquid, which should be strained.

2   Heat the oil and butter in a wok, then stir-fry the shallots and white part of the scallions for 1 minute. Toss in the soaked mushrooms and the cremini mushrooms, and stir-fry for 5 minutes. Add the garlic and ginger and cook for 1 minute longer.

3   Pour in the stock and reserved mushroom liquid and bring to a boil, then reduce the heat. Add the sugar and soy sauce and simmer for 8 minutes. Season to taste with pepper. Serve with the green part of the scallions sprinkled on top.

039 poached chicken in broth with baby vegetables

PREPARATION TIME: *15 minutes* **COOKING TIME:** *25 minutes*

6 cups chicken stock
4 tbsp Chinese rice wine
   or dry sherry
4 skinless, boneless chicken breast
   halves, about 5 oz each
2 tbsp light soy sauce
2-inch piece fresh ginger,
   peeled and cut into 8 slices

½ tsp Chinese five-spice
4 baby leeks, each cut into 3
6 baby zucchini, halved lengthwise
6 baby carrots, halved lengthwise
salt and freshly ground black pepper
4 tbsp Cilantro Pesto
   (see page 78), optional

1 Put the stock, wine or sherry, chicken, soy sauce, ginger, and five-spice powder in a wok. Bring to a boil, then reduce the heat and cover the wok. Simmer until the chicken is cooked through, 15–20 minutes.

2 Remove the chicken using a slotted spoon and keep warm. Add the leeks, zucchini, and carrots to the broth in the wok and simmer until the vegetables are tender, about 5 minutes. Season to taste with salt and pepper.

3 Slice the chicken breasts and arrange in four serving bowls, then add the vegetables and broth. Top each serving with a tablespoonful of pesto, if using, and serve.

040 thai fish noodle bowl

PREPARATION TIME: *20 minutes* **COOKING TIME:** *22 minutes*

6 cups vegetable or fish stock
2 tbsp tom yum soup paste
1-inch piece fresh ginger,
   peeled and minced
2 stalks lemongrass,
   peeled and crushed
3 kaffir lime leaves
4 scallions, finely sliced
juice of 1 lime
1 tbsp fish sauce

½ tsp sugar
½ cup coconut milk
1 lb firm white fish fillet,
   cut into pieces
8 oz cooked small shrimp, peeled
6 oz rice noodles, cooked
handful of cilantro leaves,
   roughly chopped

1 Put the stock, tom yum paste, ginger, lemongrass, and lime leaves in a wok and bring to a boil. Reduce the heat and simmer for 15 minutes, then strain and discard the solids.

2 Return the flavored broth to the wok and add the scallions, lime juice, fish sauce, sugar, coconut milk, and fish, and simmer for 3 minutes. Add the shrimp and noodles, then simmer for 2 minutes to heat through. Serve immediately, sprinkled with the chopped cilantro.

041 thai chicken & noodle broth

PREPARATION TIME: *15 minutes*   **COOKING TIME:** *30 minutes*

2-inch piece fresh ginger,
  peeled and cut into 10 slices
6 cups chicken stock
2 stalks lemongrass,
  peeled and bruised
5 kaffir lime leaves
4 tsp fish sauce
4 skinless, boneless chicken breast
  halves, about 5 oz each
4 cloves garlic, thinly sliced
5 oz fresh spinach leaves,
  tough stems removed

3 tbsp rice vinegar
3 tbsp lime juice
½ tsp sugar
2 hot Thai chilies, seeded and minced
salt
6 oz medium egg noodles,
  cooked
a large handful of Thai basil leaves,
  roughly chopped

1   Take 4 slices of the ginger, cut into fine matchsticks, and set on one side.
2   Put the stock, lemongrass, remaining ginger slices, lime leaves, and fish sauce into a wok. Add the chicken breasts and bring to a boil. Reduce the heat and simmer, covered, until the chicken is cooked, 15–20 minutes. Remove the chicken and set aside. Strain the broth, discarding the solids.
3   Return the broth to the pan and add the ginger matchsticks, garlic, spinach, rice vinegar, lime juice, sugar, and chilies, then simmer for 5 minutes. If necessary, season with salt to taste.
4   Divide the cooked noodles among four shallow serving bowls. Thinly slice the chicken and place on top. Ladle the stock over, garnish with the fresh basil, and serve.

042 miso soup with somen noodles

PREPARATION TIME: *10 minutes*   **COOKING TIME:** *10 minutes*

large handful of fine green beans,
  trimmed and thinly sliced
1 small carrot, finely shredded
2 large handfuls of fresh
  spinach leaves, shredded
3½ cups hot vegetable stock
4–6 tbsp miso paste,
  according to taste
4 nori strips, toasted and
  broken into small pieces

1-inch piece fresh ginger,
  peeled and cut into thin strips
3 scallions, white and green parts
  separated and sliced diagonally
4 tbsp dark soy sauce
6 oz somen noodles, cooked
1 tbsp toasted sesame seeds
½ tsp dried chili flakes

1   Place the green beans in a large bamboo steamer. Cover and steam over a wok of simmering water for about 2 minutes. Add the carrot and spinach, and steam for 1 minute longer. Set the steamed vegetables on one side and keep warm.
2   Discard the water in the wok and carefully pour in the hot stock. Spoon in the miso and stir until dissolved. Add the nori, ginger, and white part of the scallions. Stir in the soy sauce and simmer for 5 minutes.
3   Divide the cooked noodles among four shallow bowls. Top with the steamed vegetables, then ladle the miso broth over. Sprinkle with the green part of the scallions, the sesame seeds, and the chili flakes, and serve.

043 japanese dashi & udon soup with tuna

PREPARATION TIME: *15 minutes, plus 1 hour marinating time* **COOKING TIME:** *12 minutes*

4 thick tuna steaks, about 5 oz each
2 tbsp sunflower oil
4 scallions, sliced diagonally into
    1-inch lengths
4 tbsp dark soy sauce
6 cups hot water
1 sachet (¼ oz) dashi stock powder
    (dashi-no-moto)
2 tbsp mirin
2 carrots, sliced
sesame seeds for coating

3 cups shredded fresh spinach leaves
6 oz somen noodles, cooked
1 large cooked beet, thinly sliced
green nori flakes for garnish

MARINADE:
1 tbsp mirin
4 tbsp dark soy sauce
½ tsp sansho pepper or freshly ground
    black pepper

1. Mix together the ingredients for the marinade in a shallow dish. Add the tuna and spoon the marinade over to coat well. Let marinate for 1 hour, turning occasionally.
2. Heat ½ tablespoon of the oil in a wok. Add the scallions and stir-fry for 30 seconds. Stir in 1 tablespoon of the soy sauce, then transfer the onions to a plate and leave on one side.
3. Mix together the hot water, dashi powder, mirin, and the remaining soy sauce. Heat another ½ tablespoon of oil in the wok, add the carrots, and stir-fry for 1 minute. Pour in the prepared dashi broth and heat until it is just starting to boil. Reduce the heat and simmer for 5 minutes.
4. Meanwhile, remove the tuna from the marinade and dip both sides of each piece into sesame seeds until well coated. Heat a ridged grill pan until hot, then brush the surface with oil and pan-grill the tuna for about 1 minute on each side. Slice and set on one side, keeping warm.
5. Stir the spinach and noodles into the dashi broth in the wok until the spinach wilts, then divide among four large serving bowls. Place the beet and tuna slices on top, sprinkle with the nori flakes, and serve immediately.

CHAPTER 2

SALADS & SIDE DISHES

Salads do not usually spring to mind when considering what can be prepared in a wok, but this collection of tempting recipes, with their wide spectrum of colors, flavors, and textures, should soon have you thinking very differently and will hopefully stimulate ideas for many new and delicious combinations.

The vibrant Stir-Fried Beet and Carrot Salad makes an excellent side dish, as does Warm Pepper Salad with Crisp Basil. For something a little more substantial, look no further than Sesame Tuna and Noodle Salad, Vietnamese Hot Beef Salad, Egg Noodle Salad with Scallops, or the tastebud-tingling Thai-Style Pork Salad.

The collection of side dishes is equally varied and versatile. Included are Aromatic Cardamom Carrots, Bombay Potatoes, Broccoli in Black Bean Sauce, Chili Bean Eggplant, Vietnamese Lemongrass Vegetables, and the perennial favorite, Crisp "Seaweed."

You could combine these recipes with a selection of other Asian dishes in this book to create a spectacular feast. Many, however, may also be served to give an exciting and original twist to a classic American-style meal, such as a roast or a barbecue.

044 vietnamese baby vegetable salad

PREPARATION TIME: *15 minutes* COOKING TIME: *6 minutes*

7 oz dried rice vermicelli
1 tbsp peanut oil
1 mildly hot, long, red chili, seeded
   and chopped
2 lemongrass stalks, peeled and minced
3 Asian red shallots, thinly sliced
6 baby zucchini, sliced into rounds
6 ears baby corn, halved lengthwise
1 small head white cabbage, shredded

DRESSING:
1 tbsp toasted sesame oil
1 tbsp sunflower oil
1 tbsp soy sauce
juice of 1 lime
½ tsp sugar
salt and freshly ground black pepper

1   Cook the noodles following the package directions; drain and rinse under cold running water. Cut into shorter lengths and set on one side.

2   Mix together all the ingredients for the dressing, seasoning to taste with salt and pepper. Set on one side.

3   Heat a wok until hot. Add the oil, then the chili and lemongrass and stir-fry for a few seconds. Toss in the shallots, zucchini, baby corn, and white cabbage and stir-fry for 2 minutes. Let cool slightly, then stir in the cooked noodles and pile onto a serving platter. Pour the dressing over and serve immediately.

045 stir-fried beet & carrot salad

PREPARATION TIME: *15 minutes, plus cooling time* COOKING TIME: *6 minutes*

3 tbsp olive oil
3 Asian red shallots, sliced
14 oz raw beets, cut into thin sticks
2 carrots, cut into thin sticks
finely grated zest and juice of 1 lime
large pinch of sugar

2 tsp toasted sesame oil
salt and freshly ground black pepper
handful of alfalfa sprouts
2 scallions, thinly sliced
1 tbsp sesame seeds, toasted

1   Heat the oil in a wok. Add the shallots and stir-fry for 1 minute. Add the beets and carrots and stir-fry until tender, 3–4 minutes.

2   Add the lime zest and juice, sugar, and sesame oil, and stir until the vegetables are well coated. Transfer the vegetables to a serving bowl and let cool.

3   Just before serving, season to taste with salt and pepper and stir in the alfalfa sprouts and scallions. Sprinkle with the sesame seeds and serve.

046 spicy potato salad

PREPARATION TIME: *15 minutes* COOKING TIME: *13 minutes*

1 lb baby new potatoes, scrubbed
2 tbsp peanut oil
2 cloves garlic, chopped
2 tsp ground cumin
2 tsp ground coriander
1 tsp garam masala

1-inch piece fresh ginger, peeled
   and minced
salt and freshly ground black pepper
4–5 tbsp sour cream
large handful of cilantro leaves,
   roughly chopped

1   Cook the potatoes in plenty of boiling, salted water until tender. Drain and set on one side.

2   Heat the oil in a wok. Add the garlic, ground cumin, ground coriander, garam masala, and ginger, and stir-fry for 1 minute. Remove from the heat.

3   Toss in the potatoes and stir until they are coated in the spice mixture. Season to taste with salt and pepper, and stir in the sour cream. Sprinkle with the chopped cilantro and serve.

047 warm asian salad

PREPARATION TIME: *10 minutes*   **COOKING TIME:** *7 minutes*

2 large handfuls of fine
  green beans, trimmed
12 asparagus spears, trimmed
  and sliced diagonally
large handful of snow peas,
  trimmed

2 tbsp olive oil
1 tbsp toasted sesame oil
2-inch piece fresh ginger,
  peeled and grated
2 tbsp soy sauce
1 large clove garlic, thinly sliced

1   Place the green beans and asparagus in a bamboo steamer lined with parchment paper.
    Cover and steam over a wok of simmering water for about 3 minutes.
    Add the snow peas and steam until all the vegetables are tender,
    1–2 minutes longer. Remove from the steamer,
    arrange on a serving platter, and keep warm.

2   Pour the water out of the wok and dry
    with paper towels. Add the oils and heat
    gently. Add the ginger, soy sauce, and garlic,
    and cook until heated through, about 1 minute.
    Pour this sauce over the steamed vegetables
    and leave for a few minutes to let
    the flavors mingle,
    then serve.

048 thai-style pork salad

PREPARATION TIME: *15 minutes* **COOKING TIME:** *4 minutes*

4 lean pork medallions, about 4 oz each,
   sliced into strips
1 tbsp peanut oil
salt and freshly ground black pepper
2 small heads romaine, leaves separated
2–3 Asian red shallots, finely sliced
5 vine-ripened tomatoes, peeled,
   seeded, and diced
large handful of cilantro leaves,
   roughly chopped
large handful of basil leaves, torn

DRESSING:
juice of 1 lime
½ tsp light brown sugar
1 tbsp olive oil
1 tsp toasted sesame oil
1 large clove garlic, crushed
2 tsp Thai fish sauce
1 mildly hot, long, red chili, seeded
   and thinly sliced into rounds
1 tbsp light soy sauce

1   Put the pork in a bowl with the oil and season well with salt and pepper. Turn the pork until it is well coated. Heat a wok until hot, add half the pork and oil, and stir-fry for 4 minutes. Remove from the wok, drain on paper towels, and set on one side. Repeat with the remaining pork and oil.

2   Mix together all the ingredients for the dressing in a small bowl and set on one side.

3   Arrange the lettuce leaves on a serving platter. Scatter the shallots, tomatoes, and half of the fresh cilantro and basil leaves over the lettuce. Place the cooked pork on top. Spoon the dressing over the pork, sprinkle with the remaining cilantro and basil, and serve.

049 egg noodle salad with scallops

PREPARATION TIME: *15 minutes* **COOKING TIME:** *6 minutes*

7 oz dried thin egg noodles
1 small English cucumber, seeded
   and cut into thin sticks
2 carrots, cut into thin strips
5 medium-sized tomatoes, peeled,
   seeded, and diced
6 scallions, shredded
handful of cilantro leaves,
   roughly chopped
handful of basil leaves, torn
1 mildly hot, long, red chili, seeded
   and minced
12 sea scallops, without the roe,
   halved horizontally

salt and freshly ground black pepper
2 tsp toasted sesame oil
1 tbsp sunflower oil

DRESSING:
2 tbsp sunflower oil
2 tbsp toasted sesame oil
juice of 1 lime
large pinch of sugar
1 tbsp light soy sauce
1-inch piece fresh ginger, peeled
   and grated
2 cloves garlic, crushed

1   Cook the noodles following the package directions. Drain, refresh under cold running water, and set on one side. Mix together the ingredients for the dressing in a bowl and set on one side.

2   Put the cucumber, carrots, tomatoes, and scallions in a serving bowl. Add half the chopped cilantro and basil leaves, the chili, the cooked noodles, and the dressing, and toss together until all the ingredients are well combined. Set on one side

3   Put the scallops in a bowl, season well with salt and pepper, and stir in the sesame oil. Heat a wok until hot, then add the sunflower oil. Add half of the scallops and sear until lightly browned, about 30 seconds on each side. Remove from the wok, drain on paper towels, and set on one side. Repeat with the remaining scallops.

4   Arrange the scallops on top of the bowl of noodle salad, sprinkle the remaining chopped cilantro and basil leaves over, and serve.

050 sesame tuna & noodle salad

PREPARATION TIME: *15 minutes, plus 1 hour marinating time* **COOKING TIME:** *13 minutes*

½ cup teriyaki sauce
1 tbsp honey
1 tbsp Japanese soy sauce
4 thick tuna steaks, about 4 oz each
7 oz dried egg noodles
2 tbsp sunflower oil
1 red bell pepper, cut into strips

1 small English cucumber, seeded and
   cut into thin sticks
1 tbsp toasted sesame oil
4 tomatoes, peeled, seeded, and diced
4 scallions, sliced on the diagonal
salt and freshly ground black pepper
1 tbsp sesame seeds, toasted

1   Mix together the teriyaki sauce, honey, and soy sauce in a shallow dish. Arrange the tuna steaks in the dish and turn to coat them in the marinade. Let marinate for 1 hour. Drain, reserving the marinade.

2   Meanwhile, cook the noodles following the package directions, then drain and rinse under cold running water. Set on one side in a saucepan of cold water.

3   Heat a wok until hot, then pour in 1 tablespoon of the sunflower oil. Use a slotted spatula to carefully place two tuna steaks in the hot oil and sear until lightly browned but still a little pink inside, about 1½ minutes on each side. Remove from the wok with the spatula and set on one side. Repeat with the remaining tuna steaks.

4   Wipe the wok clean and add the remaining sunflower oil. Toss in the red pepper and stir-fry for 1 minute. Add the cucumber and stir-fry for another minute. Drain the cooked noodles and add to the wok with the reserved marinade and sesame oil. Stir until the noodles are hot.

5   Transfer to a serving bowl and mix in the tomatoes and scallions. Season to taste with salt and pepper and add a little more soy sauce, if desired. Cut the tuna into strips and place on top, sprinkle the sesame seeds over, and serve.

051 tofu noodle salad

PREPARATION TIME: *15 minutes* **COOKING TIME:** *10 minutes*

9 oz dried egg noodles
4 tbsp sunflower oil
1 tbsp toasted sesame oil
9 oz firm block tofu, patted dry
1 small English cucumber, peeled and cut
   into thin batons
1 red bell pepper, seeded and cut into
   thin strips
5 scallions, sliced diagonally
1 carrot, sliced diagonally
1 mildly hot, long, red chili, seeded and
   thinly sliced

handful of cilantro leaves, chopped
salt and freshly ground black pepper
2 tbsp toasted sesame seeds

DRESSING:
3 tbsp yellow bean sauce
5 tbsp teriyaki sauce
1 tbsp water
1 clove garlic, crushed
juice of 1 lime
1 tsp minced fresh ginger
1 tsp toasted sesame oil

1   Cook the noodles following the package directions, then drain and refresh under cold running water. Mix together the ingredients for the dressing.

2   Heat the sunflower and sesame oils in a wok and, when hot, carefully place the block of tofu in the wok. Cook the tofu until golden on all sides. Remove from the wok and drain on paper towels. Cut the tofu into slices.

3   Put the tofu, noodles, cucumber, red pepper, scallions, carrot, chili, and cilantro in a serving bowl. Pour the dressing over, season to taste, and carefully mix until the ingredients are combined. Sprinkle the sesame seeds on top before serving.

052 thai-style squid salad

PREPARATION TIME: *20 minutes* **COOKING TIME:** *5 minutes*

12 small squid, cleaned and tentacles
   separated
salt
2 tbsp olive oil
2 large handfuls of baby spinach leaves,
   tough stems removed and leaves
   shredded
2 handfuls of arugula leaves
1 mildly hot, long, red chili, seeded and
   cut into fine strips
large handful of cilantro leaves,
   roughly chopped
handful of basil leaves, torn

DRESSING:
3 tbsp lime juice
2 tbsp olive oil
2 tsp toasted sesame oil
1 tbsp light soy sauce
1-inch piece fresh ginger, peeled
   and grated
1 small clove garlic, minced
1 hot green chili, seeded and minced
½ tsp palm sugar or light brown sugar

1   Mix together the ingredients for the dressing in a small bowl and set on one side.

2   Snip along the side edge of each squid pouch using scissors and open out to make a flat piece.
Rinse and pat dry with paper towels. Cut into 1½-inch squares, then lightly score each piece in
a criss-cross pattern. Season the squid squares and the tentacles with salt and drizzle half the
olive oil over them. Set on one side.

3   Heat the remaining olive oil in a wok. Add half the squid and sear for 1½ minutes on each side.
Remove from the wok, drain on paper towels, and set on one side.
Repeat with the remaining squid.

4   Arrange the spinach and arugula leaves on a
serving platter, then pile the squid on top.
Spoon the dressing over, garnish with the
red chili, chopped cilantro and basil
leaves, and serve.

053   vietnamese hot beef salad

PREPARATION TIME: *15 minutes, plus 1 hour marinating time*   **COOKING TIME:** *10 minutes*

1 lb boneless sirloin steak, cut into thin
   strips
2 large handfuls of beansprouts
2 handfuls of snow peas, trimmed and
   sliced diagonally
1 small English cucumber, seeded and
   sliced into ribbons with a potato peeler
1 tbsp sunflower oil
4 scallions, sliced diagonally
1 mildly hot, long, red chili, seeded
   and cut into strips

DRESSING:
4 tbsp rice vinegar
4 tbsp fish sauce
2 cloves garlic, crushed
2 tbsp sunflower oil
1 tsp sugar
juice of 2 limes
1 tbsp light soy sauce

1   Mix together the ingredients for the dressing in a small bowl. Pour half of the dressing into
    a shallow dish and add the beef. Turn to coat, then let marinate for at least 1 hour. Drain.
2   Arrange the beansprouts, snow peas, and cucumber on a serving platter.
3   Heat a wok until hot. Add the oil, then half the beef and stir-fry for 4–5 minutes. Remove the
    beef from the wok with a slotted spoon, drain on paper towels, and set on one side. Repeat
    with the remaining beef. Let cool slightly.
4   Place the beef on top of the platter of vegetables, spoon the remaining dressing over, and
    sprinkle with the scallions and chili. Serve immediately.

054   warm salad with satay dressing

PREPARATION TIME: *15 minutes*   **COOKING TIME:** *5 minutes*

1 medium-sized head broccoli,
   cut into small florets
1 small head cauliflower,
   cut into small florets
2 handfuls of fine green beans,
   trimmed
2 carrots, cut into thin ribbons
   using a potato peeler
1 large, red bell pepper, cut into strips
4 scallions, sliced diagonally

SATAY DRESSING:
6 tbsp crunchy peanut butter
1 tbsp olive oil
1 tbsp light soy sauce
2 tbsp hot water
4 tbsp coconut milk
½ tsp dried chili flakes
1 large clove garlic, crushed
1-inch piece fresh ginger,
   peeled and grated

1   Put the ingredients for the satay dressing in a bowl and beat until well combined. Set on
    one side.
2   Place the broccoli, cauliflower, and beans in a bamboo steamer lined with parchment paper.
    Cover and steam over a wok of simmering water for 2 minutes. Add the carrot ribbons
    and steam until all the vegetables are tender, about 2 minutes longer.
3   Arrange the cooked vegetables on a serving platter with the red pepper and scallions, drizzle
    the satay dressing all over, and serve.

055 hokkein noodle & smoked tofu salad

PREPARATION TIME: *15 minutes* COOKING TIME: *10 minutes*

12-oz block smoked tofu
½ small head white cabbage,
   finely shredded
2 carrots, finely shredded
4 scallions, sliced diagonally
2 hot green chilies, seeded and
   finely sliced into rounds
1 lb hokkein noodles, cooked
1 tbsp sesame seeds, toasted

DRESSING:
1-inch piece fresh ginger,
   peeled and grated
2 cloves garlic, crushed
2 tbsp tahini
1½ tbsp soy sauce
1 tbsp toasted sesame oil
3 tbsp hot water
salt and freshly ground black pepper

1 Blend together all the ingredients for the dressing in a small bowl until smooth and creamy. Season to taste with salt and pepper and set on one side.
2 Place the tofu on a plate that fits snugly into a bamboo steamer. Cover and steam over a wok of simmering water for 10 minutes. Carefully remove the tofu from the wok, cut into long slices, and set on one side.
3 Mix together the cabbage, carrots, scallions, and chilies. Arrange the noodles on serving plates, then top with the vegetables and slices of tofu. Spoon the dressing over all, sprinkle with the sesame seeds, and serve.

056 soba noodle & chicken salad

PREPARATION TIME: *15 minutes* COOKING TIME: *5 minutes*

2 tbsp sunflower oil
1 lb skinless, boneless chicken breast,
   cut into strips
9 oz dried soba noodles
1 tbsp toasted sesame oil
2 tbsp light soy sauce
1-inch piece fresh ginger, grated

1 tsp palm sugar or light brown sugar
5 scallions, shredded
2 carrots, cut into thin sticks
2-inch piece English cucumber, seeded
   and cut into thin sticks
salt and freshly ground black pepper
handful of cilantro leaves

1 Heat a wok until hot. Add half the sunflower oil, then half the chicken and stir-fry until lightly browned and cooked, about 4 minutes. Remove from the wok using a slotted spoon, drain on paper towels, and set on one side. Repeat with the remaining chicken.
2 Cook the soba noodles following the package directions, then drain and refresh under cold running water. Put into a serving bowl. Mix together the remaining sunflower oil, the sesame oil, soy sauce, ginger, and sugar, and pour over the noodles. Add the scallions, carrots, and cucumber, and mix gently until combined.
3 Season the noodle salad to taste with salt and pepper, then divide among four plates. Top with the cooked chicken, sprinkle with the cilantro, and serve.

057 warm pepper salad with crisp basil

PREPARATION TIME: *5 minutes* COOKING TIME: *3 minutes*

2 tbsp olive oil
handful of basil leaves
1 large, red bell pepper, sliced
1 large, yellow bell pepper, sliced

1 large, orange bell pepper, sliced
2 tsp balsamic vinegar
salt and freshly ground black pepper

1 Heat the oil in a wok. Toss in the basil leaves and fry until crisp. Remove from the wok, drain on paper towels, and set on one side.
2 Toss the peppers into the wok and stir-fry for 2 minutes. Add the balsamic vinegar and stir briskly, then arrange the peppers and any juices on a serving plate. Season to taste with salt and pepper, sprinkle with the crisp-fried basil, and serve.

058 spinach with shredded coconut

PREPARATION TIME: *15 minutes*   **COOKING TIME:** *6 minutes*

2 tbsp peanut oil
1 large onion, chopped
1 tbsp yellow mustard seeds
1 mildly hot, long, red chili, seeded
   and chopped

10 curry leaves
1 lb spinach, tough stems removed
   and leaves shredded
grated flesh of ½ small coconut
salt and freshly ground black pepper

1   Heat a wok until hot. Add the oil, then the onion and stir-fry it for 3 minutes. Add the mustard seeds, chili, and curry leaves, and stir-fry for 1 minute longer.

2   Toss in the spinach and stir-fry until wilted, about 2 minutes, adding a little water if necessary. Stir in the coconut, season to taste with salt and pepper, and serve.

059 bok choy in oyster sauce

PREPARATION TIME: *10 minutes* COOKING TIME: *4 minutes*

2 tbsp sunflower oil
2 cloves garlic, crushed
3 tbsp oyster sauce
1 tbsp hoisin sauce

1 tbsp light soy sauce
2 tbsp water
4 small heads bok choy,
    halved lengthwise

1   Heat the oil in a wok. Add the garlic and stir-fry for a few seconds. Stir in the oyster sauce, hoisin sauce, soy sauce, water, and bok choy. Stir-fry until the bok choy is tender, 2–3 minutes, then serve immediately.

060 sesame asparagus

PREPARATION TIME: *10 minutes* COOKING TIME: *4 minutes*

1 tbsp sunflower oil
2 tsp toasted sesame oil
2-inch piece fresh ginger,
    peeled and grated

20 thin asparagus spears, trimmed
salt and freshly ground black pepper
1 tbsp sesame seeds, toasted

1   Heat a wok until hot. Add the oils, then toss in the ginger and asparagus and stir-fry them until the asparagus is just tender, 3–4 minutes.
2   Season to taste with salt and pepper and serve, sprinkled with the sesame seeds.

061 bombay potatoes

PREPARATION TIME: *10 minutes, plus about 1 hour cooling time* COOKING TIME: *20 minutes*

6 medium-sized potatoes, halved
    if large
salt
2 tbsp sunflower oil
1 large onion, sliced
1 tsp cumin seeds
1 tsp ground coriander

½ tsp hot chili powder
1 tsp turmeric
5 fenugreek leaves
3 tomatoes, peeled,
    seeded, and chopped
4 tbsp water

1   Cook the potatoes in plenty of boiling salted water until tender. Drain and let cool. When the potatoes are cool, peel and cut into bite-sized cubes. Set on one side.
2   Heat a wok until hot. Add the oil, then the onion and stir-fry it for 3 minutes. Toss in the cumin seeds, ground coriander, chili powder, turmeric, and fenugreek leaves and cook for 1 minute. Stir in the tomatoes and water, season to taste with salt, and cook until the tomatoes become very mushy.
3   Stir in the potatoes, heat through, and serve.

062 garlic & lemon chard
PREPARATION TIME: *10 minutes* **COOKING TIME:** *5 minutes*

2 tbsp olive oil
14 oz Swiss chard, trimmed, stems
  sliced, and leaves torn
2 large cloves garlic, minced

finely grated zest of ½ small lemon
juice of 1 small lemon
salt and freshly ground black pepper

1 Heat a wok until hot. Add the oil, then the chard stems and stir-fry them for 2 minutes. Add the garlic and stir-fry for 30 seconds longer.
2 Add the chard leaves to the wok and stir-fry until all the chard is tender, about 2 minutes. Stir in the lemon zest and juice, season to taste with salt and pepper, and serve.

063 spiced sweet potato
PREPARATION TIME: *15 minutes, plus about 1 hour cooling time* **COOKING TIME:** *14 minutes*

2 sweet potatoes, peeled, halved,
  and thickly sliced
2 tbsp peanut oil
2 cloves garlic, minced
1 tsp fennel seeds

1 tsp cumin seeds
1 tsp ground coriander
2 tbsp sweet chili sauce
4 tbsp water
salt and freshly ground black pepper

1 Cook the sweet potatoes in plenty of boiling salted water until tender. Drain and let cool.
2 Heat the oil in a wok. Add the garlic and fennel and cumin seeds and stir-fry for 30 seconds. Add the ground coriander and sweet potatoes, and cook over medium heat, stirring, until the potatoes are well coated with the spices and heated through.
3 Stir in the chili sauce and water, season to taste with salt and pepper, and serve.

064 sesame & tahini spinach
PREPARATION TIME: *10 minutes* **COOKING TIME:** *3 minutes*

1 tbsp toasted sesame oil
1 tbsp sunflower oil
1 large clove garlic, minced
1 tbsp mirin or dry sherry
1 tbsp light tahini

1–2 tbsp water
14 oz spinach, tough stems removed
salt and freshly ground black pepper
2 tsp sesame seeds, toasted

1 Heat the oils in a wok. Add the garlic and stir-fry for a few seconds.
2 Stir in the mirin, tahini, and water, then toss in the spinach and stir-fry until wilted, about 2 minutes. Season to taste with salt and pepper and serve, sprinkled with the sesame seeds.

065 ginger-glazed shallots

PREPARATION TIME: *10 minutes* **COOKING TIME:** *8 minutes*

1 lb shallots, peeled	2-inch piece fresh ginger,
1 tbsp sunflower oil	peeled and minced
1 tbsp soft butter	1 tbsp clear honey

1   Plunge the shallots into a saucepan of just-boiled water for 4 minutes. Drain well, rinse under cold running water, and set on one side.

2   Heat the oil in a wok. Add the shallots and stir-fry for 3 minutes, then stir in the butter. When the butter has melted, add the ginger, then the honey.

3   Continue to stir-fry the shallots for 1 minute longer, until well coated in a glossy honey glaze, then serve.

066 stir-fried celery

PREPARATION TIME: *10 minutes* **COOKING TIME:** *5 minutes*

1 tbsp sunflower oil
2 cloves garlic, chopped
½ tsp dried chili flakes

6 stalks celery, cut into
½-inch slices
2 tbsp light soy sauce

1 Heat a wok until hot. Add the oil, then the garlic and chili flakes and stir-fry for a few seconds.
2 Toss in the celery and stir-fry for 3 minutes, then pour in the soy sauce, stir well, and serve.

067 sooke aloo

PREPARATION TIME: *15 minutes, plus about 1 hour cooling time* **COOKING TIME:** *25 minutes*

6 medium-sized baking potatoes,
halved if large
6 tbsp peanut oil
1 tsp black mustard seeds
1 tsp fenugreek seeds
1 tsp cumin seeds

4 cardamom pods, split
1 tsp turmeric
1 tbsp lemon juice
salt and freshly ground black pepper
1 hot red chili, seeded and cut into
thin strips

1 Cook the potatoes in plenty of boiling salted water until tender. Drain and let cool, then peel and cut into bite-sized cubes.
2 Heat the oil in a wok. Add half the potatoes and fry until crisp and golden, 3–4 minutes, turning occasionally. Remove from the wok with a slotted spatula, drain on paper towels, and set on one side. Repeat with the remaining potatoes.
3 Pour all but 1 tablespoon of the oil out of the wok. Add the mustard, fenugreek, and cumin seeds and, when they start to pop, stir in the cardamom pods and turmeric. Return the potatoes to the wok and heat through, then stir in the lemon juice. Season to taste with salt and pepper. Serve garnished with the chili.

068 sprout & orange stir-fry

PREPARATION TIME: *10 minutes* **COOKING TIME:** *7 minutes*

1 tbsp sunflower oil
2 tsp toasted sesame oil
1 onion, sliced
1 large clove garlic, chopped
2-inch piece fresh ginger, peeled
and grated

12 oz Brussels sprouts, trimmed
and sliced
4 tbsp fresh orange juice
salt and freshly ground black pepper
1 tbsp sunflower seeds,
toasted (optional)

1 Heat a wok until hot. Add the oils, then the onion and stir-fry it for 2 minutes. Add the garlic, ginger, and sprouts, and stir-fry for about 3 minutes.
2 Pour in the orange juice and stir-fry until the sprouts are just crisp-tender, 1–2 minutes longer. Season to taste with salt and pepper and serve, sprinkled with the sunflower seeds, if using.

069 crisp "seaweed"
PREPARATION TIME: *10 minutes* **COOKING TIME:** *5 minutes*

vegetable oil for deep-frying
6 green cabbage leaves, finely shredded

salt

1   Pour oil into a large wok until it is one-third full. Heat until the oil is hot enough to brown a
    cube of day-old bread in about 30 seconds. Toss in the shredded cabbage and stir-fry for
    2 minutes. Scoop out using a slotted spoon, drain on paper towels, and set on one side.
2   Just before serving, heat the oil again, then add the cabbage and fry until really crisp, about
    1 minute. Remove from the wok with a slotted spoon, drain on paper towels, and season to
    taste with salt. Serve immediately.

070 braised leeks with ginger
PREPARATION TIME: *10 minutes* **COOKING TIME:** *6 minutes*

1 tbsp sunflower oil
10 baby leeks, halved
   lengthwise
2-inch piece fresh ginger,
   peeled and minced

1 cup vegetable stock
1 tbsp soft butter
freshly ground black pepper

1   Heat a wok until hot. Add the oil, then the leeks and ginger and stir-fry them for 1 minute.
2   Add the stock and bring to a boil, then reduce the heat, cover, and simmer until the leeks are
    tender, 2–3 minutes.
3   Remove the leeks with a slotted spoon and place on a serving platter. Stir the butter into the
    broth, then increase the heat and cook until the broth has reduced slightly. Pour the buttery
    broth over the leeks, season well with pepper, and serve.

071 japanese-style steamed greens
PREPARATION TIME: *10 minutes* **COOKING TIME:** *5 minutes*

2 tsp toasted sesame oil
2 tbsp Japanese soy sauce
1 tbsp mirin
½ tsp sugar

1 small head white cabbage, shredded
3 small heads bok choy, sliced
large handful of mizuna
   leaves, shredded

1   Mix together the sesame oil, soy sauce, mirin, and sugar in a small bowl and set on one side.
2   Place the cabbage and bok choy in a bamboo steamer lined with parchment paper. Cover and
    steam over a wok of simmering water until the vegetables are tender, about 4 minutes. Add
    the mizuna leaves and steam for 1 minute longer.
3   Transfer the vegetables to a shallow serving bowl. Pour the soy and mirin mixture over the
    vegetables and serve.

072 stir-fried sesame greens

PREPARATION TIME: *10 minutes* **COOKING TIME:** *4 minutes*

2 tbsp light soy sauce
3 tbsp Chinese cooking wine
 or dry sherry
1 tsp palm sugar or
 light brown sugar
2 tsp toasted sesame oil
1 tbsp sunflower oil

2-inch piece fresh ginger,
 peeled and chopped
1 mildly hot, long, red chili, seeded
 and thinly sliced
12 oz Savoy cabbage, shredded
 (about 4 cups)
salt and freshly ground black pepper

1 Mix together the soy sauce, wine, and sugar in a small bowl and set on one side.
2 Heat a wok until hot. Add the oils, then the ginger and chili and stir-fry them for a few seconds.
 Toss in the cabbage and sir-fry for 2 minutes.
3 Pour in the soy sauce mixture and stir-fry for 1 minute longer. Season to taste and serve.

073 honey-glazed carrots

PREPARATION TIME: *10 minutes* **COOKING TIME:** *5 minutes*

1 tbsp sunflower oil
3 carrots, cut into thin sticks
1 large clove garlic, chopped
handful of rosemary, leaves chopped

1 tbsp soft butter
1 tsp Dijon mustard
1 tbsp clear honey

1 Heat a wok until hot. Add the oil, then the carrots and stir-fry them for 2 minutes. Add the garlic
 and rosemary and cook for 1 minute longer.
2 Add the butter, mustard, and honey, and stir well to coat the carrots. Cook over medium heat
 until the carrots are tender. Serve hot.

074 cumin-spiced cauliflower

PREPARATION TIME: *5 minutes* **COOKING TIME:** *5 minutes*

2 tbsp sunflower oil
1 medium-sized head cauliflower,
 cut into small florets
 and stems sliced
2 cloves garlic, crushed
1 tsp garam masala

2 tsp cumin seeds
1 tsp mustard seeds
juice of 1 lemon
salt
2 handfuls of cilantro leaves,
 roughly chopped

1 Heat a wok until hot. Add the oil, then the cauliflower and stir-fry it for 3 minutes. Remove from
 the wok using a slotted spoon and set on one side.
2 Reduce the heat, add the garlic, garam masala, and cumin and mustard seeds, and stir-fry for
 1 minute. Return the cauliflower to the wok along with the lemon juice. Turn the cauliflower
 until it is coated with the spice mixture, then season to taste with salt.
3 Transfer the cauliflower to a serving bowl and let cool slightly. Serve sprinkled with the
 chopped cilantro.

075 aromatic cardamom carrots
PREPARATION TIME: *10 minutes* **COOKING TIME:** *3 minutes*

2 tbsp sunflower oil
3 carrots, thinly sliced diagonally
3 cardamom pods, split and seeds removed

4 tbsp fresh orange juice
salt and freshly ground black pepper

1 Heat a wok until hot. Add the oil, then the carrots and cardamom seeds and stir-fry for 2 minutes.
2 Pour in the orange juice and cook until the liquid has reduced slightly, about 1 minute. Season to taste with salt and pepper, then serve.

076 stir-fried chili mushrooms
PREPARATION TIME: *10 minutes* **COOKING TIME:** *6 minutes*

2 tbsp sunflower oil
3 cloves garlic, chopped
7 oz shiitake mushrooms,
 halved or quartered if large
7 oz cremini mushrooms,
 halved or quartered if large

1 mildly hot, long, red chili, seeded
 and thinly sliced
3 tbsp light soy sauce
1 tbsp sweet chili sauce
1 tbsp fresh lime juice
salt and freshly ground black pepper
1 tbsp chopped cilantro

1 Heat a wok until hot. Pour in the oil and swirl it around to coat the wok, then add the garlic and stir-fry for 30 seconds. Toss in both types of mushrooms and the chili. Stir-fry over high heat for 3 minutes.
2 Reduce the heat to medium-low, then pour in the soy sauce, chili sauce, and lime juice. Season to taste and stir-fry for 1 minute longer. Serve sprinkled with the cilantro.

077 chili bean eggplant
PREPARATION TIME: *10 minutes, plus 30 minutes salting time* **COOKING TIME:** *8 minutes*

1 large eggplant, quartered lengthwise
 and sliced across
salt
½ cup vegetable stock
4 tsp rice vinegar
3 tbsp Chinese cooking wine
 or dry sherry
1 tsp palm sugar or light brown sugar

2 tbsp light soy sauce
4 tbsp sunflower oil
2 cloves garlic, chopped
1-inch piece fresh ginger, peeled
 and roughly chopped
1 tbsp chili bean paste

1 Lay the eggplant on a plate, sprinkle generously with salt, cover, and let drain for 30 minutes. Rinse well to remove the salt, pat dry using paper towels, and set on one side.
2 Mix together the stock, rice vinegar, wine, sugar, and soy sauce in a small bowl and set on one side.
3 Heat a wok until hot. Add the oil, then half the eggplant and stir-fry for 5 minutes. Remove the eggplant from the wok with a slotted spoon and set on one side. Put the remaining eggplant in the wok, with more oil if necessary, and stir-fry for 5 minutes. Return the first batch of eggplant to the wok.
4 Stir in the garlic and ginger, then pour in the stock mixture and add the chili bean paste. Cook, stirring frequently, until the liquid has reduced and thickened, about 2 minutes. Serve hot.

078 zucchini in yellow bean sauce

PREPARATION TIME: *5 minutes* **COOKING TIME:** *3 minutes*

3 tbsp yellow bean sauce
1 tsp chili bean paste
1-inch piece fresh ginger,
   peeled and grated

1 tbsp sunflower oil
4 zucchini, cut into
   thin sticks

1 Mix together the yellow bean sauce, chili bean paste, and ginger in a small bowl and set on one side.
2 Heat a wok until hot. Add the oil, then toss in the zucchini and stir-fry them for 1 minute. Pour in the yellow bean mixture and stir-fry until the zucchini are tender and thoroughly coated in the sauce, about 1 minute longer. Serve hot.

079 broccoli with mustard seeds

PREPARATION TIME: *10 minutes* **COOKING TIME:** *7 minutes*

2 tbsp sunflower oil
1 tbsp yellow mustard seeds
2-inch piece fresh ginger, peeled
   and minced
2 cloves garlic, minced

12 oz broccoli, cut into small florets
   and stems sliced
⅔ cup vegetable stock
salt and freshly ground black pepper

1 Heat the oil in a wok. Add the mustard seeds and, when they start to pop, add the ginger and garlic. Stir-fry for a few seconds, then add the broccoli and stir-fry for 2 minutes longer.
2 Pour in the stock and bring to a boil. Reduce the heat, cover, and simmer until the broccoli is tender, 3–4 minutes. Season to taste with salt and pepper, and serve.

080 vietnamese lemongrass vegetables

PREPARATION TIME: *15 minutes* COOKING TIME: *4 minutes*

2 tbsp sunflower oil

2-inch piece fresh ginger,
    peeled and minced

1 stalk lemongrass, peeled
    and minced

2 cloves garlic, chopped

1 mildly hot, long, red chili, seeded
    and minced

3 zucchini, sliced diagonally

6 scallions, sliced diagonally

12 ears baby corn

2 tbsp light soy sauce

2 handfuls of Vietnamese mint
    or cilantro leaves, roughly chopped

1   Heat the oil in a wok. Add the ginger, lemongrass, garlic, and chili, and stir-fry for a few seconds over medium heat.

2   Increase the heat slightly, add the zucchini, scallions, and corn, and stir-fry until the vegetables are just tender, about 2 minutes. Add the soy sauce and toss until the vegetables are well coated. Serve with the chopped mint or cilantro sprinkled over the top.

081 chinese chili bean cucumber

PREPARATION TIME: *15 minutes, plus 30 minutes salting time* COOKING TIME: *4 minutes*

1 English cucumber

2 zucchini, halved lengthwise,
    then sliced across

salt

2 tsp chili bean paste

3 tbsp oyster sauce

2 tsp toasted sesame oil

½ tsp sugar

1 tbsp sunflower oil

4 cloves garlic, minced

2-inch piece fresh ginger,
    peeled and minced

1   Halve the cucumber lengthwise, scoop out the seeds, and slice into half-moon shapes. Combine with the zucchini on a plate and sprinkle generously with salt. Let stand for 30 minutes, then rinse well to remove all the salt. Pat dry with paper towels and set on one side.

2   Mix together the chili bean paste, oyster sauce, sesame oil, and sugar in a small bowl and set on one side.

3   Heat the oil in a wok. Add the garlic and ginger and stir-fry for 30 seconds, then add the zucchini and cucumber, and stir-fry for 3 minutes. Stir in the chili bean mixture. Stir-fry for 1 minute longer, then serve.

082 broccoli in black bean sauce

PREPARATION TIME: *10 minutes* COOKING TIME: *8 minutes*

12 oz broccoli florets

2 tsp toasted sesame oil

1 tbsp sunflower oil

2 cloves garlic, crushed

1-inch piece fresh ginger, grated

2 tbsp light soy sauce

4 tbsp black bean sauce

2 tbsp water

handful of unsalted cashew nuts,
    toasted and roughly chopped

1   Put the broccoli in a bamboo steamer lined with parchment paper. Cover and steam over a wok of simmering water until just tender, about 4 minutes. Remove the broccoli from the steamer and set on one side.

2   Empty the wok and wipe dry. Pour in the sesame and sunflower oils and heat. Add the garlic, ginger, and steamed broccoli, and stir-fry for 1 minute.

3   Stir in the soy sauce, black bean sauce, and water, and cook, tossing the broccoli in the sauce, until heated through. Serve with the cashew nuts sprinkled over the top.

083 chinese mushroom & choy sum stir-fry

PREPARATION TIME: *10 minutes, plus 20 minutes soaking time*   **COOKING TIME:** *5 minutes*

½ oz dried shiitake mushrooms
2 tbsp sunflower oil
3 heads choy sum, stems sliced
 and leaves cut into thirds

4 oz cremini mushrooms, sliced
 (about 1½ cups)
2 tbsp Shaoxing wine or Scotch whisky
2 tbsp light soy sauce

1 Put the dried mushrooms in a bowl, cover with boiling water, and let soak for 20 minutes. Drain, reserving the soaking liquid. Slice the mushrooms, discarding any tough stems. Strain the soaking liquid and set aside.

2 Heat a wok until hot. Add the oil, then the choy sum stems and soaked shiitake mushrooms and stir-fry them for 2 minutes. Toss in the cremini mushrooms and stir-fry for 1 minute longer.

3 Add the choy sum leaves and stir-fry for 1 minute. Stir in the wine or whisky, soy sauce, and a little mushroom soaking liquid. Cook briefly to heat through, then serve.

084 masala cauliflower with almonds

PREPARATION TIME: *15 minutes*   **COOKING TIME:** *10 minutes*

1 medium-sized head cauliflower,
 cut into small florets
3 tbsp sunflower oil
1 tbsp black mustard seeds
1 tbsp coriander seeds, crushed
2 cloves garlic, chopped

½ tsp dried chili flakes
3 tbsp water
1 tbsp lemon juice
salt and freshly ground black pepper
handful of sliced almonds, toasted

1 Put the cauliflower in a bamboo steamer lined with parchment paper. Cover and steam over a wok of simmering water until slightly softened, 2–3 minutes. Remove from the steamer and set on one side.

2 Empty the wok and wipe dry. Add the oil and heat, then add the mustard and coriander seeds, garlic, and chili and stir-fry for a few seconds. Toss in the steamed cauliflower and stir well to coat it with the spices.

3 Add the water, cover the wok with a lid, and cook the cauliflower until tender, about 8 minutes, stirring occasionally. Stir in the lemon juice, season to taste with salt and pepper, and serve, sprinkled with the sliced almonds.

085 napa cabbage & beansprout stir-fry

PREPARATION TIME: *10 minutes*   **COOKING TIME:** *3 minutes*

2 tsp toasted sesame oil
1 tbsp sunflower oil
1 mildly hot, long, red chili, seeded
 and minced
1 lb napa cabbage, shredded

3 handfuls of beansprouts
2 tbsp light soy sauce
juice of 1 lime
handful of cilantro leaves

1 Heat a wok until hot. Add the oils, then the chili and napa cabbage and stir-fry for 2 minutes.

2 Add the beansprouts, soy sauce, and lime juice and stir-fry for a few seconds, then serve, sprinkled with the cilantro leaves.

CHAPTER 3

NOODLES & RICE

Noodles and rice are far more than just filling accompaniments to a meal. Fluffy grains of fragrant basmati rice, hearty udon and buckwheat noodles, and silky threads of rice vermicelli shape the character of so much Asian cuisine. Without noodles and rice, many of the great dishes of Thailand, China, Japan, Vietnam, India, Indonesia, and Malaysia would be inconceivable.

This chapter will show you just how versatile and satisfying noodles and rice can be by revealing the huge range of appetizing meals that can be created around these two most basic of staples. Among the varied recipes included are well-known classics such as Chinese Egg-Fried Rice with Pork and Cashews, the Indonesian favorite Nasi Goreng, Pad Thai, and, in the Indian style, Aromatic Spicy Vegetable Rice, and Kitchiri, a vegetarian dish that combines rice with spices and red lentils.

There are also recipes that fuse European and Asian elements to create exciting new taste sensations. Chinese Mushroom Risotto combines Italian arborio rice with shiitake and oyster mushrooms and Chinese rice wine, while in Asian-Style Paella a mixture of chicken, shrimp, and rice is infused with aromatic Chinese five-spice.

086 pad thai

PREPARATION TIME: *15 minutes* **COOKING TIME:** *8 minutes*

9 oz medium rice noodles
1 tbsp sunflower oil
3 cloves garlic, minced
1 large carrot, cut into thin strips
4 scallions, white and green parts
   separated and sliced diagonally
1 mildly hot, long, red chili,
   finely sliced
juice of 1 lime

3 tbsp light soy sauce
2 tbsp rice vinegar
2 tbsp sweet chili sauce
2 eggs, lightly beaten
salt and freshly ground black pepper
handful of beansprouts
handful of roasted peanuts, crushed
large handful of cilantro leaves,
   minced

1   Cook the noodles following the package directions. Drain, refresh under cold running water, and set on one side.

2   Heat a wok until hot. Add the oil, then the garlic, carrot, white part of the scallions, and the chili and stir-fry for 1 minute. Stir in the lime juice, soy sauce, rice vinegar, and chili sauce.

3   Add the cooked noodles and mix with the other ingredients, stirring gently to avoid breaking up the noodles. Push the noodles to one side and add the eggs. Stir gently until the eggs are incorporated into the noodles and lightly set. Season to taste with salt and pepper.

4   Sprinkle the beansprouts, peanuts, cilantro, and the green parts of the scallions over the top and serve.

087 udon noodles with spiced beef & basil

PREPARATION TIME: *15 minutes, plus 1 hour marinating time* **COOKING TIME:** *10 minutes*

2 tbsp soy sauce
juice of 1 lime
salt and freshly ground black pepper
1 lb boneless sirloin steak, cut into
   strips across the grain
1 lb cooked udon noodles
7 oz fine green beans, trimmed
2 tbsp sunflower oil

2 small, hot red chilies,
   seeded and chopped
4 scallions, sliced
1 tbsp fish sauce
1 tbsp palm sugar or
   light brown sugar
handful of cilantro leaves, chopped
handful of basil leaves, torn

1   Mix together the soy sauce and lime juice in a shallow dish. Season well with salt and pepper, and add the steak. Stir until the steak is coated in the marinade. Let marinate for 1 hour. Drain, reserving the marinade.

2   Put the cooked noodles in a pan of boiling water and cook for 1 minute to separate them. Drain well, refresh under cold running water, and set on one side. Plunge the green beans into a pan of boiling water and blanch for 2 minutes, then drain, refresh under cold running water, and set on one side.

3   Heat a wok until hot. Add the oil, then toss in the beef and stir-fry it for 2–3 minutes. Remove the beef from the wok using a slotted spoon and set on one side.

4   Put the chilies, scallions, and green beans into the wok and stir-fry for 1 minute. Add the fish sauce, reserved marinade, and sugar. Stir, then return the beef to the wok along with the noodles and heat through, stirring constantly. Season to taste with salt and pepper, then mix in the cilantro and serve with the basil scattered over.

088 chiang mai noodles

PREPARATION TIME: *20 minutes* **COOKING TIME:** *20 minutes*

8 oz dried rice noodles

2 tbsp sunflower oil

3 Asian red shallots, chopped

2 zucchini, sliced

2 cloves garlic, sliced

8 cremini mushrooms, sliced

1 red bell pepper, diced

½ tsp dried chili flakes

3 heaped tbsp Thai Green Curry Paste
   (see page 15)

1 cup coconut milk

1 cup vegetable stock

1 tbsp fish sauce

1 tsp palm sugar or
   light brown sugar

1 tbsp lime juice

handful of roasted unsalted peanuts,
   chopped

handful of cilantro leaves,
   roughly chopped

1 Cook the noodles following the package directions. Drain, refresh under cold running water, and set on one side.

2 Heat a wok until hot. Add the oil, then the shallots and stir-fry them for 2 minutes. Add the zucchini, garlic, mushrooms, and red pepper, and stir-fry for 1 minute longer. Stir in the chili flakes and curry paste, and cook for 2 more minutes.

3 Pour in the coconut milk, stock, and fish sauce. Stir in the sugar and bring to a boil. Reduce the heat and simmer, covered, for 10 minutes. Add the cooked noodles and heat through, stirring gently. Divide among four warm serving bowls and serve, sprinkled with the peanuts and chopped cilantro.

089 egg noodles with chicken & water chestnuts

PREPARATION TIME: *10 minutes* **COOKING TIME:** *10 minutes*

9 oz dried medium egg noodles

2 tbsp sunflower oil

1 red bell pepper, chopped

2 cloves garlic, chopped

2-inch piece fresh ginger, peeled
   and grated

1 lb skinless, boneless chicken breast,
   cut into strips

large handful of snow peas, trimmed

5 oz canned water chestnuts,
   drained and halved

3 tbsp light soy sauce

2 tbsp oyster sauce

2 tbsp water

salt and freshly ground black pepper

2 scallions, thinly sliced

1 Cook the noodles following the package directions, then drain and refresh under cold running water. Set on one side.

2 Heat a wok until hot. Add the oil, then the red pepper, garlic, and ginger and stir-fry them for about 30 seconds. Add the chicken and stir-fry until golden and cooked through, 3–4 minutes. Toss in the snow peas and water chestnuts and stir-fry for 1 minute longer.

3 Gently stir in the cooked noodles, soy sauce, oyster sauce, and water. Heat through, tossing until everything is mixed together. Season to taste with salt and pepper and serve, topped with the scallions.

090 mee siam

PREPARATION TIME: *10 minutes, plus 20 minutes soaking time*   **COOKING TIME:** *13 minutes*

½ oz dried Chinese mushrooms
2 bundles dried rice vermicelli
3 tbsp sunflower oil
2 eggs, lightly beaten
4 shallots, sliced
3 cloves garlic, chopped

1 mildly hot, long, red chili, thinly sliced
2 carrots, cut into thin matchsticks
4 scallions, chopped
2 tsp chili bean paste
1 tbsp light soy sauce
2 tsp fish sauce

1   Put the dried mushrooms in a bowl, pour over enough boiling water to cover them, and let soak for 20 minutes. Drain the mushrooms; strain and reserve the soaking liquid.

2   While the mushrooms are soaking, cook the noodles following the package directions, then drain and refresh under cold running water. Set on one side.

3   Heat ½ tablespoon of the oil in a wok and use half the beaten egg to make a thin omelet, following the instructions on page 83. Remove from the wok and keep warm. Use the remaining egg to make a second omelet, adding more oil if necessary. Set aside with the first omelet and keep warm.

4   Heat the remaining oil in the wok. Add the shallots and stir-fry until golden and crisp. Remove using a slotted spoon, drain on paper towels, and set on one side.

5   Pour off all but 1 tablespoon of the oil. Heat the wok again, then add the garlic, chili, carrots, mushrooms, and scallions and stir-fry for 2 minutes. Stir in the chili bean paste and half of the reserved mushroom soaking liquid.

6   Add the cooked noodles, soy sauce, and fish sauce, and toss until well combined and heated through. Divide the noodles among four warm serving bowls. Cut the omelets into thin strips and place on the noodles. Top with the crisp-fried shallots and serve.

091 sticky vietnamese pork noodles

PREPARATION TIME: *15 minutes*   **COOKING TIME:** *8 minutes*

3-inch piece fresh ginger,
   peeled and grated
3 tbsp palm sugar or
   light brown sugar
1 tbsp fish sauce
3 tbsp light soy sauce
9 oz dried thin egg noodles
2 tbsp peanut oil

1 lb boneless pork loin, trimmed and cut
   into thin slices across the grain
4 Asian red shallots, thinly sliced
8 scallions, white and green part
   separated and sliced diagonally
salt and freshly ground black pepper
handful of unsalted roasted peanuts,
   chopped

1   Mix together the ginger, sugar, fish sauce, and soy sauce in a small bowl and set on one side.

2   Cook the noodles following the package directions. Drain, refresh under cold running water, and set on one side.

3   Heat a wok until hot. Add the oil, then toss in the pork and sear it until lightly browned, about 1 minute. Remove from the wok using a slotted spoon and set on one side. Put the shallots and the white part of the scallions into the wok and stir-fry for 2 minutes. Stir in the ginger mixture, then return the pork to the wok and stir-fry until the sauce becomes sticky and the pork golden, about 3 minutes. Lower the heat.

4   Stir the cooked noodles into the pork mixture until combined and heated through. Season to taste with salt and pepper. Divide among four warm serving bowls. Sprinkle with the peanuts and the green part of the scallions, and serve.

092 chicken chow mein

PREPARATION TIME: *15 minutes, plus 30 minutes marinating time*   **COOKING TIME:** *14 minutes*

3 tbsp mirin

3 tbsp light soy sauce

2 tsp cornstarch

1¼ lb skinless, boneless chicken
   thighs, cut into bite-sized pieces

10 oz dried medium egg noodles

3 tbsp sunflower oil

2 cloves garlic, chopped

2-inch piece fresh ginger,
   peeled and minced

1 carrot, diced

2 large handfuls of snow peas, trimmed

3 leaves napa cabbage, sliced

5 scallions, sliced

⅔ cup chicken stock

2 tbsp oyster sauce

2 tbsp light soy sauce

large handful of beansprouts

1   Mix together the mirin, soy sauce, and cornstarch in a shallow dish. Add the chicken and turn
    to coat in the marinade. Let marinate for 30 minutes, then drain, reserving the marinade.

2   Meanwhile, cook the noodles following the package directions. Drain, refresh under cold
    running water, and set on one side.

3   Heat a wok until hot. Add the oil, then toss in the chicken and stir-fry it until golden, 3–4
    minutes. Remove the chicken from the wok using a slotted spoon, drain on paper towels, and
    set on one side. Put the garlic, ginger, carrot, snow peas, napa cabbage, and scallions into the
    wok and stir-fry for 2 minutes.

4   Return the chicken to the wok and pour in the stock, oyster sauce, soy sauce, and reserved
    marinade. Stir-fry until the liquid has reduced and thickened, about 2 minutes. Stir in the
    cooked noodles and beansprouts. Heat through and serve immediately.

093 mee krob

PREPARATION TIME: *10 minutes* COOKING TIME: *10 minutes*

6 tbsp Chinese rice wine or dry sherry

2 tbsp light soy sauce

1 tsp sugar

juice of 2 limes

peanut oil for deep-frying

1 bundle dried rice vermicelli

10 oz skinless, boneless chicken breast,
   sliced into thin strips

2 cloves garlic, chopped

10 oz raw tiger shrimp, peeled

2-inch piece fresh ginger, peeled
   and minced

1 lb spinach, tough stems removed
   and shredded

½–1 tsp dried chili flakes

4 tbsp water

salt

1   Mix together the wine, soy sauce, sugar, and lime juice in a small bowl and set on one side.

2   Heat enough oil in a large wok to deep-fry the noodles. Add half the noodles and cook until
    they puff up and become light and crisp—this takes a matter of seconds. Remove from the wok
    using a slotted spoon, drain on paper towels, and
    set on one side. Repeat with the remaining noodles.

3   Pour all but 2 tablespoons of the oil out of the
    wok and reheat. Add the chicken and stir-fry for
    3–4 minutes, then remove using a slotted spoon,
    drain on paper towels, and set on one side.

4   Add the garlic, shrimp, and ginger to the wok and
    stir-fry for 1 minute, then toss in the spinach with
    the wine mixture, followed by the chicken and the
    chili flakes. Pour in the water and stir-fry for
    2 minutes. Season to taste with salt.

5   Divide the stir-fry among four shallow
    serving bowls, top each with some
    of the crisp noodles, and serve.

094 egg-fried noodles

PREPARATION TIME: *10 minutes* **COOKING TIME:** *8 minutes*

9 oz dried wide rice noodles
2 tbsp peanut oil
12 cremini mushrooms, sliced
2 handfuls of snow peas,
    trimmed and halved diagonally
4 scallions, green and white parts
    separated and sliced

2 tbsp light soy sauce
1 tsp sugar
2 eggs, lightly beaten
1 onion, roughly chopped
    and fried until crisp

1   Cook the noodles following the package directions. Drain, refresh under cold running water, and set on one side.
2   Heat a wok until hot. Add the oil, then toss in the mushrooms and stir-fry them for 2 minutes. Add the snow peas and scallions and stir-fry for 1 minute longer.
3   Stir in the soy sauce and sugar, followed by the cooked noodles. Heat, tossing frequently, until the noodles are warmed through. Pour in the eggs and let them cook slightly, then stir them into the noodles until well combined. Divide among four warm serving bowls, sprinkle with the crisp-fried onion, and serve.

095 pork & lemon noodles

PREPARATION TIME: *15 minutes* **COOKING TIME:** *10 minutes*

grated zest of 1 lemon
juice of 2 lemons
2 tbsp light soy sauce
1 tbsp rice vinegar
1 tbsp palm sugar or
    light brown sugar
¼ cup water

1 tbsp sunflower oil
1¼ lb pork tenderloin, thinly sliced
    across the grain
2 cloves garlic, chopped
6 cups shredded napa cabbage
4 scallions, sliced
1¼ lb cooked hokkein noodles

1   Mix together the lemon zest and juice, soy sauce, rice vinegar, sugar, and water in a small bowl and set on one side.
2   Heat the oil in a wok. Add the pork and stir-fry for 2 minutes. Add the garlic and napa cabbage, and stir-fry for 1 minute longer. Remove the pork and vegetables from the wok using a slotted spoon and set on one side.
3   Pour the lemon juice mixture into the wok. Bring to a boil, then reduce the heat and simmer until reduced and slightly sticky, 1–2 minutes. Return the pork and vegetables to the wok along with the scallions and noodles. Stir until hot, then serve.

096 garlic noodles with spinach

PREPARATION TIME: *10 minutes* **COOKING TIME:** *7 minutes*

9 oz dried medium egg noodles
1 tbsp sunflower oil
3 cloves garlic, thinly sliced
8 oz spinach, tough stems removed and
    leaves shredded (about 3½ cups)

3 tbsp water
handful of basil leaves, torn
handful of mint leaves, chopped
1 tsp toasted sesame oil
salt and freshly ground black pepper

1   Cook the noodles following the package directions. Drain, refresh under cold running water, and set on one side.
2   Heat a wok until hot. Add the oil, then toss in the garlic and stir-fry it for 30 seconds. Add the spinach and stir-fry for 2 minutes. Add the cooked noodles, water, basil, and mint, and toss until heated through. Stir in the sesame oil, season to taste with salt and pepper, and serve.

097 chinese egg noodles with crab

PREPARATION TIME: *10 minutes, plus 15 minutes marinating time* **COOKING TIME:** *5 minutes*

2 tbsp light soy sauce

1 tsp sugar

12 oz fresh or canned white
    crab meat (about 3 cups)

1 tbsp cornstarch

3 tbsp Chinese rice wine
    or dry sherry

5 tbsp water

9 oz dried medium egg noodles

3 tbsp sunflower oil

4 large leaves napa cabbage,
    shredded

2 handfuls of snow peas, trimmed

2-inch piece fresh ginger,
    peeled and chopped

4 scallions, white and green parts
    separated and sliced diagonally

salt and and freshly ground
    black pepper

handful of cilantro leaves

1   Mix together the soy sauce and sugar in a small bowl and set on one side. Put the crab meat
    in another bowl with the cornstarch, wine, and water and let marinate for 15 minutes.

2   Cook the noodles following the package directions, then drain, refresh under cold running
    water, and set on one side.

3   Heat a wok until hot. Add the oil, then the napa cabbage and snow peas and stir-fry them for
    1 minute. Add the ginger and white part of the scallions and stir-fry for 30 seconds.

4   Reduce the heat slightly and stir in the crab meat mixture and cooked noodles. Pour in the
    soy sauce mixture and heat through, adding more water if necessary. Season to taste with
    salt and pepper and serve, with the cilantro leaves and green part of the scallions sprinkled
    over the top.

098 thai chili squid noodles

PREPARATION TIME: *20 minutes* **COOKING TIME:** *14 minutes*

4 Asian red shallots, sliced

2 stalks lemongrass,
    peeled and chopped

3 cloves garlic, crushed

1-inch piece fresh ginger,
    peeled and grated

2 hot, red Thai chilies,
    minced

1 tbsp palm sugar or
    light brown sugar

juice of 1 lime

2 tbsp tomato paste

2 tsp fish sauce

7 oz dried rice stick noodles

6 oz fine green beans, trimmed

2 tbsp sunflower oil

1½ lb cleaned squid, sliced into rounds

large handful of cilantro leaves,
    roughly chopped

1   Put the shallots, lemongrass, garlic, ginger, and chilies in a blender or food processor and
    process to form a coarse paste. Add a little oil if the mixture is too dry to blend.

2   Mix together the sugar, lime juice, tomato paste, and fish sauce in a small bowl and set
    on one side.

3   Cook the noodles following the package directions, adding the green beans to the cooking
    water at the same time. Drain, refresh the noodles and beans under cold running water, and
    set on one side.

4   Heat a wok until hot. Add the oil, then toss in half the squid and stir-fry it for 1½ minutes.
    Remove the squid from the wok using a slotted spoon and set on one side. Repeat with the
    remaining squid.

5   Put the paste in the wok and fry for 5 minutes. Add the squid, the lime juice mixture, and the
    cooked noodles and beans. Toss until heated through and well combined. Stir in the chopped
    cilantro and serve.

099 japanese-style salmon noodles

PREPARATION TIME: *20 minutes* **COOKING TIME:** *8 minutes*

4 tbsp Japanese soy sauce
1 tbsp rice vinegar
½ cup mirin
4 tbsp water
1 tsp sugar
9 oz dried soba noodles
2 tbsp all-purpose flour
2 tsp wasabi powder or
    English mustard powder

1 lb salmon fillet, skinned and cut into
    large bite-sized pieces
2–3 tbsp sunflower oil
2 cloves garlic, chopped
10 oz spinach, tough stems removed and
    leaves shredded (about 4 cups)
salt and freshly ground black pepper
2 tbsp toasted sesame seeds
1 English cucumber, sliced into thin
    ribbons using a potato peeler

1 Mix together the soy sauce, vinegar, mirin, water, and sugar in a small bowl and set on one side.

2 Cook the noodles following the package directions, then drain, refresh under cold running water, and set on one side.

3 Combine the flour and wasabi powder on a plate and dip the salmon pieces into the mixture until lightly dusted.

4 Heat 2 tablespoons of the oil in a wok. Add half the salmon and fry over medium-high heat until golden, about 1 minute on each side. Remove from the wok with a slotted spatula, set on one side, and keep warm. Repeat with the remaining salmon, adding more oil if necessary.

5 Wipe the wok and add another tablespoon of oil. Add the garlic and stir-fry for 30 seconds, then pour in the soy sauce mixture. Toss in the spinach and cook until wilted, about 1 minute. Carefully stir in the cooked noodles until heated through.

6 Divide the noodles and vegetables among four warm serving bowls. Top with the salmon, season to taste with salt and pepper, sprinkle the sesame seeds and cucumber over, and serve.

100 coconut chicken noodles

PREPARATION TIME: *15 minutes* **COOKING TIME:** *12 minutes*

7 oz dried rice stick noodles
2 tbsp sunflower oil
1¼ lb skinless, boneless chicken thighs,
    cut into thin strips
1 red bell pepper, diced
4 small heads bok choy, leaves and
    stems separated
2 large cloves garlic, chopped

1 tsp turmeric
1 tbsp garam masala
1 tsp dried chili flakes
½ cup hot vegetable stock
3 heaped tbsp smooth peanut butter
1½ cups coconut milk
2 tbsp light soy sauce
3 scallions, shredded

1 Cook the noodles following the package directions, then drain and refresh under cold running water. Set on one side.

2 Heat a wok until hot. Add the oil, then toss in half the chicken and stir-fry it for 3–4 minutes. Remove the chicken from the wok using a slotted spoon, drain on paper towels, and set on one side. Repeat with the remaining chicken.

3 Put the red pepper, bok choy stems, and garlic into the wok and stir-fry for 1 minute. Add the turmeric, garam masala, chili flakes, and bok choy leaves, and stir-fry for 1 minute longer. Return the chicken to the wok.

4 Mix together the hot stock and peanut butter, then pour into the stir-fry along with the coconut milk and soy sauce. Add the cooked noodles. Gently toss the noodles until coated in the sauce and heated through. Serve garnished with the scallions.

101 rainbow vegetable noodles
PREPARATION TIME: *10 minutes* **COOKING TIME:** *12 minutes*

9 oz dried thick egg noodles
1 tbsp sunflower oil
2 tsp toasted sesame oil
8 medium-sized broccoli florets,
   cut into smaller florets
   and stems thinly sliced
2 handfuls of fine green beans,
   trimmed and sliced

1 carrot, finely shredded
1 red bell pepper, diced
2 cloves garlic, chopped
2-inch piece fresh ginger,
   peeled and grated
2 tbsp light soy sauce
4 tbsp fresh apple juice
2 tbsp sesame seeds, toasted

1   Cook the noodles following the package directions. Drain, refresh under cold running water, and set on one side.

2   Heat a wok until hot. Add the oils, then toss in the broccoli and green beans and stir-fry them for 2 minutes. Add the carrot and red pepper and stir-fry for 2 minutes, then add the garlic and ginger and stir-fry for 1 minute longer.

3   Pour in the soy sauce and apple juice and add the cooked noodles. Stir-fry for 2 minutes, gently tossing the noodles and adding a little water if the noodles appear too dry. Serve sprinkled with the toasted sesame seeds.

102 eggplant & mushroom noodles
PREPARATION TIME: *10 minutes* **COOKING TIME:** *10 minutes*

9 oz dried medium egg noodles
3 tbsp sunflower oil
1 eggplant, diced
5 oz shiitake mushrooms, sliced
   (about 2 cups)
3 cloves garlic, chopped
2-inch piece fresh ginger,
   peeled and minced

2 scallions, white and green parts
   separated and thinly sliced
4 tsp chili bean paste
4 tbsp oyster sauce
½ tsp sugar
6 tbsp water
1 tsp toasted sesame oil
handful of basil leaves

1   Cook the noodles following the package directions. Drain, refresh under cold running water, and set on one side.

2   Heat a wok until hot. Add the oil, then toss in the eggplant and stir-fry it for 4 minutes. Add the mushrooms and stir-fry until golden, about 2 minutes. Remove the eggplant and mushrooms from the wok using a slotted spoon and set on one side.

3   Put the garlic, ginger, and white part of the scallions into the wok and stir-fry for 30 seconds. Add the chili bean paste, oyster sauce, sugar, water, and sesame oil and stir-fry for 1 minute.

4   Return the eggplant, mushooms, and cooked noodles to the wok and toss until the noodles are heated through and coated with the sauce, adding a little more water if the sauce appears too dry. Serve topped with the green part of the scallions and the basil leaves.

103 yellow bean noodles with shrimp

PREPARATION TIME: *15 minutes* **COOKING TIME:** *13 minutes*

9 oz dried ho fun noodles
4 tbsp yellow bean paste
1 tbsp fish sauce
2 tbsp light soy sauce
1 tsp sugar
2 tbsp Chinese rice wine or dry sherry
3 tbsp water
2 tbsp sunflower oil

4 shallots, sliced
2 zucchini, diced
2 cloves garlic, crushed
2-inch piece fresh ginger,
  peeled and grated
10 oz raw tiger shrimp, peeled
large handful of cilantro leaves,
  roughly chopped

1 Cook the noodles following the package directions, then drain, refresh under cold running water, and set on one side.
2 Mix together the yellow bean paste, fish sauce, soy sauce, sugar, wine, and water in a small bowl and set on one side.
3 Heat a wok until hot. Add the oil, then toss in the shallots and stir-fry for 2 minutes. Add the zucchini, garlic, and ginger, and stir-fry for another 2 minutes. Pour in the yellow bean mixture.
4 Stir in the shrimp and cook until the sauce has reduced and thickened and the shrimp are pink, about 2 minutes. Stir in the noodles and cilantro, heat through, and serve.

104 thai pork with rice noodles

PREPARATION TIME: *15 minutes* **COOKING TIME:** *22 minutes*

3 tbsp lime juice
2 tbsp fish sauce
1 tbsp palm sugar or
  light brown sugar
4 tbsp light soy sauce
9 oz dried medium rice noodles
2 tbsp sunflower oil
7 oz fine green beans, trimmed

4 scallions, minced
2 hot red chilies, minced
2 stalks lemongrass, minced
4 tbsp sesame seeds, for coating
4 pork loin steaks, about 5 oz each
1 tbsp toasted sesame oil
handful of basil leaves

1 Mix together the lime juice, fish sauce, sugar, and soy sauce in a small bowl and set on one side.
2 Cook the noodles following the package directions. Drain, refresh under cold running water, and set on one side.
3 Heat a wok until hot. Add half the sunflower oil, then toss in the beans and stir-fry them for 2–3 minutes. Add the scallions, chilies, and lemongrass, and stir-fry for 1 minute. Pour in the lime juice mixture and heat through, stirring, then transfer to a bowl and set on one side.
4 Spread the sesame seeds on a plate. Dip the pork steaks into the sesame seeds and turn until they are coated. Heat the remaining sunflower oil with the sesame oil in the wok. Add two of the pork steaks and fry for 2–3 minutes on each side. Remove from the wok, set on one side, and keep warm. Repeat with the remaining two pork steaks.
5 Put the cooked noodles, basil leaves, and reserved bean mixture into the wok and turn gently until combined and heated through. Divide among four warm serving bowls. Slice the pork, place on top of the vegetables and noodles, and serve.

111 spiced thai noodles with tuna

PREPARATION TIME: *15 minutes, plus 1 hour marinating time* **COOKING TIME:** *7 minutes*

4 thick tuna steaks, about 4 oz each,
  sliced into strips
7 oz dried medium rice noodles
2 tbsp sunflower oil
4 garlic cloves, chopped
3 mildly hot, long, red chilies, seeded
  and minced
2 handfuls of snow peas, trimmed
2 tbsp fish sauce

2 tbsp light soy sauce
2 tsp sugar
4 scallions, sliced diagonally
2 limes, cut into wedges

MARINADE:
1 tbsp toasted sesame oil
1 tbsp light soy sauce
1 tbsp honey

1 Mix together the ingredients for the marinade in a shallow dish. Add the tuna and turn to coat it with the marinade. Let marinate for 1 hour. Drain, reserving the marinade.

2 Cook the noodles according to the package directions. Drain, refresh under cold running water, and set on one side.

3 Heat a wok until hot. Add half the oil, then half of the tuna and sear it for 1 minute, turning halfway through the cooking time. Remove the tuna from the wok with a slotted spoon and set on one side. Cook the remaining tuna in the same way, but leave in the wok and add the first batch to it. Stir in the reserved marinade and cook the tuna until golden and glossy, about 1 minute longer, turning once. Remove from the wok, set on one side, and keep warm.

4 Wipe the wok clean and pour in the remaining oil. When it is hot, stir in the garlic, chilies, and snow peas and stir-fry for 1 minute, then add the fish sauce, soy sauce, sugar, and noodles, and toss until heated through.

5 Divide the vegetables and noodles among four warm serving bowls. Arrange the tuna on top, scatter the scallions over, and serve with wedges of lime.

112 soba noodles with tofu & asparagus

PREPARATION TIME: *15 minutes, plus 1 hour marinating time* **COOKING TIME:** *20 minutes*

8 oz firm tofu
9 oz dried soba noodles
2 tbsp sunflower oil
12 asparagus spears, trimmed
  and cut into thirds
1 red bell pepper, sliced
1 carrot, cut into matchsticks
2 scallions, cut into thin strips

2 tbsp toasted sesame seeds
½ tsp dried chili flakes

MARINADE:
4 tbsp mirin
4 tbsp Japanese soy sauce
4 tbsp sake
1 tsp sugar

1 Mix together the ingredients for the marinade in a shallow dish. Add the tofu and spoon the marinade over until it is well coated. Let marinate for 1 hour, turning the tofu occasionally. Drain, reserving the marinade.

2 Cook the noodles following the package directions. Drain, refresh under cold running water, and set on one side.

3 Heat the oil in a wok. Add the block of tofu and fry, turning occasionally, until golden all over, 8–10 minutes. Remove from the wok with a slotted spoon, drain on paper towels, and set on one side, keeping warm.

4 Toss the asparagus, red pepper, and carrot into the wok and stir-fry until they are tender, about 3 minutes. Pour in the reserved marinade, then add the noodles and toss until heated through and coated with the sauce.

5 Cut the tofu into ½-inch slices. Divide the noodles and vegetables among four warm serving bowls. Top with the tofu slices, scatter the scallions, sesame seeds, and chili flakes over each bowl, and serve.

113 yakisoba noodles

PREPARATION TIME: *15 minutes, plus 1 hour marinating time* **COOKING TIME:** *20 minutes*

12 oz firm tofu, cubed
9 oz dried ramen noodles
2 tbsp rice vinegar
1 tbsp ketchup
2 tbsp oyster sauce
1 tsp light brown sugar
1 tbsp sunflower oil
1 tbsp toasted sesame oil
2-inch piece fresh ginger,
    peeled and minced
1 red bell pepper, sliced
1 carrot, sliced diagonally

2 zucchini, sliced diagonally
3½ cups shredded napa cabbage
6 scallions, white and green parts
    separated and sliced diagonally
handful of toasted sesame seeds

MARINADE:
4 tbsp Japanese soy sauce
3 cloves garlic, minced
2 tbsp sweet chili sauce
3 tbsp mirin

1   Mix together the ingredients for the marinade in a shallow dish. Add the tofu and stir to coat with the marinade. Let marinate for 1 hour, turning the tofu occasionally. Drain, reserving the marinade.

2   Preheat the oven to 350°F. Put the tofu on a lightly oiled baking sheet and roast, turning over halfway, until crisp and golden, about 20 minutes.

3   Meanwhile, cook the noodles following the package directions. Rinse, refresh under cold running water, and set on one side. Mix together the rice vinegar, ketchup, oyster sauce, and sugar in a small bowl and set on one side.

4   Heat a wok until hot. Add the oils, then toss in the ginger, red pepper, and carrot and stir-fry for 1 minute. Add the zucchini, napa cabbage, and the white part of the scallions, and stir-fry for 2 minutes longer.

5   Mix the rice vinegar mixture and the reserved marinade together and add to the wok with the cooked noodles. Toss over medium heat until combined and heated through, then serve with the tofu, sesame seeds, and the green part of the scallions sprinkled over the top.

114 noodles with cilantro pesto

PREPARATION TIME: *20 minutes* **COOKING TIME:** *10 minutes*

9 oz dried medium egg noodles
1 tbsp sunflower oil
1 red bell pepper, sliced
12 ears baby corn, halved lengthwise
handful of beansprouts
2 tbsp sesame seeds, toasted
handful of cilantro leaves

CILANTRO PESTO:
2 handfuls of cilantro leaves,
   roughly chopped
3 cloves garlic, chopped
1 mildly hot, long, red chili, chopped
5 tbsp sunflower oil
2-inch piece fresh ginger,
   peeled and grated
grated zest and juice of 2 limes
2 tbsp light soy sauce
1 tbsp sugar
1 tbsp toasted sesame oil

1   Put all the ingredients for the pesto in a food processor or blender and process to form a
thick paste.
2   Cook the noodles following the package directions. Drain, refresh under cold running water,
and set on one side.
3   Heat a wok until hot. Add the oil, then toss in the red pepper and baby corn and stir-fry for
2 minutes. Add the cooked noodles and 4–6 tablespoons of the pesto. Toss the noodles
until they are coated with the pesto and heated through.
4   Remove from the heat and stir in the beansprouts. Serve immediately, with the sesame
seeds and cilantro leaves scattered over the top.

115 vegetable udon pot

PREPARATION TIME: *15 minutes* **COOKING TIME:** *18 minutes*

4 tbsp light soy sauce

2 tsp sugar

3 cloves garlic, minced

½–1 tsp dried chili flakes

1¼ cups vegetable stock

½ cup water

2 tbsp light tahini paste

2 tbsp peanut oil

1 tsp toasted sesame oil

1 large onion, sliced

2 cups sliced shiitake mushrooms

large handful of fine green beans, trimmed

2 carrots, cut into thin strips

4 small heads bok choy, halved lengthwise

8 leaves napa cabbage, shredded

1¼ lb cooked udon noodles

salt and freshly ground black pepper

1   Put the soy sauce, sugar, garlic, chili flakes, stock, and water in a saucepan and bring to a boil. Stir in the tahini, reduce the heat, and simmer until the tahini has dissolved. Set on one side.

2   Heat a wok until hot. Add the oils, then toss in the onion and stir-fry it for 4 minutes. Add the mushrooms and stir-fry for 2 minutes longer. Remove the onion and mushrooms from the wok using a slotted spoon and set on one side.

3   Reheat the wok and add a little more oil, if necessary. Toss in the beans and carrots and stir-fry for 3 minutes. Add the bok choy and napa cabbage, and stir-fry for 2 minutes.

4   Return the mushrooms and onion to the wok along with the noodles and tahini stock. Bring to a boil, stirring well but gently to loosen the noodles. Cover, reduce the heat, and simmer for 3 minutes. Season to taste with salt and pepper, and serve.

116 chili-fried noodles with tuna

PREPARATION TIME: *15 minutes, plus 1 hour marinating time* **COOKING TIME:** *12 minutes*

4 thick tuna steaks, about 5 oz each

9 oz dried ho fun noodles

2 tbsp sunflower oil

2 mildly hot, long, red chilies, seeded
   and minced

1-inch piece fresh ginger, peeled and
   cut into thin strips

2 large handfuls of snow peas, trimmed

4 cups shredded napa cabbage

3 scallions, shredded

handful of cilantro leaves

MARINADE:

4 tbsp light soy sauce

4 tsp palm sugar or light brown sugar

4 tbsp Chinese rice wine or dry sherry

2 tbsp rice vinegar

1 tbsp toasted sesame oil

1   Mix together the ingredients for the marinade in a shallow dish. Add the tuna and spoon the marinade over until it is well coated. Let marinate for 1 hour. Drain, reserving the marinade.

2   Cook the noodles following the package directions, then drain, refresh in cold running water, and set on one side.

3   Heat a wok until hot. Add the oil, then toss in the chilies, ginger, snow peas, and napa cabbage, and stir-fry for 1 minute. Remove the vegetables from the wok using a slotted spoon and set on one side.

4   Heat the wok again. Add two of the tuna steaks and fry for 1 minute on each side. Remove from the wok with a slotted spatula and keep warm. Repeat with the remaining tuna steaks.

5   Return the vegetables to the wok along with the marinade and cooked noodles. Toss until heated through. Slice the warm tuna.

6   Divide the noodles and vegetables among four warm serving bowls, then top with the sliced tuna, scallions, and cilantro leaves, and serve.

121 rice sticks with shrimp

PREPARATION TIME: *20 minutes* COOKING TIME: *14 minutes*

7 oz dried rice stick noodles
2 tbsp sunflower oil
4 shallots, minced
2 cloves garlic, chopped
large handful of fine green beans,
   trimmed and sliced
3 small heads bok choy, stems sliced
   and leaves torn
12 oz raw tiger shrimp, peeled
2 tbsp fish sauce
1 tbsp palm sugar or light brown sugar

1 tbsp tamarind paste
juice of 1½ limes
2 tbsp light soy sauce
2 eggs, lightly beaten
2 handfuls of beansprouts
handful of cilantro leaves,
   roughly chopped
salt
1 mildly hot, long, red chili, seeded
   and thinly sliced

1   Cook the noodles following the package directions, then drain and refresh under cold running water. Set on one side.
2   Heat a wok until hot. Add the oil, then the shallots and stir-fry them for 2 minutes. Toss in the garlic and green beans, and stir-fry for another 2 minutes. Add the bok choy and shrimp, and stir-fry for 1 minute.
3   Stir in the fish sauce, sugar, tamarind paste, lime juice, and soy sauce, then pour in the eggs. Let the eggs set slightly before combining with the rest of the ingredients in the wok.
4   Gently mix in the cooked noodles, beansprouts, and cilantro, and heat through. Season to taste with salt and serve, with the chili scattered on top.

122 udon with chili peanut sauce

PREPARATION TIME: *15 minutes* COOKING TIME: *8 minutes*

1 heaped cup unsalted peanuts
3 cloves garlic
3-inch piece fresh ginger,
   peeled and minced
1¼ cups coconut milk
3 tbsp dark soy sauce
1½ tsp hot chili sauce
1 tbsp sunflower oil
2 mildly hot, long, red chilies, seeded
   and chopped

1¼ lb cooked udon noodles
1 cup water
juice of 2 limes
1 tbsp toasted sesame oil
2 handfuls of beansprouts
handful of cilantro leaves,
   roughly chopped
1 onion, chopped and fried
   until crisp and golden

1   Roast the peanuts in a dry wok, tossing frequently, until beginning to color and smell toasted. Let cool slightly, then put into a food processor or blender and process until finely ground. Transfer the peanuts to a bowl and stir in the garlic, ginger, coconut milk, soy sauce, and chili sauce to make the sauce.
2   Heat the oil in a wok. Add the chilies and stir-fry for 30 seconds. Add the noodles, peanut sauce, water, lime juice, and sesame oil. Stir gently to loosen the noodles and heat through for about 2 minutes.
3   Remove from the heat and stir in the beansprouts and cilantro. Divide among four warm serving bowls, scatter the crisp-fried onions on top, and serve.

123 crispy noodle stir-fry

PREPARATION TIME: *15 minutes*   **COOKING TIME:** *8 minutes*

8 broccoli florets, cut into smaller florets
2 tbsp light soy sauce
½ tsp sugar
2 tbsp lime juice
2 tbsp Shaoxing wine or medium sherry
peanut oil for deep-frying
5 oz dried medium egg nooodles

1 large onion, sliced
3 cloves garlic, chopped
1 yellow bell pepper, sliced
12 shiitake mushrooms, sliced
2 zucchini, sliced diagonally
2 mildly hot, long, red chilies, seeded
   and thinly sliced (optional)

1   Plunge the broccoli into a pan of boiling water for 1 minute; drain and set on one side. Mix
    together the soy sauce, sugar, lime juice, and wine in a small bowl and set on one side.
2   Heat enough oil in a large wok to deep-fry the noodles. Add half the noodles and deep-fry
    until golden and crisp. Remove from the oil using a slotted spoon, drain on paper towels, and
    set on one side. Repeat with the remaining noodles.
3   Pour off all but 1 tablespoon of the oil from the wok. Reheat the wok, add the onion, and
    stir-fry for 3 minutes. Toss in the garlic, yellow pepper, mushrooms, and zucchini, and stir-fry
    for 2 minutes. Add the broccoli, pour in the soy sauce mixture, and stir-fry for 1 more minute.
4   Toss the vegetables with the crispy noodles, then divide among four warm serving bowls.
    Scatter on the chilies, if using, and serve.

124 black bean noodles with omelet

PREPARATION TIME: *15 minutes*   **COOKING TIME:** *15 minutes*

7 oz dried medium rice noodles
2 tbsp sunflower oil
2 cloves garlic, chopped
2-inch piece fresh ginger,
   peeled and grated
2 cups sliced cremini mushrooms
9 oz spinach, tough stems removed and
   leaves shredded (about 4 cups)
6 tbsp black bean sauce

2 tbsp light soy sauce
3 tbsp water
salt and freshly ground black pepper
2 tbsp sesame seeds, toasted

OMELET:
4 eggs, lightly beaten
a little butter
1 tbsp sunflower oil

1   To make the omelets, melt a little butter and oil in a wok, add one-quarter of the beaten egg
    and swirl it around until it coats the bottom of the wok, then let set. Slide the omelet out of the
    wok and set on one side. Repeat with the remaining egg to make three more omelets. Keep
    warm while preparing the stir-fry
2   Cook the noodles following the package directions. Drain, refresh under cold running water,
    and set on one side.
3   Heat the wok until hot. Add the oil, then toss in the garlic, ginger, and mushrooms and stir-fry
    them for 1 minute. Add the spinach and stir-fry until wilted.
4   Pour in the black bean sauce, soy sauce, and water, followed by the cooked noodles. Toss until
    the noodles are heated through and coated with the sauce. Season to taste with salt and
    pepper and divide among four warm serving bowls.
5   Cut the omelets into strips and place on top of the noodles. Sprinkle the sesame seeds over
    and serve.

125 kitchiri

PREPARATION TIME: *15 minutes* **COOKING TIME:** *30 minutes*

2 tbsp dried red lentils
1 cup basmati rice, rinsed
1 bay leaf
3 cloves
2 cups water
salt and freshly ground black pepper
1 tbsp peanut oil

3 tbsp butter
1 onion, sliced
1 tbsp garam masala
½–1 tsp dried chili flakes
handful of cilantro leaves,
    roughly chopped
4 hard-cooked eggs, quartered

1   Put the lentils in a saucepan and cover with water. Bring to a boil, skimming off any foam, then reduce the heat, cover, and simmer until tender, 20–25 minutes. Drain well and set on one side.

2   Meanwhile, put the rice in a saucepan with the bay leaf and cloves and cover with the water. Season to taste with salt and bring to a boil, then reduce the heat, cover, and simmer until the water is absorbed and the rice is tender, 10–12 minutes. Remove the pan from the heat and fluff up the rice with a fork, then let cool slightly.

3   Heat the oil and butter in a wok. Add the onion and fry for 4 minutes. Add the garam masala and chili flakes and stir-fry for 30 seconds. Add the cooked rice and lentils and mix thoroughly but gently until they are coated with the spiced butter. Season to taste with salt and pepper, stir in the chopped cilantro, and serve, topped with the quarters of hard-cooked egg.

126 simple lime rice with peanuts

PREPARATION TIME: *8 minutes* **COOKING TIME:** *20 minutes*

1½ cups basmati rice, rinsed
3 cups water
salt
large handful of unsalted peanuts
1 tbsp peanut oil
1 tsp mustard seeds
1 tsp fenugreek seeds

3 cardamom pods, split
    and seeds removed
6 curry leaves
3 hot red chilies
1 tsp turmeric
grated zest of 1 lime
juice of 3 limes

1   Put the rice in a saucepan and cover with the water. Season to taste with salt and bring to a boil. Reduce the heat, cover, and simmer until the water is absorbed and the rice is tender, 10–12 minutes. Remove from the heat and set aside for 5 minutes, then fluff up the rice with a fork and let cool slightly.

2   Meanwhile, dry-roast the peanuts in a wok until beginning to brown and they smell toasted. Transfer to a plate and roughly chop.

3   Heat the oil in the wok. Add the mustard seeds, fenugreek seeds, and cardamom seeds and stir-fry until they start to pop. Add the curry leaves, chilies, and turmeric, and stir-fry for 1 more minute.

4   Remove from the heat and stir in the cooked rice and lime zest and juice. Sprinkle with the peanuts and serve.

127 asian-style paella

PREPARATION TIME: *20 minutes* **COOKING TIME:** *35 minutes*

2 tbsp vegetable oil

2 handfuls of fine green beans,
trimmed and halved

1 red bell pepper, diced

1½ cups thickly sliced shiitake
mushrooms

1 onion, minced

2 cloves garlic, chopped

2-inch piece fresh ginger,
peeled and minced

1 tsp turmeric

½ tsp Chinese five-spice

1⅔ cups paella or risotto rice, rinsed

2 tbsp Chinese rice wine or dry sherry

4 cups hot chicken or vegetable
stock

⅔ cup frozen petit pois (petite
green peas)

1½ cups roughly chopped
napa cabbage

7 oz cooked tiger shrimp, peeled

10 oz cooked skinless, boneless
chicken breast, cut into
bite-sized pieces

2 tsp toasted sesame oil

salt and freshly ground black pepper

1 Heat a wok until hot. Add the vegetable oil, then toss in the green beans, red pepper, and mushrooms and stir-fry them for 3 minutes. Remove from the wok using a slotted spoon and set on one side.

2 Put the onion into the wok and stir-fry for 4 minutes. Add the garlic, ginger, tumeric, and five-spice, and stir-fry for 30 seconds. Tip in the rice and stir-fry until translucent, about 2 minutes.

3 Stir in the wine and cook until most has evaporated, then add 1 cup of the stock. Bring to a boil, then reduce the heat and simmer, stirring frequently, until most of the stock has been absorbed by the rice, about 3 minutes. Continue to simmer, adding the stock in batches and stirring frequently, until the rice is cooked but still has some bite, 15–20 minutes in total.

4 Just before you stir in the last batch of stock, add the peas, napa cabbage, shrimp, chicken, and reserved vegetables, and stir in the sesame oil. Cover and let cook until the rice is tender, about 3 minutes longer. Add a little more water if necessary to keep the rice moist but not sloppy. Season to taste with salt and pepper, and serve.

128 chinese fried rice
with pineapple & chicken

PREPARATION TIME: *15 minutes* **COOKING TIME:** *22 minutes*

1½ cups basmati rice, rinsed

3 cups water

salt and freshly ground black pepper

2 tbsp sunflower oil

14 oz skinless, boneless chicken breast,
  cut into long strips

2-inch piece fresh ginger, peeled
  and minced

2 cloves garlic, chopped

12 ears baby corn, sliced lengthwise

1½ cups sliced fine green beans

1 tsp Chinese five-spice

1 small pineapple, peeled,
  cored, and cut into chunks

2 tbsp light soy sauce

3 scallions, sliced diagonally

1   Put the rice in a saucepan and cover with the water. Season to taste with salt and bring to a
    boil. Cover, then reduce the heat and simmer until the water has been absorbed and the rice is
    tender, 10–12 minutes. Remove the pan from the heat and let stand, covered, for 5 minutes.
    Transfer the rice to a bowl and let cool, fluffing it up occasionally with a fork.

2   Heat a wok until hot. Add the oil, then toss in the chicken and stir-fry it until golden and cooked
    through, 3–4 minutes. Remove from the wok using a slotted spoon and set on one side.

3   Put the ginger and garlic into the wok and stir-fry for 30 seconds. Toss in the corn and green
    beans and cook for 3 minutes longer, stirring constantly. Return the chicken to the wok along
    with the five-spice and pineapple.

4   Stir in the cooked rice with the soy sauce, and toss until it is heated through. Season to taste
    with salt and pepper and serve with the scallions scattered over the top.

129   mango fried rice with almonds

PREPARATION TIME: *10 minutes* **COOKING TIME:** *20 minutes*

1 cup basmati rice, rinsed

2 cups water

salt and freshly ground black pepper

2 tbsp sliced almonds

1 tbsp peanut oil

1 tbsp butter

1 onion, chopped

2 cloves garlic, chopped

2 tsp ground cumin

2 tsp ground coriander

1 tsp ground cinnamon

3 cardamom pods, split

1 large mango, peeled,
  pitted, and cut into chunks

1   Put the rice in a saucepan and cover with the water. Season to taste with salt and bring to a
    boil, then reduce the heat, cover, and simmer until the water has been absorbed and the rice is
    tender, 10–12 minutes. Remove the pan from the heat and let stand, covered, for 5 minutes.
    Transfer the rice to a bowl and let cool, fluffing it up occasionally with a fork.

2   Toast the almonds in a wok until lightly golden. Remove and set on one side.

3   Heat the oil and butter in the wok. Add the onion and fry until golden and softened, about
    5 minutes. Add the garlic, cumin, coriander, cinnamon, and cardamom, and stir-fry for
    30 seconds. Add the cooked rice and mango, and toss until the rice is heated through. Season
    to taste with salt and pepper and serve with the toasted almonds scattered over the top.

130   nasi goreng

PREPARATION TIME: *15 minutes*   **COOKING TIME:** *8 minutes*

2 tbsp sunflower oil
4 shallots, minced
2 mildly hot, long, red chilies, seeded
  and chopped
1-inch piece fresh ginger, peeled
  and minced
1 tsp paprika
3 cups shredded white cabbage
2 cups sliced cremini mushrooms

1 large carrot, diced
1 tbsp tomato paste or ketchup
2 tbsp light soy sauce
3½ cups cooked, cold long-grain rice
salt and freshly ground black pepper
7 oz tofu puffs or crisp-fried tofu
1 onion, roughly chopped and fried until
  crisp and golden

1   Heat a wok until hot. Add the oil, then toss in the shallots and stir-fry them for 2 minutes. Add
    the chilies, ginger, and paprika and stir-fry for 30 seconds. Add the cabbage, mushrooms, and
    carrot and stir-fry for 4 minutes, adding a little more oil if necessary.
2   Stir in the tomato paste or ketchup, soy sauce, and rice, and mix until the rice is heated through
    and coated with the sauce. Season to taste with salt and pepper, then stir in the tofu. Scatter
    the crisp-fried onion over the top and serve hot.

131   stir-fried rice with seafood

PREPARATION TIME: *20 minutes*   **COOKING TIME:** *25 minutes*

1½ cups long-grain rice, rinsed
3 cups water
salt and freshly ground black pepper
2 tbsp light soy sauce
2 tbsp ketchup
2 tbsp fish sauce
2 tbsp peanut oil
3 shallots, minced
2-inch piece fresh ginger,
  peeled and grated

2 hot red chilies, seeded
  and thinly sliced
10 oz thick white fish fillet,
  cut into large bite-sized pieces
16 raw jumbo shrimp, peeled
6 squid, cleaned and cut into rings
handful of cilantro leaves,
  roughly chopped

1   Put the rice in a saucepan and cover with the water. Season to taste with salt and bring to a
    boil, then reduce the heat, cover, and simmer until the water has been absorbed and the rice is
    tender, 10–12 minutes. Remove the pan from the heat and let stand, covered, for 5 minutes.
    Transfer the rice to a bowl and let cool, fluffing it up occasionally with a fork.
2   Mix together the soy sauce, ketchup, and fish sauce in a small bowl and set on one side.
3   Heat a wok until hot. Add half the oil, then toss in the shallots and stir-fry them for 2 minutes.
    Mix in the ginger and chilies and stir-fry for 30 seconds. Add the cooked rice and the soy sauce
    mixture and heat through, stirring frequently. Remove from the wok, season to taste with salt
    and pepper, and keep warm.
4   Heat the remaining oil in the wok, add the fish, and cook for 3 minutes, turning occasionally
    and gently to avoid breaking up the fish. Remove from the wok. Add the shrimp and squid to the
    wok, with a little more oil, if necessary, and stir-fry for 2 minutes. Combine the seafood with
    the warm rice, stir in the cilantro, and serve.

132 egg-fried rice with pork & cashews

PREPARATION TIME: *15 minutes* **COOKING TIME:** *18 minutes*

1½ cups basmati rice, rinsed

3 cups water

salt and freshly ground black pepper

2 tbsp peanut oil

1 clove garlic, chopped

1-inch piece fresh ginger, peeled
and minced

4 scallions, sliced diagonally

8 ears baby corn, sliced lengthwise

10 oz Chinese barbecued pork, diced

2 tbsp Chinese cooking wine
or dry sherry

2 tbsp light soy sauce

2 tsp toasted sesame oil

2 eggs, lightly beaten

large handful of roasted unsalted
cashew nuts, chopped

1   Put the rice in a saucepan and cover with the water. Season to taste with salt and bring to a
boil, then reduce the heat, cover, and simmer until the water has been absorbed and the rice is
tender, 10–12 minutes. Remove the pan from the heat and let stand, covered, for 5 minutes.
Transfer the rice to a bowl and let cool, fluffing it up occasionally with a fork.

2   Heat the oil in a wok. Add the garlic, ginger, and scallions and stir-fry for 30 seconds. Add the
baby corn and pork, and stir-fry for 2 minutes.

3   Add the cooked rice and stir-fry for 1 minute, then pour in the wine, soy sauce, and sesame oil.
Add the eggs and leave for a few seconds to let them start to set, then stir-fry until mixed
throughout the rice. Season to taste with salt and pepper and serve, topped with the toasted
cashew nuts.

133 aromatic spicy vegetable rice

PREPARATION TIME: *15 minutes* **COOKING TIME:** *25 minutes*

2 tbsp peanut oil

2 onions, chopped

1 tbsp mustard seeds

1 tsp cumin seeds

2 cloves garlic, chopped

2-inch piece fresh ginger,
   peeled and chopped

1 tsp ground coriander

1 tsp turmeric

6 curry leaves

1 yellow bell pepper, diced

8 cremini mushrooms, sliced

1½ cups basmati rice, rinsed

½ cup frozen petit pois (petite
   green peas)

3 cups vegetable stock

3 tomatoes, peeled, seeded,
   and diced

1 tbsp lemon juice

2 mildly hot, long, red chilies, seeded
   and chopped

handful of cilantro leaves,
   roughly chopped

salt and freshly ground black pepper

4 hard-cooked eggs,
   halved

1   Heat a wok until hot. Add the oil, then toss in the onions and stir-fry for 4 minutes. Add the mustard and cumin seeds and, when they start to pop and smell aromatic, stir in the garlic, ginger, ground coriander, turmeric, and curry leaves. Stir-fry for 1 minute.

2   Toss in the yellow pepper and mushrooms and stir-fry for 2–3 minutes, then add the rice and peas, and stir until they are coated with the spice mixture.

3   Add the stock and tomatoes and bring to a boil, then reduce the heat, cover, and simmer for 10 minutes. Stir in the lemon juice, chilies, and half of the cilantro. Cover and cook until the liquid has been absorbed and the rice is tender, about 5 minutes longer. Remove from the heat and let stand for 5 minutes before fluffing up the rice with a fork.

4   Season to taste with salt and pepper and serve with the halved eggs on top and the remaining cilantro sprinkled over.

134 vegetable pilau

PREPARATION TIME: *10 minutes* **COOKING TIME:** *20 minutes*

1½ cups basmati rice, rinsed

3 cups vegetable stock

salt and freshly ground black pepper

1 tbsp peanut oil

1 tbsp butter

2 tsp cumin seeds

1 tsp coriander seeds, crushed

1 onion, chopped

⅔ cup frozen petit pois (petite
   green peas)

1   Put the rice in a saucepan and cover with the stock. Season to taste with salt and bring to a boil, then reduce the heat, cover, and simmer until the stock has been absorbed and the rice is tender, 10–12 minutes. Remove the pan from the heat and let stand, covered, for 5 minutes. Transfer the rice to a bowl and let cool, fluffing it up occasionally with a fork.

2   Heat the oil and butter in a wok. Add the cumin and coriander seeds and stir-fry for 30 seconds. Add the onion and stir-fry for 5 minutes, then toss in the peas and stir-fry for 1 more minute. Mix in the cooked rice and heat through. Season to taste with salt and pepper and serve immediately.

135 stir-fried yellow bean rice

PREPARATION TIME: *10 minutes* **COOKING TIME:** *18 minutes*

1½ cups long-grain rice, rinsed
3 cups water, plus 3 tbsp
salt and freshly ground
    black pepper
2 tbsp sunflower oil
3 cloves garlic, chopped
3-inch piece fresh ginger, peeled
    and minced

5 leaves napa cabbage, shredded
1 small head Savoy cabbage, cored
    and shredded
5 tbsp yellow bean sauce
2 tbsp light soy sauce

1   Put the rice in a saucepan and cover with the 3 cups water. Season to taste with salt and bring
    to a boil, then reduce the heat, cover, and simmer until the water has been absorbed and the
    rice is tender, 10–12 minutes. Remove the pan from the heat and let stand, covered, for
    5 minutes. Transfer the rice to a bowl and let cool, fluffing it up occasionally with a fork.
2   Heat a wok until hot. Add the oil, then toss in the garlic and ginger and stir-fry for 30 seconds.
    Add the napa cabbage and Savoy cabbage and stir-fry for 2 minutes longer.
3   Add the cooked rice and spoon in the yellow bean sauce, 3 tablespoons water, and the soy
    sauce. Stir well until the rice is coated with the sauce and heated through. Season to taste
    with salt and pepper, then serve immediately.

136 thai-style rice with egg

PREPARATION TIME: *10 minutes* **COOKING TIME:** *10 minutes*

2 tbsp sunflower oil
1 tsp toasted sesame oil
2 handfuls of fine green beans, trimmed
4 Asian red shallots, sliced
3 cloves garlic, chopped
1 mildly hot, long, red chili, seeded
    and thinly sliced

12 shiitake mushrooms, sliced
3 small heads bok choy, sliced
2 tbsp sweet chili sauce
3 tbsp dark soy sauce
3 heaped cups cooked brown rice
4 eggs, fried
handful of Thai basil leaves

1   Heat a wok until hot. Add the oils, then toss in the green beans and stir-fry them for 2 minutes.
    Remove from the wok using a slotted spoon and drain on paper towels. Set on one side and
    keep warm.
2   Put the shallots into the wok and stir-fry for 2 minutes. Add the garlic, chili, mushrooms, and
    bok choy, and stir-fry for 2 more minutes.
3   Stir in the sweet chili sauce, soy sauce, and rice. Toss until the rice is heated through. Divide
    among four warm serving bowls. Top each serving with a spoonful of green beans and a fried
    egg. Scatter the basil over the bowls and serve.

137 spiced coconut rice

PREPARATION TIME: *10 minutes* **COOKING TIME:** *20 minutes*

1 cup basmati rice, rinsed
⅔ cup coconut cream
1¼ cups water
1 tsp salt
1 tbsp peanut oil
1 tsp cumin seeds
1 tsp fenugreek seeds

3 cardamom pods, split
  and seeds crushed
1-inch piece fresh ginger, peeled
  and minced
1 hot red chili, minced
2 tbsp dried shredded coconut
handful of cilantro leaves,
  roughly chopped

1   Put the rice in a saucepan. Mix together the coconut cream and water and pour into the pan,
    then add the salt. Bring to a boil, then reduce the heat, cover, and simmer until the liquid is
    absorbed and the rice is tender, 10–12 minutes. Remove from the heat and set aside for
    5 minutes, then fluff up the rice with a fork and let cool slightly.
2   Heat the oil in a wok. Add the cumin, fenugreek, and cardamom seeds and stir-fry them for
    30 seconds. Stir in the ginger, chili, and half of the shredded coconut.
3   Add the coconut rice and mix thoroughly until well combined. Serve with the remaining coconut
    and chopped cilantro sprinkled over.

138 tandoori chicken with rice

PREPARATION TIME: *10 minutes* **COOKING TIME:** *20 minutes*

1½ cups basmati rice, rinsed
3 cups water
salt and freshly ground black pepper
1 tbsp peanut oil
2 tbsp butter

1 onion, minced
1 tbsp tandoori curry powder
1 lb cooked tandoori chicken pieces

1   Put the rice in a saucepan and cover with the water. Season to taste with salt and bring to a
    boil, then reduce the heat, cover, and simmer until the water has been absorbed and the rice is
    tender, 10–12 minutes. Remove the pan from the heat and let stand, covered, for 5 minutes.
    Transfer the rice to a bowl and let cool, fluffing it up occasionally with a fork.
2   Heat the oil and butter in a large wok, add the onion, and stir-fry for 5 minutes, then stir in
    the curry powder.
3   Mix in the cooked rice and heat through, stirring constantly to coat with the buttery spice
    mixture. Season to taste with salt and pepper, then transfer to a serving bowl and keep warm.
4   Pour a little extra oil into the wok and add the chicken. Stir-fry until heated through. Lift out of
    the wok with a slotted spoon, put on top of the rice, and serve.

142 shrimp & coconut pilaff

PREPARATION TIME: *10 minutes* **COOKING TIME:** *24 minutes*

1½ cups basmati rice, rinsed
1 cinnamon stick
2 whole cloves
3 cups water, plus 5 tbsp
salt and freshly ground
   black pepper
2 tbsp peanut oil
1 onion, minced
1 tbsp cumin seeds
3 cloves garlic, chopped

3-inch piece fresh ginger, peeled
   and grated
10 curry leaves
1 tsp turmeric
8 cremini mushrooms, sliced
14 oz canned coconut milk
10 oz raw tiger shrimp, peeled
6 oz spinach, tough stems removed
   and leaves shredded (about 3 cups)

1. Put the rice, cinnamon stick, and cloves in a saucepan and cover with the 3 cups water. Season to taste with salt and bring to a boil, then reduce the heat, cover, and simmer until the water has been absorbed and the rice is tender, 10–12 minutes. Remove the pan from the heat and let stand, covered, for 5 minutes. Transfer the rice to a bowl and let cool, fluffing it up occasionally with a fork.

2. Heat a wok until hot. Add the oil, then toss in the onion and stir-fry it for 3 minutes. Add the cumin seeds, garlic, ginger, curry leaves, and turmeric and stir-fry for 30 seconds. Add the mushrooms and cook for 1 minute longer.

3. Pour in the coconut milk and the remaining 5 tablespoons of water. Bring to a boil, then reduce the heat and simmer for 5 minutes. Stir in the cooked rice, shrimp, and spinach, and cook, stirring frequently, for a few more minutes until the rice is heated through, the shrimp are pink, and the spinach has wilted. Season to taste with salt and pepper, and serve.

143 thai fried rice with chicken

PREPARATION TIME: *15 minutes* **COOKING TIME:** *20 minutes*

2 tsp fish sauce
1 tsp palm sugar or light brown sugar
3 tbsp light soy sauce
juice of 1 lime
1½ cups Thai jasmine rice, rinsed
3 cups water
2 tbsp sunflower oil
12 oz skinless, boneless chicken
   breast, cut into strips

4 Asian red shallots, sliced
2 cloves garlic, chopped
2 hot red chilies, thinly sliced
1 large red bell pepper, diced
10 cremini mushrooms, sliced
8 ears baby corn, sliced lengthwise
salt and freshly ground black pepper
handful each of basil and cilantro leaves,
   roughly chopped

1. Mix together the fish sauce, sugar, soy sauce, and lime juice in a small bowl and set on one side.

2. Put the rice in a saucepan and cover with the water. Bring to a boil, then reduce the heat, cover, and simmer until the water has been absorbed and the rice is tender, 10–12 minutes. Remove the pan from the heat and let stand, covered, for 5 minutes. Transfer the rice to a bowl and let cool, fluffing it up occasionally with a fork.

3. Heat a wok until hot. Add the oil, then toss in the chicken and stir-fry it until golden and cooked through, 3–4 minutes. Remove from the wok using a slotted spoon and set on one side.

4. Put the shallots, garlic, chilies, and red pepper into the wok and stir-fry for 1 minute. Add the mushrooms and baby corn and stir-fry for 2 minutes longer. Return the chicken to the wok, then stir in the fish sauce mixture. Mix in the cooked rice and heat through. Season to taste with salt and pepper, stir in the chopped basil and cilantro, and serve immediately.

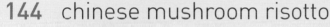

144 chinese mushroom risotto

PREPARATION TIME: *15 minutes, plus 20 minutes soaking time* **COOKING TIME:** *35 minutes*

12 dried shiitake mushrooms
2 tbsp sunflower oil
1 large onion, minced
2 cloves garlic, chopped
2-inch piece fresh ginger, peeled
   and minced
1½ cups sliced cremini mushrooms
2 cups sliced oyster mushrooms
2½ cups risotto rice

¾ cup Chinese rice wine
   or dry sherry
5 cups hot vegetable stock
salt and freshly ground black pepper
2 handfuls of basil leaves, torn
2 handfuls of cilantro leaves,
   roughly chopped
2 handfuls of Chinese chives, snipped
soy sauce for sprinkling

1 Put the dried shiitake mushrooms in a bowl, pour in enough hot water to cover, and let soak until softened, about 20 minutes. Drain, reserving the soaking liquid. Remove the mushroom stems and discard them. Slice the caps and set on one side.

2 Heat a wok until hot. Add the oil, then toss in the onion and stir-fry it for 4 minutes. Add the garlic, ginger, and all the mushrooms, and stir-fry for 3 minutes. Mix in the rice and cook until the grains are translucent, about 1 more minute.

3 Pour in the wine and bring to a boil, then reduce the heat and cook, stirring, until the wine has been absorbed. Strain the mushroom soaking liquid and combine with the stock. Add the stock a little at a time and simmer, stirring, until all the liquid is absorbed and the rice is tender, 20–25 minutes. Season to taste with salt and pepper and stir in the basil, cilantro, and chives. Sprinkle a little soy sauce over the top and serve.

CHAPTER 4

MEAT

India, Thailand, China, Japan, Malaysia, and Indonesia are just a few of the Asian countries that have inspired the recipes in this chapter. Each national cuisine has its own distinctive characteristics, but they all demonstrate the subtle balance of taste sensations—sweet, sour, hot, and salty—that are key to fine Asian cooking.

Asia's many tempting meat dishes clearly demonstrate the diversity of food from this corner of the world. Quickly prepared stir-fries and slow-cooked stews are created by infusing carefully selected cuts of beef, pork, lamb, and other meats with flavorings such as tamarind, lime, lemongrass, chilies, soy sauce, mirin, garlic, ginger, and coconut. Try the classic Indian curry, Lamb Rogan Josh, in which succulent chunks of meat are simmered in a spicy yogurt sauce, or travel to China for fragrant Five-Spice Pork with Choy Sum, or to Japan for appetizing Beef with Lime and Sesame Marinade.

Always choose meat that suits the cooking technique being used (see pages 12–13). Successful stir-frying demands really lean, tender meat, preferably cut across the grain to prevent it from drying out. Marinating meat before cooking helps to tenderize it and will add flavor, too.

145 braised beef with butternut squash

PREPARATION TIME: *15 minutes* **COOKING TIME:** *35 minutes*

3 tbsp sunflower oil

1¼ lb boneless beef chuck steak,
   cut into ¾-inch cubes

2 onions, sliced

1 medium-sized butternut squash,
   peeled and cubed

3 star anise

1 tsp Chinese five-spice

2-inch piece fresh ginger,
   peeled and finely sliced

2 cups water

5 tbsp dark soy sauce

5 tbsp Chinese rice wine or dry sherry

2 tsp sugar

1   Heat a wok until hot. Add 2 tablespoons of the oil, then add half of the beef and sear it until
    browned all over. Remove the beef using a slotted spoon and set on one side. Repeat with
    the remaining beef.

2   Put the onions in the wok and cook over medium heat for about 4 minutes. Add the squash, star
    anise, five-spice, and ginger, and stir-fry for 1 minute.

3   Add the water, soy sauce, wine, and sugar, then add the beef. Bring to a boil, reduce the heat,
    cover, and simmer for 15 minutes. Uncover and cook until the liquid has reduced slightly.
    Season to taste with salt and pepper, and serve.

146 sweet & sour pork

PREPARATION TIME: *15 minutes* **COOKING TIME:** *15 minutes*

5 tbsp fresh orange juice

3 tbsp light soy sauce

1 tbsp honey

2 tbsp rice vinegar

2 tsp cornstarch

2 tbsp vegetable oil

1¼ lb boneless pork loin, thinly sliced
   across the grain

1 large onion, thinly sliced

8 cremini mushrooms, sliced

2 carrots, sliced diagonally

2 zucchini, sliced diagonally

large handful of beansprouts

1   Mix together the orange juice, soy sauce, honey, rice vinegar, and cornstarch in a small bowl
    and set on one side.

2   Heat a wok until hot. Add the oil, then add half the pork and stir-fry it until browned all over,
    3–4 minutes. Remove from the wok using a slotted spoon and set on one side. Repeat with the
    remaining pork.

3   Put the onion into the wok and stir-fry for 2 minutes. Add the mushrooms, carrots, and zucchini,
    and stir-fry for 2–3 minutes longer.

4   Return the pork to the wok and stir in the beansprouts. Pour in the orange juice mixture and
    let it bubble, stirring, until the sauce has thickened. Add a little water if the sauce becomes
    too thick, then serve.

147 pork, napa cabbage & peanuts

PREPARATION TIME: *15 minutes, plus 30 minutes marinating time* **COOKING TIME:** *8 minutes*

1 egg white, lightly beaten
4 tbsp Chinese rice wine or dry sherry
2 tbsp light soy sauce
4 tbsp water
1 tbsp cornstarch
1¼ lb boneless pork loin, thinly sliced
  across the grain
2 tbsp sunflower oil

4 scallions, sliced diagonally
2 cloves garlic, chopped
2-inch piece fresh ginger,
  peeled and minced
5 leaves napa cabbage, shredded
handful of unsalted peanuts, toasted

1 Mix together the egg white, half the wine, the soy sauce, water, and cornstarch in a bowl. Add the pork and stir until well coated. Let marinate for 30 minutes.

2 Heat a wok until hot. Add the oil, then toss in the scallions, garlic, ginger, and cabbage, and stir-fry for 30 seconds. Lift the pork out of the marinade using a slotted spoon, add to the wok, and stir-fry until browned on both sides, 3–4 minutes.

3 Pour in the remaining wine and the marinade and stir-fry until reduced and thickened. Serve sprinkled with the toasted peanuts.

148 vietnamese beef with peppers

PREPARATION TIME: *15 minutes* **COOKING TIME:** *11 minutes*

2 tbsp vegetable oil
1¼ lb boneless sirloin steak, thinly
  sliced across the grain
4 Asian red shallots, chopped
1 yellow bell pepper, sliced
3 cloves garlic, chopped
2 hot red chilies, seeded and thinly
  sliced into rounds

4 tbsp dark soy sauce
1 tbsp fish sauce
2 tbsp lime juice
2 tbsp palm sugar or light
  brown sugar
2 scallions, shredded
1 large carrot, cut into ribbons using
  a potato peeler

1 Heat a wok until hot. Add the oil, then add half of the beef and stir-fry it until browned on both sides, 1–2 minutes. Remove from the wok using a slotted spoon and set on one side. Repeat with the remaining beef.

2 Put the shallots and yellow pepper in the wok and stir-fry for 2 minutes. Add the garlic and chilies and stir-fry for about 30 seconds.

3 Stir in the soy sauce, fish sauce, lime juice, and sugar, then return the beef to the wok. Toss the beef until it is mixed with the sauce, then cover the wok and simmer, stirring occasionally, until the beef is coated in a thick, glossy sauce, about 4 minutes. Serve sprinkled with the scallions and carrot ribbons.

149 lamb kofta in spiced tomato sauce

PREPARATION TIME: *10 minutes, plus 30 minutes chilling time* COOKING TIME: *45 minutes*

1 lb lean ground lamb
2 onions, minced
large handful of cilantro leaves, roughly
    chopped, plus extra for garnish
2-inch piece fresh ginger,
    peeled and grated
1 tsp hot chili powder
salt and freshly ground black pepper

2–3 tbsp sunflower oil
2 cloves garlic, chopped
2 tsp garam masala
1 tsp ground coriander
1 tsp ground cumin
14 oz canned crushed tomatoes
1¼ cups water
4 tbsp plain yogurt

1   Put the ground lamb, 1 onion, the cilantro, ginger, chili powder, and salt and pepper to taste in
    a food processor or blender and process to form a coarse paste. Form the mixture into 16 balls,
    place on a plate, cover, and chill for 30 minutes.
2   Heat 2 tablespoons of the oil in a wok and fry half the lamb balls (kofta), turning them
    occasionally, until golden all over, about 10 minutes. Remove from the wok with a slotted spoon
    and drain on paper towels. Repeat with the remaining kofta.
3   Add the extra oil to the wok, if necessary, and stir-fry the remaining onion for 4 minutes, then
    add the garlic, garam masala, and ground coriander and cumin. Pour in the tomatoes and water
    and bring to a boil, then reduce the heat, cover, and simmer until the sauce has reduced and
    thickened, 10–15 minutes.
4   Season to taste with salt and pepper and stir in the yogurt. Add the kofta and heat through
    gently for a few minutes. Sprinkle with some cilantro leaves and serve.

150 thai-style beef with broccoli

PREPARATION TIME: *15 minutes* COOKING TIME: *10 minutes*

12 oz broccoli, cut into
    small florets
2 tbsp sunflower oil
2 tsp toasted sesame oil
1¼ lb boneless sirloin steak,
    thinly sliced across the grain
2 stalks lemongrass,
    peeled and crushed

4 kaffir lime leaves
4 cloves garlic, minced
3-inch piece fresh ginger,
    peeled and minced
1 red bell pepper, sliced
4 scallions, sliced diagonally
1 tsp dried chili flakes
4 tbsp light soy sauce

1   Plunge the broccoli into a pan of boiling water. Cook for 2 minutes, then drain and rinse under
    cold running water. Set on one side.
2   Heat a wok until hot. Add the oils, then add half of the beef and stir-fry it until browned on both
    sides, 1–2 minutes. Remove from the wok with a slotted spoon and set on one side. Repeat
    with the remaining beef.
3   Put the lemongrass, lime leaves, garlic, and ginger into the wok and stir-fry for 30 seconds. Add
    the red pepper, scallions, chili flakes, and broccoli, and stir-fry for 2 minutes. Return the beef to
    the wok, add the soy sauce, and stir-fry for 1 more minute. Remove the lemongrass and kaffir
    lime leaves and serve.

151 pork jungle curry

PREPARATION TIME: *20 minutes* **COOKING TIME:** *22 minutes*

2 tbsp vegetable oil
1½ lb boneless pork loin, cut
    into ¾-inch cubes
1 large onion, finely sliced
10 oz broccoli florets
    (about 3 cups)
2 cloves garlic, chopped
1 recipe quantity Jungle Curry Paste
    (see page 14)
1½ cups chicken stock

1 tbsp fish sauce
3½ tbsp ground candlenuts
    or almonds
½ cup canned bamboo shoots,
    drained and rinsed
juice of 1 lime
salt and freshly ground
    black pepper

1   Heat a wok until hot. Add the oil, then add half of the pork and stir-fry it until browned all over, 3–4 minutes. Remove from the wok with a slotted spoon and set on one side. Repeat with the remaining pork.

2   Add the onion to the wok and stir-fry for 3 minutes, then toss in the broccoli and cook, stirring, for 2 minutes longer. Stir in the garlic and curry paste and cook, stirring, for 3 minutes.

3   Return the pork to the wok along with the stock, fish sauce, nuts, and bamboo shoots, and bring to a boil. Reduce the heat and simmer, covered, for 5 minutes. Stir in the lime juice, season to taste with salt and pepper, and serve.

152 stir-fried lamb with scallions

PREPARATION TIME: *15 minutes, plus 1 hour marinating time* **COOKING TIME:** *8 minutes*

5 tbsp Chinese rice wine or dry sherry
3 tbsp light soy sauce
2 tsp toasted sesame oil
1½ lb boneless lamb loin, thinly sliced
   across the grain
2 tbsp sunflower oil
3 cloves garlic, chopped

2-inch piece fresh ginger, peeled
   and grated
6 scallions, white and green parts
   separated and sliced diagonally
12 oz gai lan (Chinese kale), trimmed
salt and freshly ground black pepper

1   Mix together the wine, soy sauce, and sesame oil in a shallow dish. Add the lamb and turn until coated. Let marinate for at least 1 hour. Drain, reserving the marinade.

2   Heat a wok until hot. Add the sunflower oil, then add half of the lamb and stir-fry it over high heat for 2 minutes until well browned. Remove using a slotted spoon and set on one side. Repeat with the remaining lamb.

3   Reduce the heat to medium, toss in the garlic, ginger, and white part of the scallions, and stir-fry for 30 seconds. Add the gai lan and stir-fry for 2 minutes longer.

4   Return the lamb to the wok and pour in the marinade. Stir-fry for 1 more minute. Season to taste with salt and pepper and serve, sprinkled with the green part of the scallions.

153 pork & pineapple red curry

PREPARATION TIME: *20 minutes* **COOKING TIME:** *26 minutes*

2 tbsp sunflower oil
1½ lb boneless pork loin, cut into
   ¾-inch cubes
1 large onion, sliced
1 recipe quantity Thai Red Curry Paste
   (see page 15)
1¼ cups coconut milk
1 cup water

1 tbsp palm sugar or
   light brown sugar
1 tbsp fish sauce
2 tbsp light soy sauce
juice of 1 lime
1 small pineapple, peeled,
   cored, and cut into chunks
salt

1   Heat a wok until hot. Add the oil, then add half of the pork and stir-fry it until browned all over, 3–4 minutes. Remove using a slotted spoon and set aside. Repeat with the remaining pork.

2   Put the onion into the wok and stir-fry for 3 minutes, then stir in the curry paste and cook for 2 minutes longer. Pour in the coconut milk and water and stir, then add the sugar, fish sauce, and soy sauce. Return the pork to the wok. Bring to a boil, then reduce the heat and simmer over low heat for 10 minutes. Cover the wok if the curry becomes too dry.

3   Add the lime juice and pineapple and simmer for 2 minutes longer. Season to taste with salt and serve.

154   singapore pork

PREPARATION TIME: *15 minutes, plus 30 minutes marinating time*   **COOKING TIME:** *16 minutes*

1½ lb boneless pork loin, cut into ½-inch
   slices across the grain
4 tbsp dark soy sauce
3 tbsp sunflower oil
2 onions, thinly sliced
2–3 mildly hot, red chilies, seeded and
   thinly sliced

2 tbsp palm sugar or light
   brown sugar
½ cup water
juice of 2 limes
handful of cilantro leaves,
   roughly chopped

1   Put the pork and the soy sauce in a bowl and turn to coat the pork well, then let marinate for
   30 minutes. Remove the pork from the marinade using tongs.

2   Heat a wok until hot. Add the oil, then add half of the pork and stir-fry it until browned,
   3–4 minutes. Remove using a slotted spoon and set aside. Repeat with the remaining pork.

3   Put the onions into the wok and stir-fry for 3 minutes, then add the chilies and stir-fry for
   30 seconds longer.

4   Return the pork to the wok and stir in the sugar, water, and soy sauce marinade. Stir-fry until
   the sauce has thickened and reduced, about 4 minutes. Stir in the lime juice and serve,
   sprinkled with chopped cilantro.

155   korean-style marinated pork

PREPARATION TIME: *12 minutes, plus 1 hour marinating time*   **COOKING TIME:** *20 minutes*

1½ lb boneless pork loin, sliced into
   strips across the grain
2 tbsp peanut oil
3 scallions, white and green parts
   separated and shredded
2 tbsp sesame seeds
Asian chili sauce for serving

MARINADE:
4 tbsp light soy sauce
3 tbsp dark soy sauce
2 tbsp palm sugar or light brown sugar
2 cloves garlic, sliced
2-inch piece fresh ginger, peeled
   and minced
1 tbsp toasted sesame oil

1   Mix together the ingredients for the marinade in a shallow dish. Add the pork and turn until
   coated. Let marinate for at least 1 hour. Drain, reserving the marinade.

2   Heat a wok until hot. Add the oil, then add half of the pork and stir-fry it until browned,
   3–4 minutes. Remove with a slotted spoon and set aside. Repeat with the remaining pork.

3   Put the white part of the scallions into the wok and stir-fry for 30 seconds, then pour in the
   reserved marinade and heat through. Return the pork to the wok and stir-fry until the meat is
   coated in a glossy sauce, 1–2 minutes. Serve sprinkled with the green part of the scallions and
   sesame seeds, with a bowl of chili sauce on the side.

156 five-spice pork with choy sum

PREPARATION TIME: *15 minutes* **COOKING TIME:** *45 minutes*

2½ cups chicken stock
4 tbsp light soy sauce
6 tbsp Chinese rice wine
   or dry sherry
2-inch piece fresh ginger, peeled
   and minced
2 star anise
1 tsp Chinese five-spice
4 large strips of orange zest

1½ tbsp palm sugar or
   light brown sugar
1½ tbsp sunflower oil
1¼ lb pork tenderloin
5 scallions, sliced diagonally
1 large red bell pepper, sliced
12 oz choy sum (Chinese flowering
   cabbage), stems sliced and
   leaves left whole

1   Put the stock, soy sauce, wine, ginger, star anise, five-spice, and orange zest in a large saucepan. Bring to a boil, then stir in the sugar. Reduce the heat and simmer for 5 minutes, then strain and set on one side.

2   Heat a large wok until hot. Add the oil, then add the pork and fry it over high heat until it is browned on all sides. Pour in the stock, cover, and simmer for 25 minutes, turning the pork from time to time.

3   Remove the pork from the wok with a slotted spoon; set on one side and keep warm. Add the scallions, red pepper, and choy sum to the wok and simmer until tender, about 4 minutes.

4   Slice the pork and divide among four warm serving bowls. Spoon the vegetables and stock over the pork and serve.

157 black bean & scallion pork

PREPARATION TIME: *15 minutes* **COOKING TIME:** *12 minutes*

6 tbsp black bean sauce
3 tbsp light soy sauce
2 tbsp Chinese rice wine or dry sherry
4 tbsp water
1 tbsp sunflower oil
2 tsp toasted sesame oil
1½ lb lean pork tenderloin,
   thinly sliced across the grain

2-inch piece fresh ginger,
   peeled and minced
2 cloves garlic, chopped
5 scallions, white and green parts
   separated and sliced diagonally
large handful of snow peas, trimmed

1 Mix together the black bean sauce, soy sauce, wine, and water in a small bowl and set
   on one side.
2 Heat a wok until hot. Add the oils, then add half of the pork and stir-fry it until browned,
   3–4 minutes. Remove from the wok using a slotted spoon and set on one side. Repeat with
   the remaining pork.
3 Toss the ginger, garlic, white part of the scallions and the snow peas into the wok and stir-fry
   for 1 minute, then return the pork to the wok along with the black bean sauce mixture. Stir-fry
   until the sauce has thickened, about 1–2 minutes. Scatter the green part of the scallions over
   the top and serve.

158 simple lamb curry

PREPARATION TIME: *20 minutes* **COOKING TIME:** *1 hour, 18 minutes*

1½ lb boneless leg of lamb, cut into
   ¾-inch cubes, fat trimmed
2 tbsp peanut oil
1 large onion, chopped
2 cloves garlic, chopped
1-inch piece fresh ginger, peeled
   and grated
2 mildly hot, long, red chilies,
   minced

1 tsp salt
1 tsp turmeric
1 tbsp ground coriander
1 tbsp garam masala
1 cup tomato purée or sauce
3¼ cups hot water
juice of 1 lime
2 handfuls of cilantro leaves,
   roughly chopped

1 Gently heat a wok until hot. Add the lamb and cook over medium to low heat until well
   browned. Remove the lamb using a slotted spoon and set on one side. Wipe the wok clean.
2 Heat the oil in the wok, add the onion, and stir-fry for 4 minutes. Stir in the garlic, ginger,
   chilies, salt, turmeric, ground coriander, and garam masala. Pour in the tomato purée and half
   the water and heat until the oil begins to separate out from the liquid. Add the lamb and cook
   for 5 minutes longer.
3 Add the rest of the water, the lime juice, and one handful of cilantro. Bring to a boil,
   then reduce the heat, cover, and simmer for 1 hour. Serve sprinkled with the remaining
   chopped cilantro.

159 spicy lamb stir-fry with coconut relish

PREPARATION TIME: *20 minutes, plus 1 hour chilling time* **COOKING TIME:** *12 minutes*

2 tbsp sunflower oil
1¼ lb boneless lamb loin, thinly
   sliced across the grain
1 large onion, sliced
1 red bell pepper, sliced
3 cloves garlic, chopped
1 tbsp cumin seeds
1 tbsp mustard seeds
salt and freshly ground black pepper

COCONUT RELISH:
½ cup dried shredded coconut
2 hot green chilies, minced
2 handfuls of cilantro leaves,
   roughly chopped
⅔ cup plain yogurt
juice of 1 lemon
½ tsp salt

1 Put the relish ingredients in a food processor and process until combined. Transfer to a bowl and leave in the refrigerator for 1 hour to let the relish thicken.

2 Heat a wok until hot. Add the oil, then add half of the lamb and stir-fry it for 2 minutes. Remove from the wok using a slotted spoon and set on one side. Repeat with the remaining lamb.

3 Put the onion into the wok and stir-fry for 3 minutes. Add the red pepper, garlic, and cumin and mustard seeds and stir-fry for 2 minutes longer. Return the lamb to the wok and stir-fry for 2 more minutes, adding a little water if the stir-fry is too dry. Season to taste with salt and pepper and serve with the chilled coconut relish.

160 pork stir-fry with sweet & spicy sauce

PREPARATION TIME: *15 minutes* **COOKING TIME:** *14 minutes*

5 tbsp light soy sauce
5 tbsp Chinese rice wine
   or dry sherry
2 tbsp palm sugar or
   light brown sugar
juice of 1 lime
1 tbsp sunflower oil
1 tbsp toasted sesame oil
1¼ lb lean pork tenderloin,
   thinly sliced across the grain

2 handfuls of fine green beans,
   trimmed and halved diagonally
2-inch piece fresh ginger,
   peeled and minced
2 large, mildly hot, red chilies, seeded
   and finely sliced
2 cloves garlic, sliced
½ tsp Chinese five-spice

1 Mix together the soy sauce, wine, sugar, and lime juice in a small bowl and set on one side.

2 Heat a large wok until hot. Add the oils, then add half of the pork and stir-fry it until well browned, 3–4 minutes. Remove from the wok using a slotted spoon and set on one side. Repeat with the remaining pork.

3 Toss the beans into the wok and stir-fry for 2 minutes. Add the ginger, chilies, and garlic and stir-fry for 30 seconds. Return the pork to the wok along with the five-spice and soy sauce mixture. Stir-fry until the sauce has thickened slightly, about 2 minutes, then serve.

161 beef rendang

PREPARATION TIME: *25 minutes* **COOKING TIME:** *2 hours, 25 minutes*

2 tbsp peanut oil
1 large onion, minced
1¼ lb boneless beef chuck or brisket,
　　cut into 1-inch cubes
5 cloves garlic, chopped
2-inch piece fresh ginger,
　　peeled and minced
2 stalks lemongrass, peeled and bruised
3 small, hot red chilies, seeded
　　and minced

4 cardamom pods, split
2 tsp ground turmeric
1 tsp ground coriander
1 tsp hot chili powder
1 tsp ground cumin
1¾ cups water
1½ cups coconut milk
2 tbsp ground almonds
salt
2 tbsp dried shredded coconut, toasted

1　Heat a wok until hot. Add the oil, then toss in the onion and stir-fry it until softened, about
　4 minutes. Add half of the beef and sear it on each side for 1–2 minutes. Remove from the wok
　with a slotted spoon and set aside.
2　Sear the remaining beef, then return the first batch of beef to the wok. Add the garlic, ginger,
　lemongrass, chilies, and spices and cook, stirring, for 1 minute.
3　Pour in the water and coconut milk. Bring to a boil, then reduce the heat to very low, cover, and
　simmer for 2 hours. Stir occasionally and add extra water if the curry seems too dry.
4　Uncover, stir in the almonds, and cook for 5–10 minutes. Season to taste with salt and serve,
　sprinkled with the toasted coconut.

162 red-cooked beef

PREPARATION TIME: *10 minutes, plus 5 minutes infusing time* **COOKING TIME:** *25 minutes*

1¼ cups dark soy sauce
6 tbsp Shaoxing wine or medium sherry
4 star anise
½-inch piece fresh ginger,
　peeled and sliced
4 whole cloves

2 cinnamon sticks
grated zest of ½ lemon or orange
juice of 2 lemons or oranges
2 tsp sugar
1½ lb lean flank or skirt steak, cut
　into ¾-inch cubes

1 Put the soy sauce, wine, star anise, ginger, cloves, cinnamon, zest, juice, and sugar into a wok and bring to a boil. Remove from the heat and set aside for 5 minutes so the flavors can infuse.
2 Add the beef to the wok and spoon the soy mixture over the meat. Bring to a boil, then reduce the heat and simmer, covered, for 15–20 minutes, turning the meat halfway through the cooking time and occasionally spooning the sauce over.
3 Serve with a little of the sauce. The remaining sauce can be chilled or frozen for later use. It makes a good base for many meat and poultry dishes.

163 beef & shiitake stir-fry

PREPARATION TIME: *15 minutes* **COOKING TIME:** *10 minutes*

2 tbsp sunflower oil
1¼ lb boneless sirloin steak, thinly
　sliced across the grain
4 cloves garlic, minced
2-inch piece fresh ginger,
　peeled and minced

2 tsp Szechuan peppercorns,
　roasted and crushed
3½ cups sliced shiitake mushrooms
1 green bell pepper, sliced
4 scallions, sliced on the diagonal
3 tbsp light soy sauce
4 tbsp water

1 Heat a wok until hot. Add the oil, then add half of the beef and stir-fry it until browned, 1–2 minutes. Remove using a slotted spoon and set aside. Repeat with the remaining beef.
2 Add the garlic, ginger and Szechuan pepper to the wok and stir-fry for 30 seconds. Add more oil if necessary, then put the mushrooms, green pepper, and half the scallions into the wok and stir-fry for 2 minutes.
3 Return the beef to the wok along with the soy sauce and water. Stir-fry until the liquid has reduced, about 2 minutes. Serve immediately, sprinkled with the remaining scallions.

164 shredded beef in oyster sauce

PREPARATION TIME: *15 minutes* **COOKING TIME:** *8 minutes*

2 tbsp light soy sauce
4 tbsp oyster sauce
2 tbsp Chinese rice wine or dry sherry
2 tbsp sunflower oil
1¼ lb boneless sirloin steak, cut into
　fine strips

1 large onion, thinly sliced
2-inch piece fresh ginger, peeled
　and minced
1 mildly hot, long, red chili, seeded and
　thinly sliced
2 scallions, sliced diagonally

1 Mix together the soy sauce, oyster sauce, and rice wine in a small bowl.
2 Heat a wok until hot. Add half of the oil, then add half of the beef and stir-fry it until browned, about 1 minute, breaking up the meat if it sticks together. Remove from the wok with a slotted spoon and set on one side. Repeat with the remaining beef.
3 Heat the remaining oil in the wok, add the onion, and stir-fry for 3 minutes. Stir in the ginger and chili, then return the beef to the wok along with the soy sauce mixture and stir-fry for 2 minutes. Scatter the scallions over the beef and serve.

165 malaysian marinated chili pork

PREPARATION TIME: *10 minutes, plus 1 hour marinating time* COOKING TIME: *9 minutes*

1 lb boneless pork loin, thinly sliced
   across the grain
2 tbsp sunflower oil
1 onion, finely sliced

MARINADE:
1 tbsp sunflower oil
3 tbsp sambal oelek (Indonesian
   chili sauce)
juice of 1 lime
2-inch piece fresh ginger, peeled
   and minced
½ tsp turmeric

1 Mix together all the ingredients for the marinade in a shallow dish. Add the pork and turn until coated, then let marinate for 1 hour. Drain, reserving the marinade.

2 Heat a wok until hot. Add the oil, then add half of the pork and stir-fry it until browned, 3–4 minutes. Remove using a slotted spoon and set aside. Repeat with the remaining pork.

3 Add the onion to the wok and stir-fry for 3 minutes. Return the pork to the wok, pour in the reserved marinade, and stir-fry for 1 minute longer, then serve.

166 japanese beef with lime & sesame marinade

PREPARATION TIME: *15 minutes, plus 30 minutes marinating time* COOKING TIME: *3 minutes*

1½ lb lean beef tenderloin, thinly sliced
   across the grain
1½ tbsp sunflower oil
2 handfuls of beansprouts
2 tbsp sesame seeds

MARINADE:
1 tsp sansho pepper or ground
   black pepper
2 tsp toasted sesame oil
4 tbsp Japanese soy sauce
2 tbsp mirin or dry sherry
juice of 2 limes

1 Mix together the ingredients for the marinade in a shallow dish. Add the strips of beef and turn to coat them with the marinade. Let marinate for 30 minutes.

2 Heat a wok until hot, then add the sunflower oil. Lift the beef out of the marinade with a slotted spoon, add to the wok, and stir-fry until browned, 1–2 minutes. Add the beansprouts and the marinade and stir-fry for 1 minute longer. Serve with the sesame seeds sprinkled over.

167 lamb stir-fry with mixed peppers

PREPARATION TIME: *15 minutes* COOKING TIME: *11 minutes*

2 tbsp peanut oil
1 tbsp toasted sesame oil
1 lb boneless lamb loin, thinly sliced
   across the grain
1 red bell pepper, sliced
1 yellow bell pepper, sliced

4 cloves garlic, sliced
2-inch piece fresh ginger, peeled and
   cut into thin matchsticks
6 tbsp fresh orange juice
3 tbsp light soy sauce
freshly ground black pepper

1 Heat a wok until hot. Add the oils, then add half of the lamb and stir-fry it until browned, about 2 minutes. Remove from the wok using a slotted spoon and set on one side. Repeat with the remaining lamb.

2 Put the red and yellow peppers, garlic, and ginger into the wok and stir-fry for 2 minutes. Return the lamb to the wok, then pour in the orange juice and soy sauce and stir-fry for 2 minutes longer. Season to taste with pepper and serve.

168 aromatic chili bean lamb

PREPARATION TIME: *15 minutes, plus 1 hour marinating time* **COOKING TIME:** *9 minutes*

1 tbsp black vinegar

6 tbsp Chinese rice wine or dry sherry

1 tbsp palm sugar or light brown sugar

3 tbsp light soy sauce

1½ lb boneless lamb loin, thinly sliced
   across the grain

2 tbsp sunflower oil

12 oz napa cabbage, sliced
   (about 4 cups)

3 cloves garlic, chopped

2-inch piece fresh ginger, peeled
   and chopped

6 tbsp water

2 tbsp chili bean paste

1   Mix together the black vinegar, wine, sugar, and soy sauce in a shallow dish. Add the lamb and
    turn until coated. Let marinate for at least 1 hour. Drain, reserving the marinade.

2   Heat a wok until hot. Add the oil, then add half of the lamb and stir-fry it until browned, about
    2 minutes. Remove using a slotted spoon and set on one side. Repeat with the remaining lamb.

3   Add the napa cabbage, garlic, and ginger to the wok and stir-fry for 2 minutes. Pour in the
    reserved marinade and water, then add the bean paste and cook, stirring frequently, until the
    liquid has reduced and thickened, about 2 minutes longer. Serve immediately.

169 beef satay with snow peas

PREPARATION TIME: *15 minutes* **COOKING TIME:** *8 minutes*

3 tbsp smooth peanut butter
2 tbsp light soy sauce
1 tbsp fish sauce
6 tbsp hot water
¾ cup coconut milk
1 tbsp palm sugar or
   light brown sugar
1 tbsp sunflower oil
1½ lb boneless sirloin steak, cut into
   ½-inch strips across the grain

2 mildly hot, long, red chilies, seeded
   and thinly sliced into rounds
2 handfuls of snow peas
2-inch piece fresh ginger,
   peeled and minced
2 cloves garlic, minced
3 scallions, white and green parts
   separated and sliced diagonally
salt and freshly ground black pepper
handful of cilantro leaves,
   roughly chopped

1 Mix together the peanut butter, soy sauce, fish sauce, water, coconut milk, and sugar.
2 Heat a wok until hot. Add the oil, then add half of the beef and stir-fry it until browned,
   1–2 minutes. Remove with a slotted spoon and set aside. Repeat with the remaining beef.
3 Put the chilies and snow peas into the wok and stir-fry for 1 minute. Add the ginger, garlic, and
   the white part of the scallions, and stir-fry for another minute.
4 Return the beef to the wok, add the peanut butter mixture and season to taste with salt and
   pepper. Bring to a boil. Reduce the heat and simmer, covered, until the sauce has reduced and
   thickened, about 3 minutes. Add extra water if the sauce appears too thick. Sprinkle with the
   green part of the scallions and the chopped cilantro and serve.

170 thai coconut pork

PREPARATION TIME: *20 minutes* **COOKING TIME:** *30 minutes*

2 tbsp peanut oil
1½ lb boneless pork loin,
   cut into ¾-inch cubes
6 Asian red shallots, chopped
2 stalks lemongrass, peeled
   and bruised
4 kaffir lime leaves
4 garlic cloves, chopped
2-inch piece fresh ginger,
   peeled and grated

2 hot red chilies, seeded and chopped
1 red bell pepper, sliced
12 cremini mushrooms,
   halved or quartered if large
1 tbsp fish sauce
1¾ cups coconut milk
juice of 1 lime
salt
handful of cilantro leaves,
   roughly chopped

1 Heat a wok until hot. Add the oil, then add half of the pork and stir-fry it until browned,
   3–4 minutes. Remove from the wok using a slotted spoon, drain on paper towels, and set
   on one side. Repeat with the remaining pork.
2 Put the shallots into the wok and stir-fry for 2 minutes. Add the lemongrass, kaffir lime leaves,
   garlic, ginger, chilies, red pepper, and mushrooms, and stir-fry for 2 minutes longer.
3 Return the pork to the wok and pour in the fish sauce and coconut milk. Bring to a boil, then
   lower the heat and simmer until the sauce has reduced and thickened, 12–15 minutes. Stir
   in the lime juice, season to taste with salt, and serve sprinkled with the chopped cilantro.

171 pork & pineapple stir-fry
PREPARATION TIME: *20 minutes* **COOKING TIME:** *15 minutes*

2 tbsp sunflower oil
1¼ lb pork tenderloin,
    thinly sliced across the grain
4 Asian red shallots, finely sliced
2 cloves garlic, chopped
2 hot Thai chilies, seeded
    and minced
2 stalks lemongrass, peeled and bruised

10 oz gai lan (Chinese kale),
    stems trimmed
juice of 2 limes
2 tbsp fish sauce
1 small pineapple, peeled, cored,
    and cut into bite-sized pieces
2 handfuls of cilantro leaves,
    roughly chopped

1   Heat a wok until hot. Add the oil, then add half of the pork and stir-fry it until browned, 3–4 minutes. Remove using a slotted spoon and set aside. Repeat with the remaining pork.

2   Toss the shallots into the wok and stir-fry for 2 minutes. Add the garlic, chilies, lemongrass, and gai lan, and stir-fry for another 2 minutes. Add the lime juice, fish sauce, and pineapple, and stir-fry for 2 minutes longer. Serve immediately, sprinkled with the chopped cilantro.

172 pork with lime & ginger
PREPARATION TIME: *15 minutes* **COOKING TIME:** *11 minutes*

2 tbsp sunflower oil
1¼ lb boneless pork loin, thinly sliced
    across the grain
6 scallions, sliced diagonally
2-inch piece fresh ginger, peeled
    and minced
4 small, hot red chilies, seeded and
    minced

3 cloves garlic, minced
2 tbsp fish sauce
2 tsp sugar
grated zest of 1 lime and juice of 2
handful of cilantro leaves,
    roughly chopped
handful of unsalted cashew nuts,
    toasted and chopped

1   Heat a wok until hot. Add the oil, then add half of the pork and stir-fry it until browned, 3–4 minutes. Remove with a slotted spoon and set aside. Repeat with the remaining pork.

2   Add the scallions, ginger, chilies, and garlic to the wok and stir-fry for 30 seconds. Return the pork to the wok along with the fish sauce, sugar, and lime zest and juice. Stir until combined and heated through.

3   Mix in the cilantro and serve immediately with the cashew nuts sprinkled over the top.

173 thai beef red curry
PREPARATION TIME: *15 minutes* **COOKING TIME:** *28 minutes*

2 tbsp sunflower oil
1½ lb boneless beef chuck steak,
    cut into ¾-inch cubes
3 heaped tbsp Thai Red Curry Paste
    (see page 15)
1–2 hot Thai chilies, seeded
    and chopped

1½ cups coconut milk
1¼ cups chicken stock
12 oz baby new potatoes
3 cups shredded spinach leaves
salt and freshly ground black pepper
2 large handfuls of cilantro leaves,
    roughly chopped

1   Heat a wok until hot. Add the oil, then add half of the beef and stir-fry it until browned, 1–2 minutes. Remove using a slotted spoon and set aside. Repeat with the remaining beef.

2   Put the red curry paste and chilies into the wok and cook for 3 minutes, stirring. Pour in the coconut milk and stock and simmer, covered, for 5 minutes.

3   Return the beef to the wok, add the potatoes, and cook until the potatoes are tender, 10–15 minutes. Stir in the spinach and cook for 2 minutes longer. Season to taste with salt and pepper. Stir in the cilantro and serve.

174 ginger beef dumplings

PREPARATION TIME: *20 minutes, plus 30 minutes chilling time*   **COOKING TIME:** *25 minutes*

1 lb ground beef
4 scallions, chopped
3 cloves garlic, chopped
2 handfuls of cilantro leaves
1 mildly hot, long, red chili, seeded
   and chopped

2 stalks lemongrass, peeled and chopped
3-inch piece fresh ginger, peeled
   and chopped
salt and freshly ground black pepper
1 recipe quantity Nuac Cham (see
   page 149) for serving

1 Put all the ingredients, except the nuac cham dip, into a food processor or blender and process
   to form a coarse paste.
2 Tip the paste into a bowl and shape into 20 walnut-sized balls. Place on a plate, cover with
   plastic wrap, and chill for 30 minutes.
3 Put the beef dumplings into a large bamboo steamer. Cover and steam over a wok of simmering
   water until cooked through, about 6 minutes. You may need to steam the dumplings in batches,
   keeping them warm while the remainder cook. Serve with a dish of nuac cham.

175 stir-fried spicy lamb with chickpeas

PREPARATION TIME: *15 minutes*   **COOKING TIME:** *17 minutes*

2 tbsp peanut oil
1¼ lb boneless lamb loin,
   thinly sliced across the grain
1 large onion, thinly sliced
3 cloves garlic, chopped
1 large red bell pepper, sliced
4 tbsp curry paste

1 tbsp tomato paste
¾ cup water
14 oz canned chickpeas, drained
   and rinsed
juice of ½ lemon
salt and freshly ground black pepper

1 Heat a wok until hot. Add the oil, then add half of the lamb and stir-fry it until browned, about
   2 minutes. Remove using a slotted spoon and set on one side. Repeat with the remaining lamb.
2 Put the onion into the wok and stir-fry for 4 minutes. Add the garlic and red pepper and stir-fry
   for 1 minute longer.
3 Return the lamb to the wok and stir in the curry paste and tomato paste, then add the water
   and chickpeas. Cook, stirring frequently, for 5 minutes. Add the lemon juice, season to taste
   with salt and pepper, and serve.

176 sweet thai pork

PREPARATION TIME: *15 minutes, plus 30 minutes marinating time*   **COOKING TIME:** *12 minutes*

1¼ lb boneless pork loin,
   cut into ¾-inch cubes
2 tbsp light soy sauce
2 tbsp sunflower oil
1 onion, minced
2 carrots, sliced diagonally

1 tbsp palm sugar or
   light brown sugar
1 tbsp fish sauce
½ tsp freshly ground black pepper
½ cup water
2 handfuls of cilantro leaves,
   roughly chopped

1 Put the pork and soy sauce in a shallow dish and turn to coat the meat. Let marinate for
   30 minutes. Lift the pork out of the marinade using tongs. Reserve the marinade.
2 Heat a wok until hot. Add the oil, then toss in the onion and stir-fry it for 3 minutes. Add the
   carrots and cook for 2 minutes longer.
3 Add the pork, sugar, and fish sauce and stir-fry over high heat for 3 minutes. Add the soy sauce
   marinade, pepper, and water, and stir-fry until heated through, about 3 minutes. Serve sprinkled
   with the chopped cilantro.

177 teriyaki-style beef

PREPARATION TIME: *15 minutes, plus 1 hour marinating time* **COOKING TIME:** *6 minutes*

5 tbsp light soy sauce

2 tbsp sake

4 tbsp mirin or dry sherry

1 tbsp sugar

1¼ lb boneless sirloin steak, thinly
  sliced across the grain

2 tbsp sunflower oil

1 tsp toasted sesame oil

2 cloves garlic, chopped

2-inch piece fresh ginger, peeled
  and minced

10 oz fresh spinach leaves, tough
  stems removed

4 scallions, white and green parts
  separated and sliced diagonally

1 tbsp sesame seeds

1 Mix together the soy sauce, sake, mirin, and sugar in a shallow bowl. Add the beef and stir
  well until it is coated, then let marinate for 1 hour. Remove the beef from the marinade using
  a slotted spoon and reserve the marinade.

2 Heat a wok until hot. Add the oils, then add half of the beef and stir-fry it until browned,
  1–2 minutes. Remove from the wok using a slotted spoon and set on one side. Repeat with the
  remaining beef. While the second batch of beef is cooking, simmer the marinade in a small
  saucepan until reduced and slightly syrupy, stirring occasionally.

3 Add the garlic, ginger, spinach, and white part of the scallions to the hot wok and stir-fry for
  1 minute. Return the beef to the wok along with the marinade. Toss well until the beef is
  coated with the glossy sauce, then serve immediately, sprinkled with the sesame seeds and
  the green part of the scallions.

178 sticky pork with pepper

PREPARATION TIME: *15 minutes, plus 1 hour marinating time* **COOKING TIME:** *10 minutes*

1¼ lb boneless pork loin,
  thinly sliced across the grain

2 tbsp sunflower oil

1 large, green bell pepper, seeded and
  cut into bite-sized pieces

2 scallions, sliced into thin strips

MARINADE:

2 tbsp honey

4 tbsp Shaoxing wine or medium sherry

2-inch piece fresh ginger, peeled
  and minced

2 cloves garlic, chopped

3 tbsp light soy sauce

1 Mix together the ingredients for the marinade in a shallow dish. Add the pork and turn until
  coated, then let marinate for 1 hour. Drain, reserving the marinade.

2 Heat the oil in a wok until hot. Add half the pork and stir-fry until browned, 3–4 minutes.
  Remove the pork from the wok using a slotted spoon and set on one side. Repeat with the
  remaining pork.

3 Put the green pepper into the wok and stir-fry for 2 minutes. Pour in the marinade, then return
  the pork to the wok and stir-fry until the marinade has reduced and thickened. Serve with the
  scallions sprinkled over the top.

179 stir-fried beef in lettuce wrap

PREPARATION TIME: *15 minutes, plus 1 hour marinating time* **COOKING TIME:** *3 minutes*

1¼ lb boneless sirloin steak, thinly sliced
　across the grain
4 large iceberg lettuce leaves
4 scallions, shredded
2 handfuls of cilantro leaves, minced
4-inch piece English cucumber, seeded
　and thinly sliced
2 tsp toasted sesame oil
freshly ground black pepper

MARINADE:
2 tbsp light soy sauce
4 tbsp fresh orange juice
4 tbsp Chinese rice wine or dry sherry
2 tsp Sichuan pepper, toasted and ground
3 cloves garlic, chopped

1　Mix together the ingredients for the marinade in a shallow dish and add the beef. Stir, then let marinate for at least 1 hour.
2　Heat a wok over high heat. Add the beef and the marinade and stir-fry until the marinade has reduced and thickened, 1–2 minutes.
3　Open out the lettuce leaves and divide the beef and any sauce among them. Top with the scallions, cilantro, cucumber slices, and a sprinkling of sesame oil. Season to taste with pepper and serve.

180 golden honey pork

PREPARATION TIME: *15 minutes, plus 1 hour marinating time* **COOKING TIME:** *13 minutes*

1¼ lb boneless pork loin, thinly sliced
　across the grain
2 tbsp sunflower oil
2 handfuls of snow peas, trimmed
4 scallions, white and green parts
　separated and sliced diagonally
salt and freshly ground black pepper

MARINADE:
3 tbsp honey
2 tbsp light soy sauce
1 tbsp tomato paste
1-inch piece fresh ginger,
　peeled and grated

1　Mix together the ingredients for the marinade in a shallow dish. Add the pork and turn until coated, then let marinate for 1 hour. Drain, reserving the marinade.
2　Heat a wok until hot. Add the oil, then add half of the pork and stir-fry it until browned, 3–4 minutes. Remove from the wok using a slotted spoon and set on one side. Repeat with the remaining pork.
3　Put the snow peas and white part of the scallions into the wok and stir-fry for 1 minute. Return the pork to the wok along with the marinade and stir-fry until the pork is golden and glossy, 2–3 minutes longer. Season to taste with salt and pepper and serve, sprinkled with the green part of the scallions.

181 lamb korma

PREPARATION TIME: *20 minutes*   COOKING TIME: *35 minutes*

4 cardamom pods, split and
    seeds removed
1 tsp coriander seeds
1 tsp cumin seeds
4 tbsp ground almonds
2 hot green chilies, seeded and chopped
2 cloves garlic, chopped
1-inch piece fresh ginger,
    peeled and chopped
2 tbsp water
2 tbsp peanut oil
1 large onion, diced
3 cloves

1 cinnamon stick
1 tsp turmeric
1½ lb boneless leg of lamb, fat trimmed and
    cut into ¾-inch cubes
1½ cups beef stock
3 cups shredded fresh spinach leaves
1 cup frozen petit pois (petite
    green peas)
½ cup light cream
juice of ½ lemon
salt and freshly ground black pepper
handful of cilantro leaves,
    roughly chopped

1   Lightly toast the cardamom seeds, coriander seeds, and cumin seeds in a dry wok, then grind to
    a coarse powder using a mortar and pestle. Put the ground almonds, chilies, garlic, ginger, and
    water into a food processor or blender and process to form a coarse paste.
2   Heat a wok until hot. Add the oil, then toss in the onion and stir-fry it for 3 minutes. Add the
    ground spices, almond paste, cloves, cinnamon, and turmeric, and stir-fry for 1 more minute.
3   Add the lamb and stir-fry until browned, 3–4 minutes. Pour in the stock and bring to a boil.
    Reduce the heat to low, cover, and simmer for 20 minutes.
4   Stir in the spinach and peas, and cook until the liquid has reduced, about 2 minutes. Stir in the
    cream and lemon juice and heat gently. Season to taste with salt and pepper, and serve with
    the chopped cilantro sprinkled over.

182 spiced meatballs in red curry sauce

PREPARATION TIME: *25 minutes, plus 30 minutes chilling time*   COOKING TIME: *26 minutes*

4 shallots, chopped
2 cloves garlic, chopped
2-inch piece fresh ginger, peeled
    and minced
1 tsp ground cumin
juice of 1 lemon
large handful of cilantro leaves,
    minced
1 medium egg, lightly beaten
1 lb lean ground beef
salt and freshly ground black pepper

RED CURRY SAUCE:
2 tbsp sunflower oil
1 large onion, chopped
2 tbsp Tandoori curry powder
14 oz canned crushed tomatoes
1¼ cups coconut milk
6 tbsp water

1   Place the shallots, garlic, ginger, cumin, lemon juice, cilantro, egg, and ground beef in a food
    processor and process to form a coarse paste. Season well with salt and pepper, then shape
    the mixture into about 20 walnut-sized balls. Place these on a plate and chill in the refrigerator
    for about 30 minutes.
2   To make the sauce, heat the oil in a wok, add the onion, and stir-fry for 5 minutes. Add the
    curry powder and cook for 30 seconds, stirring. Stir in the canned tomatoes, coconut milk,
    and water. Season to taste with salt and pepper and bring to a boil, then reduce the heat.
3   Add the prepared meatballs to the sauce, cover, and simmer, turning occasionally, until the
    meatballs are cooked, about 20 minutes. Serve hot.

183 crisp pork balls with spinach

PREPARATION TIME: *20 minutes, plus 30 minutes chilling time* **COOKING TIME:** *17 minutes*

1 lb boneless pork loin,
   roughly chopped
2 hot Thai chilies, seeded
   and thinly sliced
2-inch piece fresh ginger, peeled
   and chopped
handful of cilantro leaves,
   roughly chopped
2 stalks lemongrass, peeled
   and minced
4 scallions, chopped

salt and freshly ground black pepper
4 tbsp peanut oil
3 cloves garlic, minced
2 tsp mustard seeds
½ tsp hot chili powder
1 lb fresh spinach leaves, tough
   stems removed
4 tbsp Chinese rice wine or dry sherry
3 tbsp light soy sauce
1 tsp sugar
juice of 2 limes

1 Put the pork, Thai chilies, ginger, cilantro leaves, lemongrass, and scallions in a food processor and process to form a coarse paste. Season to taste with salt and pepper, then form into 16 walnut-sized balls and chill in the refrigerator for 30 minutes.

2 Heat half of the oil in a wok and fry the pork balls, four at a time, until golden all over, about 4 minutes, turning occasionally. Add more oil, if necessary, before cooking the next batch, and keep the cooked balls warm while cooking the remainder.

3 Wipe the wok clean, then pour in the remaining oil and heat. Add the garlic and mustard seeds and sir-fry for 30 seconds, then add the chili powder, spinach, rice wine, soy sauce, and sugar. Stir-fry for 2 minutes, then add the lime juice. Season to taste with salt and pepper and serve, topped with the warm pork balls.

190 malaysian pork with bamboo shoots

PREPARATION TIME: *20 minutes* **COOKING TIME:** *23 minutes*

4 tbsp peanut oil
1½ lb boneless pork loin,
  sliced into ¾-inch strips
  across the grain
1 large onion, finely sliced
2 stalks lemongrass, peeled
  and minced
3 cloves garlic, chopped

½ tsp dried chili flakes
1 recipe quantity Rempeh Paste
  (see page 14)
2 carrots, sliced diagonally
1½ cups canned bamboo shoots,
  drained and rinsed
1¼ cups coconut milk
salt

1 Heat a wok until hot. Add the oil, then add half the pork and stir-fry it until browned,
   3–4 minutes. Remove from the wok using a slotted spoon, drain on paper towels, and set on
   one side. Repeat with the remaining pork.

2 Pour off all but 2 tablespoons of the oil, put the onion into the wok, and stir-fry for 3 minutes.
   Add the lemongrass, garlic, and chili flakes and stir-fry for 30 seconds longer. Add the rempeh
   paste, then the carrots and stir-fry for 2 minutes, then toss in the bamboo shoots and stir-fry for
   1 more minute.

3 Pour in the coconut milk and return the pork to the wok. Bring to a boil. Reduce the heat and
   simmer, covered, for 8 minutes, adding a little water if the sauce appears too dry. Season to
   taste with salt and serve.

191 massaman beef curry

PREPARATION TIME: *25 minutes* **COOKING TIME:** *1 hour 15 minutes*

2 tbsp peanut oil

2 onions, chopped

1½ lb boneless beef chuck or

    brisket, cut into

    ¾-inch cubes

2 kaffir lime leaves

grated zest and juice of 1 lime

2 stalks lemongrass,

    peeled and crushed

2 whole cloves

1 cinnamon stick

5 tbsp Massamun Curry Paste

    (see page 15)

2½ cups beef stock

1½ cups coconut milk

1 tsp tamarind paste

1 tbsp soy sauce

2 tsp palm sugar or

    light brown sugar

14 oz new potatoes, cooked

    and halved or quartered if large

handful of unsalted peanuts, roasted

1 Heat a wok until hot. Add the oil, then toss in the onions and stir-fry until softened, about 4 minutes. Add half the beef and stir-fry until browned, 2–3 minutes. Remove from the wok with a slotted spoon and set on one side. Brown the remaining beef, then return the first batch of beef to the wok.

2 Stir in the lime leaves, lime zest, lemongrass, cloves, and cinnamon, followed by the curry paste. Stir-fry for 2 minutes, then add the stock. Bring to a boil. Reduce the heat, cover, and simmer until the beef is tender, about 40 minutes. Add extra water if the curry appears too dry.

3 Add the coconut milk, tamarind paste, soy sauce, and palm sugar. Simmer until the sauce has reduced and thickened, 15–20 minutes. Stir in the lime juice and potatoes and heat through. Serve hot, sprinkled with the roasted peanuts.

192 lamb mumbai

PREPARATION TIME: *20 minutes* **COOKING TIME:** *55 minutes*

2 tbsp peanut oil

2 onions, minced

3 cloves garlic, chopped

4 whole cloves

4 cardamom pods, split and

    seeds removed

1 tsp mustard seeds

½ tsp ground cinnamon

2-inch piece fresh ginger,

    peeled and minced

1 tsp turmeric

1 tsp hot chili powder

1 tsp garam masala

1½ lb boneless leg of lamb, fat trimmed

    and cut into ¾-inch cubes

2½ cups water

1 cup chopped tomatoes

⅔ cup plain yogurt

salt

1 Heat a wok until hot. Add the oil, then toss in the onions and stir-fry them until softened, about 5 minutes. Add the garlic, cloves, and cardamom and mustard seeds, and cook for 30 seconds, then stir in the ground cinnamon, ginger, turmeric, chili powder, and garam masala.

2 Add the lamb and stir-fry until browned, about 4 minutes. Pour in the water and chopped tomatoes and bring to a boil. Reduce the heat, cover, and simmer until the meat is tender, 35–40 minutes. Add extra water if the curry looks too dry. Stir in the yogurt, season to taste with salt, and heat through gently, then serve.

193 hot & sour beef

PREPARATION TIME: *20 minutes, plus 30 minutes marinating time* **COOKING TIME:** *6 minutes*

4 tbsp light soy sauce
1 lb boneless sirloin steak, thinly sliced
   across the grain
2 tbsp sunflower oil
2 carrots, sliced
2-inch piece fresh ginger, peeled
   and minced

6 scallions, white and green parts
   separated and sliced diagonally
2 cloves garlic, minced
1 tsp dried chili flakes
2 tsp tamarind paste
6 tbsp water
juice of 1 lime
salt and freshly ground black pepper

1 Place the soy sauce in a large, shallow dish, add the beef, and let marinate for 30 minutes. Drain, reserving the soy sauce.
2 Heat a wok until hot. Add the oil, then add half of the beef and stir-fry until browned, 1–2 minutes. Remove using a slotted spoon and set aside. Repeat with the remaining beef.
3 Put the carrots into the wok and stir-fry for 2 minutes. Add the ginger, white part of the scallions, garlic, and chili flakes. Stir-fry for 1 minute, then add the tamarind paste and water.
4 Return the beef to the wok along with the soy sauce and lime juice and heat through, stirring. Season to taste with salt and pepper, scatter the scallion greens over, and serve.

194 sweet chili lamb

PREPARATION TIME: *15 minutes* **COOKING TIME:** *9 minutes*

2 tbsp sunflower oil
1½ lb boneless lamb loin, cut into
   ¾-inch cubes
2 handfuls of sugarsnap peas
2-inch piece fresh ginger, peeled
   and minced
4 scallions, white and green parts
   separated and sliced diagonally

3 cloves garlic, minced
4 kaffir lime leaves
juice of 2 limes
1 tbsp palm sugar or light
   brown sugar
3 tbsp sweet chili sauce
1 tbsp light soy sauce
salt and freshly ground black pepper

1 Heat a wok until hot. Add the oil, then add half of the lamb and stir-fry it until browned, about 2 minutes. Remove using a slotted spoon and set on one side. Repeat with the remaining lamb.
2 Add the sugarsnap peas, ginger, white part of the scallions, garlic, and lime leaves to the wok and stir-fry for 1 minute.
3 Add the lime juice, sugar, and chili and soy sauces. Stir until starting to thicken, then add the lamb and stir-fry for 1 minute. Season to taste, sprinkle with the scallion greens, and serve.

195 marinated ginger pork

PREPARATION TIME: *10 minutes, plus 1 hour marinating time* **COOKING TIME:** *8 minutes*

1¼ lb boneless pork loin, thinly sliced
   across the grain
2 tbsp sunflower oil
salt and freshly ground black pepper
2 handfuls of cilantro leaves,
   roughly chopped

MARINADE:
4 tbsp light soy sauce
2 tsp toasted sesame oil
2-inch piece fresh ginger, peeled
   and minced
2 cloves garlic, sliced

1 Mix together the marinade ingredients in a shallow dish. Add the pork and turn to coat well on both sides. Let marinate for at least 1 hour. Drain, reserving the marinade.
2 Heat a large wok until hot. Add the oil, then add the pork and stir-fry it until browned, 3–4 minutes. Pour in the reserved marinade and stir-fry for 2 minutes longer. Season to taste with salt and pepper and serve, sprinkled with the chopped cilantro.

196 hoisin beef stir-fry

PREPARATION TIME: *10 minutes* **COOKING TIME:** *14 minutes*

6 tbsp hoisin sauce
2 tbsp oyster sauce
¾ cup water
2–3 tbsp sunflower oil
1 lb ground beef
1 large onion, minced

2 carrots, diced
handful of fine green beans, trimmed
   and sliced diagonally
2 cloves garlic, chopped
2-inch piece fresh ginger, peeled
   and minced

1 Mix together the hoisin sauce, oyster sauce, and water in a small bowl.
2 Heat a wok until hot. Add the oil, then add the beef and stir-fry it until browned. Remove from the wok using a slotted spoon and set on one side.
3 Add more oil to the wok, if necessary, then toss in the onion and stir-fry for 4 minutes. Add the carrots and beans and stir-fry for 2 minutes, then add the garlic and ginger and stir-fry for 1 minute longer.
4 Pour in the hoisin sauce mixture, stir in the beef, and cook for 3 minutes. Serve immediately.

CHAPTER 5

POULTRY

Poultry, particularly chicken, is perfect for stir-frying in a wok, as it is quick to cook, low in fat, and usually mild enough in taste to readily take on the flavors of any aromatics that are cooked with it. The fragrant scent of herbs, such as basil and cilantro, as well as the tang of lemongrass and garlic and the warming intensity of ginger and other pungent spices, all work well with chicken.

In this chapter, alongside classics such as Chicken and Cashew Stir-Fry, Sweet and Sour Turkey, and Chili Chicken and Black Bean Stir-Fry, you will find interesting twists on traditional combinations, such as Teriyaki-Style Chicken with Scallion, and Sticky Duck and Orange Stir-Fry.

Lighter dishes are represented by Poached Chicken and Vegetables, in which the meat is cooked in a fragrant broth with asparagus, snow peas, and carrots, and by the simple Steamed Ginger Chicken, infused with the sweetness of fresh basil. And curry-lovers will find plenty to tempt them too, with variants of this richly aromatic dish drawn from all corners of Asia. They can choose from favorites such as the red and green curries of Thailand, jungle curries, and kormas, as well as a scattering of less familiar types from Sri Lanka, Vietnam, Laos, Malaysia, and Indonesia.

197 chili chicken & black bean stir-fry

PREPARATION TIME: *15 minutes, plus 10 minutes soaking time* **COOKING TIME:** *10 minutes*

4 tbsp black beans
1 tbsp cornstarch
1 tbsp light soy sauce
½ cup hot chicken stock
2 tbsp sunflower oil
1½ lb skinless, boneless chicken breast,
   cut into large, bite-sized pieces
1 onion, sliced
3 scallions, sliced
2 cloves garlic, chopped

2-inch piece fresh ginger,
   peeled and cut into thin strips
2 medium-sized, mildly hot, red chilies,
   seeded and minced
1 green bell pepper, cut into
   bite-sized pieces
½ tsp Chinese five-spice
1 tsp toasted sesame oil
salt and freshly ground black pepper

1   Put the black beans into a bowl, cover with hot water, and let soak for 10 minutes. Drain and set on one side. Mix the cornstarch and soy sauce into the hot stock and set on one side.

2   Heat a wok until hot. Add the oil, then toss in the chicken and stir-fry it until browned, about 4 minutes. Add the onion and stir-fry for 3 minutes, then add the scallions, garlic, ginger, chilies, and green pepper and stir-fry for 1 minute, taking care that the garlic does not burn.

3   Add the soaked black beans, the five-spice, and the stock and soy sauce mixture. Cook gently, stirring, until the sauce has thickened, then stir in the sesame oil. Season to taste with salt and pepper and serve.

198 sticky duck & orange stir-fry

PREPARATION TIME: *15 minutes* **COOKING TIME:** *30 minutes*

grated zest and juice of 2 oranges
3 tbsp water
2 tbsp palm sugar or light brown sugar
1-inch piece fresh ginger, peeled
   and minced
1 mildly hot, long, red chili, seeded
   and cut into rounds
2 star anise

1 tbsp sweet chili sauce
4 tbsp rice vinegar
1 tbsp sunflower oil
4 duck breast halves, about 6 oz each,
   skin pricked
handful of cilantro leaves
3 scallions, shredded

1   Mix together the orange zest and juice, water, sugar, ginger, chili, star anise, sweet chili sauce, and rice vinegar. Pour the mixture into a large wok and bring to a boil. Lower the heat and simmer until thickened and syrupy. Pour into a cup and set on one side. Wipe the wok clean.

2   Heat the oil in the wok. Add the duck breasts, skin side down first, and sear for 6 minutes on each side. Remove from the wok and let rest for 5 minutes in a warm place, then slice.

3   Pour off all but 1 tablespoon of oil from the wok, then add the orange sauce and heat gently until hot. Spoon the sauce over the sliced duck, sprinkle with the cilantro and scallions, and serve immediately.

199 shredded chicken with cilantro

PREPARATION TIME: *10 minutes, plus 1 hour marinating time* **COOKING TIME:** *10 minutes*

1½ lb skinless, boneless chicken breast,
   sliced into strips
2 tbsp peanut oil
6 oz fine green beans,
   trimmed and halved
large handful of cilantro leaves

MARINADE:
2 tbsp peanut oil
2 tsp cumin seeds, toasted
2 cloves garlic, crushed
grated zest and juice of 2 limes
salt and freshly ground black pepper

1   Mix together the ingredients for the marinade and season well with salt and pepper. Add
the chicken and spoon the marinade over the strips. Let marinate for at least 1 hour. Drain,
reserving the marinade.

2   Heat a wok until hot. Add the oil, then toss in half of the chicken and stir-fry it until lightly
browned, 3–4 minutes. Remove the chicken using a slotted spoon, drain on paper towels, and
keep warm. Repeat with the remaining chicken.

3   Put the green beans into the wok and stir-fry for 2–3 minutes. Pour in the reserved marinade,
then return the chicken to the wok and heat through over medium heat. Add a little water if the
mixture becomes too dry. Serve sprinkled with the cilantro leaves.

200 steamed ginger chicken

PREPARATION TIME: *10 minutes, plus 30 minutes marinating time* **COOKING TIME:** *23 minutes*

2 tbsp toasted sesame oil
3-inch piece fresh ginger, peeled
   and grated
½ tsp Chinese five-spice
3 tbsp light soy sauce

4 skinless, boneless chicken breast
   halves, about 6 oz each
2 tbsp sunflower oil
16 large basil leaves
salt and freshly ground black pepper

1   Mix together the sesame oil, ginger, five-spice, and soy sauce in a shallow dish. Place the chicken breasts in the dish and spoon the marinade over them to coat well. Let marinate for at least 30 minutes.

2   Meanwhile, heat the oil in a wok and fry the basil leaves for a few seconds until beginning to crisp. Remove the leaves from the wok using a slotted spoon, drain on paper towels, and set on one side.

3   Take four pieces of parchment paper, each large enough to wrap around a chicken breast. Place a chicken breast on each piece of paper. Spoon the marinade over the chicken and season well with salt and pepper. Fold up the paper around the chicken to make four loosely wrapped packets, sealing well.

4   Place the packets in a large bamboo steamer. Cover and steam over a wok of simmering water until the chicken is cooked, 15–20 minutes.

5   Remove the chicken packets from the steamer and place on four warm serving plates. Open each packet, sprinkle with the crisp basil leaves, and serve.

201 chicken in coconut & peanut sauce

PREPARATION TIME: *15 minutes* **COOKING TIME:** *10 minutes*

2 tbsp crunchy peanut butter
2 tbsp soy sauce
2 tsp fish sauce
6 tbsp hot water
½ cup coconut cream
1 tbsp palm sugar or light brown sugar
1 tbsp sunflower oil
1½ lb skinless, boneless chicken breast,
   cut into ½-inch strips
2 mildly hot, long, red chilies, seeded and
   thinly sliced into rounds

2 large handfuls of fine green beans,
   trimmed and cut into thirds
2-inch piece fresh ginger,
   peeled and minced
2 cloves garlic, minced
2 scallions, sliced
salt and freshly ground black pepper
handful of cilantro leaves,
   roughly chopped

1   Mix together the peanut butter, soy sauce, fish sauce, hot water, coconut cream, and sugar in a small bowl and set on one side.

2   Heat a large wok until hot. Add the oil, then toss in the chicken and chilies and stir-fry them until the chicken is beginning to color, 3–4 minutes. Add the beans and stir-fry for 1 minute, then add the ginger, garlic, and scallions and stir-fry for 1 minute longer.

3   Stir in the peanut butter mixture, season to taste with salt and pepper, and stir-fry until the sauce has reduced and thickened, 1–2 minutes. Add more water if the sauce appears too dry. Serve hot, sprinkled with the cilantro.

202 asian turkey & mushroom packets

PREPARATION TIME: *20 minutes, plus 30 minutes marinating time* **COOKING TIME:** *25 minutes*

1 tbsp toasted sesame oil	1½ tbsp sunflower oil
1-inch piece fresh ginger,	2 cups sliced shiitake mushrooms
peeled and grated	3 scallions, sliced diagonally
3 tbsp light soy sauce	salt and freshly ground black pepper
4 skinless turkey breast cutlets,	handful of basil leaves
about 6 oz each	

1 Mix together the sesame oil, ginger, and soy sauce in a shallow dish. Add the turkey cutlets and spoon the marinade over them. Let marinate for at least 30 minutes, then drain, reserving the marinade.

2 Heat a wok until hot. Add the oil, then toss in the mushrooms and stir-fry them for 2 minutes. Add the scallions and stir-fry for 30 seconds, then pour in the marinade, stir, and remove from the heat. Season to taste with salt and pepper.

3 Make a long slit down the length of each turkey cutlet and cut in to make a pocket. Place each cutlet on a piece of parchment paper large enough to enclose it. Spoon one-quarter of the mushroom mixture into the pocket in each turkey cutlet, then drizzle any juices left in the wok over the top and season to taste with salt and pepper. Fold the paper loosely around the turkey to make four packets, sealing well.

4 Place the turkey packets in a large bamboo steamer. Cover and steam over a wok of simmering water until the turkey is cooked and there is no trace of pink in the center, 15–20 minutes. Remove the packets from the steamer and place on warmed serving plates. Open the packets, sprinkle the basil over the top, and serve.

203 fragrant chicken with spring vegetables

PREPARATION TIME: *20 minutes* **COOKING TIME:** *20 minutes*

4 skinless, boneless chicken breast	handful of basil leaves
halves, about 6 oz each	3 handfuls of fine green beans, trimmed
1 large onion, coarsely chopped	12 spears asparagus, trimmed
3 kaffir lime leaves	2 zucchini, sliced diagonally
2 stalks lemongrass, crushed	3 tbsp sweet chili sauce
2 tbsp light soy sauce	1 tsp harissa paste
3⅓ cups chicken stock	2 tbsp mayonnaise

1 Put the chicken in a wok with the onion, lime leaves, lemongrass, and soy sauce. Pour in enough of the stock to cover the chicken. Add the basil. Bring to a boil, then reduce the heat and simmer, half covered, until the chicken is cooked, 15–20 minutes.

2 Meanwhile, in a separate pan, steam the green beans, asparagus, and zucchini until just tender, then set on one side and keep warm. Mix together the sweet chili sauce, harissa, and mayonnaise in a small bowl and set on one side.

3 Remove the chicken from the cooking liquid and slice. Arrange the vegetables on four warm serving plates, top with the sliced chicken, spoon the chili mayonnaise over, and serve.

204 poached chicken & vegetables

PREPARATION TIME: *15 minutes*　**COOKING TIME:** *27 minutes*

4 skinless, boneless chicken breast
　halves, about 6 oz each
6 tbsp Chinese rice wine or dry sherry
6 tbsp chicken stock
1 large onion, quartered
3 cloves garlic, sliced
2-inch piece fresh ginger, peeled
　and sliced

2 handfuls of snow peas, trimmed
12 spears asparagus, trimmed
2 carrots, sliced into ribbons using
　a potato peeler
light soy sauce, to taste
3 scallions, shredded
1 hot red chili, seeded and
　thinly sliced

1　Put the chicken in a large wok with the wine, stock, onion, garlic, and ginger. Bring to a boil,
　then reduce the heat and simmer, covered, until the chicken is cooked and there is no trace of
　pink in the center, 15–20 minutes. Remove the chicken from the wok with a slotted spoon, set
　on one side, and keep warm.
2　Add the vegetables to the poaching liquid in the wok and simmer until they are tender,
　4–5 minutes. Scoop out the vegetables with a slotted spoon and divide among four warm,
　shallow serving bowls.
3　Slice the chicken breasts and place on top of the vegetables, then spoon any remaining
　poaching liquid over. Sprinkle with soy sauce to taste, then garnish with the scallions and
　chili slices and serve.

205 nonya chicken

PREPARATION TIME: *10 minutes* **COOKING TIME:** *10 minutes*

3 tbsp sunflower oil
2 onions, thinly sliced
2–3 medium-sized, mildly hot, red chilies,
    seeded and thinly sliced
1½ lb skinless, boneless chicken breast,
    cut into ½-inch slices
2 tbsp palm sugar or light brown sugar

½ cup water
4 tbsp dark soy sauce
juice of 2 limes
handful of cilantro leaves,
    roughly chopped

1   Heat a large wok until hot. Add the oil, then toss in the onions and stir-fry for 2 minutes. Add
    the chilies and stir-fry for 30 seconds longer. Toss in the chicken and stir-fry for 2 minutes.
2   Add the palm sugar, water, and soy sauce and continue to stir-fry until the chicken is cooked
    through and the sauce has thickened, about 5 minutes.
3   Stir in the lime juice and serve, sprinkled with the chopped cilantro.

206 turkey with roasted cashews

PREPARATION TIME: *10 minutes* **COOKING TIME:** *10 minutes*

3 tbsp sunflower oil
large handful of unsalted cashew nuts
1¼ lb skinless, boneless turkey thighs,
    cut into bite-sized pieces
2 cloves garlic, chopped

3-inch piece fresh ginger,
    peeled and minced
2 handfuls of snow peas, trimmed
4 tbsp rice wine or dry sherry
2 tbsp light soy sauce

1   Heat 1 tablespoon of the oil in a wok. Add the cashews and stir-fry until golden. Remove using
    a slotted spoon, drain on paper towels, and set on one side.
2   Pour in the rest of the oil and heat until hot. Add half the turkey and stir-fry until cooked
    through and lightly browned, 3–4 minutes. Remove from the wok using a slotted spoon, drain
    on paper towels, and keep warm. Repeat with the remaining turkey
3   Add the garlic, ginger, and snow peas to the wok and stir-fry for 1 minute. Add the cooked
    turkey, pour in the wine and soy sauce, and stir-fry for 1–2 minutes longer. Serve with the
    cashew nuts sprinkled over the top.

207 vietnamese-style sticky chicken

PREPARATION TIME: *15 minutes* **COOKING TIME:** *17 minutes*

2 tbsp vegetable oil
1½ lb skinless, boneless chicken breast,
    cut into 1-inch cubes
4 Asian red shallots, chopped
3 cloves garlic, chopped
2 hot red chilies, seeded and chopped
3 tbsp dark soy sauce

juice of 1 lime
1 tbsp palm sugar or light brown sugar
2 scallions, shredded
½ English cucumber, cut into ribbons
    using a potato peeler

1   Heat a wok until hot. Add the oil, then add half of the chicken and stir-fry it until lightly
    browned, 3–4 minutes. Remove the chicken from the wok using a slotted spoon, drain on paper
    towels, and keep warm. Repeat with the remaining chicken.
2   Add the shallots to the wok and stir-fry for 2 minutes, then add the garlic and chilies and
    stir-fry for 30 seconds. Stir in the soy sauce, lime juice, and sugar. Return the chicken to the
    wok and toss until it is mixed with the sauce.
3   Cover and simmer, stirring occasionally, until the chicken is coated in a thick, glossy sauce,
    about 5 minutes. Scatter the scallions and cucumber ribbons over the top and serve.

208 japanese wok-fried chicken
PREPARATION TIME: *10 minutes* **COOKING TIME:** *10 minutes*

5 tbsp Japanese soy sauce
5 tbsp sake or dry sherry
3 tbsp sugar
2 tbsp sunflower oil

1½ lb skinless, boneless chicken breast,
   sliced into ½-inch strips
2 scallions, shredded

1   Mix together the soy sauce, sake, and sugar in a small bowl and set on one side.
2   Heat a wok until hot. Add the oil, then toss in the chicken and stir-fry it until lightly browned,
     3–4 minutes. Add the soy sauce mixture and stir-fry until most of the liquid has evaporated and
     the chicken is golden and glossy, 2–3 minutes. Sprinkle with the scallions and serve.

209 hoisin-style duck with pancakes
PREPARATION TIME: *10 minutes* **COOKING TIME:** *25 minutes*

⅔ cup hoisin sauce
4 tbsp dark soy sauce
2 tbsp palm sugar or light brown sugar
2 tbsp Chinese rice wine or dry sherry
4 duck breast halves, about 6 oz each

8–10 Chinese pancakes, warmed
½ English cucumber, peeled, seeded, and
   cut into thin sticks
4–6 scallions, shredded

1   Mix together the hoisin sauce, soy sauce, sugar, and wine in a small bowl. Spoon half of the
     mixture into a wok and warm over low heat for 1 minute.
2   Add 2 duck breasts and cook, spooning the sauce over the duck, until the breasts are cooked
     and glossy, about 6 minutes on each side, and the sauce has thickened. Add a little water if the
     sauce becomes too dry. Transfer the duck to a plate and spoon any sauce into a bowl.
3   Repeat with the remaining sauce and duck breasts. Let the duck breasts rest for 5 minutes,
     then slice thinly.
4   Spread a little of the sauce on one side of each warm pancake, then place a few strips of duck,
     cucumber, and scallion on top. Fold over the pancakes and serve.

210 malaysian spiced chicken
PREPARATION TIME: *15 minutes* **COOKING TIME:** *20 minutes*

4 tbsp peanut oil
1½ lb skinless, boneless chicken breast,
   cut into bite-sized pieces
2 stalks lemongrass, peeled
   and minced
3 cloves garlic, chopped
½ tsp dried chili flakes

4 heaped tbsp Rempeh Paste (see page 14)
2 zucchini, sliced diagonally
8 ears baby corn, halved lengthwise
3 cups shredded fresh spinach
1 cup coconut milk
salt

1   Heat a wok until hot. Add the oil, then add half of the chicken and stir-fry it until lightly
     browned, 3–4 minutes. Remove from the wok using a slotted spoon, drain on paper towels, and
     set on one side. Repeat with the remaining chicken.
2   Pour all but 2 tablespoons of the oil out of the wok. Add the lemongrass, garlic, and chili flakes
     and stir-fry for 30 seconds. Stir in the rempeh paste, followed by the zucchini and baby corn,
     and stir-fry for 2 minutes. Toss in the spinach and cook for 1 minute longer.
3   Return the chicken to the wok along with the coconut milk. Bring to a boil, lower the heat, and
     simmer for 8 minutes, adding more water if it becomes too dry. Season with salt and serve.

211 thai chicken bites with bok choy

PREPARATION TIME: *25 minutes, plus 30 minutes chilling time* **COOKING TIME:** *40 minutes*

1 lb skinless, boneless chicken breast,
  chopped
3 cloves garlic, chopped
2-inch piece fresh ginger, peeled
  and grated
5 scallions, chopped
1 tbsp fish sauce
1 mildly hot, long, red chili, minced

2 tbsp fresh bread crumbs
handful of cilantro leaves,
  roughly chopped
salt and freshly ground black pepper
4 small heads bok choy, sliced
  lengthwise
2 scallions, shredded
4 tbsp sweet chili sauce

1   Place the chicken, garlic, ginger, chopped scallions, fish sauce, chili, bread crumbs, and cilantro
    in a food processor or blender and process to form a coarse paste. Season well with salt and
    pepper. Form the paste into 20 walnut-sized balls. Put the balls on a plate, cover, and chill in
    the refrigerator for 30 minutes.
2   Place a lightly oiled plate in a large bamboo steamer. Place half of the balls on the plate, cover,
    and steam over a wok of simmering water until thoroughly cooked, 15–20 minutes. Remove
    from the steamer and keep warm. Repeat with the remaining balls.
3   Meanwhile, steam the bok choy in a separate pan until tender, 2–3 minutes.
4   Serve the chicken balls sprinkled with the shredded scallions and accompanied by the
    bok choy and sweet chili sauce.

212 asian turkey with sugarsnaps

PREPARATION TIME: *15 minutes* **COOKING TIME:** *10 minutes*

1 heaped tbsp cornstarch	large handful of sugarsnap peas
½ tsp Chinese five-spice	16 shiitake mushrooms, sliced
1 lb skinless, boneless turkey breast,	4 scallions, sliced diagonally
cut into thin strips	5 tbsp Chinese rice wine or dry sherry
2 tbsp sunflower oil	2 tbsp light soy sauce
2 cloves garlic, chopped	salt and freshly ground black pepper
1-inch piece fresh ginger,	handful of Chinese chives,
peeled and grated	roughly chopped

1   Mix together the cornstarch and five-spice in a shallow bowl. Add the turkey strips and toss until evenly coated.

2   Heat a wok until hot. Add the oil, then add half of the turkey and stir-fry it over high heat until cooked through and lightly browned, 3–4 minutes. Remove from the wok using a slotted spoon; set on one side and keep warm. Repeat with the remaining turkey.

3   Reduce the heat to medium, toss in the garlic and ginger, and stir-fry for 30 seconds. Add the sugarsnaps, mushrooms, and scallions and stir-fry for 2 minutes.

4   Return the turkey to the wok and add the wine and soy sauce. Toss until combined and heated through. Season to taste with salt and pepper and serve sprinkled with the chopped chives.

213 javanese chicken curry

PREPARATION TIME: *15 minutes* **COOKING TIME:** *25 minutes*

1 tsp dried shrimp paste	2-inch piece fresh ginger,
½ cup peanut oil	peeled and minced
1¼ lb skinless, boneless chicken breast,	3 hot red chilies, seeded and chopped
cut into 1-inch cubes	⅔ cup coconut milk
2 onions, minced	1 cup water
4 Asian red shallots, minced	1 cup canned crushed tomatoes
7 oz fine green beans,	2 tbsp light soy sauce
trimmed and halved	1 tbsp palm sugar or light brown sugar
4 cloves garlic, minced	salt and freshly ground black pepper

1   Wrap the shrimp paste in foil. Place under a hot broiler for 1 minute, then turn and cook for 1 minute on the other side. Unwrap the shrimp paste and set on one side.

2   Heat the oil in a large wok. Add the cubes of chicken and fry them until lightly browned all over, 3–4 minutes. Remove the chicken from the wok using a slotted spoon, drain on paper towels, and set on one side.

3   Pour all but 2 tablespoons of the oil out of the wok. Add the onions and shallots and stir-fry for 3 minutes. Toss in the green beans, garlic, ginger, chilies, and shrimp paste and stir-fry for 2 minutes longer.

4   Return the chicken to the wok and pour in the coconut milk, water, tomatoes, and soy sauce. Bring to a boil. Stir in the sugar, then reduce the heat, cover, and simmer for 10 minutes, stirring from time to time. Season to taste with salt and pepper and serve.

214 goan chicken curry

PREPARATION TIME: *20 minutes* **COOKING TIME:** *15 minutes*

2 tbsp vegetable oil

1 lb skinless, boneless chicken thighs, cut
   into bite-sized pieces

2 onions, chopped

3 cloves garlic, chopped

2 hot green chilies, sliced

2 tsp turmeric

2 tsp ground coriander

½ cup coconut milk

6 tbsp water

5 cups shredded fresh spinach

juice of 1 lemon

salt and freshly ground black pepper

handful of cilantro leaves

1 Heat a wok until hot. Add half of the chicken and stir-fry it until lightly browned, 3–4 minutes.
Remove from the wok using a slotted spoon, drain on paper towels, and set on one side.
Repeat with the remaining chicken.

2 Add the onions to the wok and stir-fry for 3 minutes, then add the garlic and chilies and stir-fry
for 30 seconds. Stir in the turmeric and ground coriander and stir-fry for 30 seconds over
medium heat.

3 Pour in the coconut milk and water, then stir in the spinach and cooked chicken. Bring to a boil.
Reduce the heat and simmer for 2–3 minutes.

4 Stir in the lemon juice and add a little more water if the curry is too dry. Season to taste with
salt and pepper and serve, garnished with the cilantro leaves.

215 turkey korma

PREPARATION TIME: *20 minutes* **COOKING TIME:** *25 minutes*

4 cardamom pods, split and seeds removed

1 tsp coriander seeds

1 tsp cumin seeds

4 tbsp ground almonds

2 hot green chilies, seeded and chopped

2 cloves garlic, chopped

1-inch piece fresh ginger,
   peeled and chopped

2 tbsp water

2 tbsp peanut oil

1¼ lb skinless, boneless turkey breast,
   cut into large bite-sized pieces

1 large onion, diced

3 whole cloves

1 cinnamon stick

1 tsp turmeric

1¼ cups chicken stock

4 cups shredded fresh spinach

½ cup light cream

juice of ½ lemon

salt and freshly ground black pepper

handful of cilantro leaves

1 Lightly toast the cardamom, coriander, and cumin seeds in a large, dry wok, then crush with
a mortar and pestle and set on one side. Put the ground almonds, chilies, garlic, ginger, and
water in a food processor or blender and process to form a coarse paste.

2 Reheat the wok. Add the oil, then toss in the turkey and stir-fry it until lightly browned,
3–4 minutes. Add the onion and stir-fry for 2 minutes, then stir in the crushed spices and
almond paste, followed by the cloves, cinnamon, and turmeric. Stir-fry for 1 minute longer.

3 Pour in the stock and bring to a boil. Reduce the heat, cover, and simmer for 10 minutes. Stir in
the spinach and cook until it has wilted and the liquid has reduced, 3–4 minutes.

4 Stir in the cream and lemon juice and heat through gently for 2–3 minutes. Season to taste
with salt pepper and serve with the cilantro leaves sprinkled over the top.

216 fragrant chicken & spinach curry

PREPARATION TIME: *15 minutes* COOKING TIME: *14 minutes*

2 tbsp sunflower oil
1 lb skinless, boneless chicken thighs, cut
    into bite-sized pieces
1 recipe quantity Thai Red Curry Paste
    (see page 15)
1¾ cups coconut milk

4 cups shredded fresh spinach
20 basil leaves, torn
large handful of cilantro leaves, chopped,
    plus extra for garnish
salt and freshly ground black pepper

1   Heat a wok until hot. Add the oil, then add half of the chicken and stir-fry it until lightly
browned, 3–4 minutes. Remove from the wok, drain on paper towels, and set on one side.
Repeat with the remaining chicken.

2   Put the curry paste into the wok and cook, stirring, for 1 minute, then add the coconut milk.
Bring to a boil. Reduce the heat. Return the chicken to the wok and simmer for 3 minutes.

3   Toss in the spinach and cook for 1–2 minutes. Add the basil leaves and chopped cilantro and
cook for 1 minute, adding a little water if the sauce is too dry. Season to taste with salt and
pepper and serve sprinkled with extra cilantro.

217 turkey & mango stir-fry

PREPARATION TIME: *10 minutes* COOKING TIME: *10 minutes*

2 tbsp sunflower oil
1 lb skinless, boneless turkey breast, cut
    into thin strips
2 cloves garlic, chopped
2 hot Thai chilies, seeded and
    minced
juice of 2 limes

1½ tbsp Thai fish sauce
4 scallions, sliced diagonally
4 small heads bok choy, sliced
1 large mango, peeled, pitted, and sliced
salt
large handful of cilantro leaves,
    roughly chopped

1   Heat a wok until hot. Add the oil, then add half of the turkey and stir-fry it until cooked through
and lightly browned, 3–4 minutes. Remove from the wok with a slotted spoon and keep warm.
Repeat with the remaining turkey.

2   Add the garlic to the wok along with the chilies, lime juice, fish sauce, scallions, and bok choy,
and stir-fry for 2 minutes.

3   Return the turkey to the wok along with the mango and stir to combine. Season to taste with
salt and serve sprinkled with the chopped cilantro.

218 hot chili chicken

PREPARATION TIME: *15 minutes, plus 1 hour marinating time* COOKING TIME: *8 minutes*

1½ lb skinless, boneless chicken breast,
    cut into ½-inch strips
2 tbsp sunflower oil
salt and freshly ground black pepper

MARINADE:
1 red bell pepper, chopped
2 hot red chilies, minced
2 tsp paprika
4 tbsp red wine vinegar
6 tbsp peanut oil

1   Put all the marinade ingredients in a blender or food processor and purée. Put into a shallow
dish and add the chicken. Turn the chicken to coat, then let marinate for 1 hour.

2   Heat a large wok until hot, then add the oil. Remove the chicken from the marinade using a
slotted spoon, add to the wok, and stir-fry it for 3–4 minutes.

3   Reduce the heat and add the marinade. Season to taste with salt and pepper and cook the
chicken until there is no trace of pink in the center, about 3 minutes longer. Serve hot.

219 sweet & sour turkey

PREPARATION TIME: *15 minutes* **COOKING TIME:** *10 minutes*

juice of 3 oranges
3 tbsp light soy sauce
1 tbsp honey
2 tbsp rice vinegar
2 tsp cornstarch
2 tbsp vegetable oil
1 onion, sliced

1¼ lb skinless, boneless turkey breast,
    cut into thin strips
8 cremini mushrooms, sliced
1 large carrot, sliced diagonally
handful of snow peas, trimmed
handful of beansprouts

1 Mix the orange juice, soy sauce, honey, rice vinegar, and cornstarch together. Set on one side.
2 Heat a wok until hot. Add the oil, then toss in the onion and stir-fry it for 2 minutes. Add the turkey and stir-fry for 2–3 minutes. Toss in the mushrooms, carrot, and snow peas and stir-fry for 2–3 minutes longer. Add the beansprouts and then the orange juice mixture. Cook, stirring, until the sauce has thickened. Serve immediately.

220 hot & spicy turkey stir-fry

PREPARATION TIME: *10 minutes* **COOKING TIME:** *13 minutes*

3 tbsp peanut oil
1 large onion, sliced
8 cremini mushrooms, sliced
1 green bell pepper, sliced
3 cloves garlic, crushed
2-inch piece fresh ginger,
    peeled and grated

1 lb skinless, boneless turkey breast,
    cut into thin strips
1 tsp hot chili powder
1 tsp ground coriander
handful of cilantro leaves, roughly chopped
juice of ½ lemon
salt

1 Heat a wok until hot. Add half of the oil, then toss in the onion and stir-fry it for 3 minutes. Add the mushrooms, green pepper, garlic, and ginger and stir-fry for 2 minutes longer. Remove from the wok and set on one side.
2 Add the remaining oil to the wok, then add the turkey and stir-fry until golden, 3–4 minutes. Stir in the chili powder and ground coriander. Add the reserved mushroom mixture along with half of the cilantro and the lemon juice and stir-fry for 2 minutes, adding a little water if too dry. Season to taste with salt and serve sprinkled with the remaining cilantro.

221 simple turkey curry with spinach

PREPARATION TIME: *10 minutes* **COOKING TIME:** *35 minutes*

2 tbsp peanut oil
2 onions, chopped
4 cloves garlic, chopped
1 lb ground turkey
6 tbsp curry paste
14 oz canned crushed tomatoes
1¼ cups chicken stock

14 oz canned chickpeas,
    drained and rinsed
4 cups shredded fresh spinach
juice of ½ lemon
salt and freshly ground black pepper
handful of cilantro leaves,
    roughly chopped

1 Heat a wok until hot. Add the oil, then toss in the onions and stir-fry for 4 minutes. Add the garlic and turkey and stir-fry for 5 minutes. Stir in the curry paste and cook for 1 more minute.
2 Pour in the tomatoes, stock, and chickpeas and bring to a boil. Reduce the heat and simmer, covered, until the sauce has reduced and thickened, 15–20 minutes.
3 Toss in the spinach and cook until wilted, 2–3 minutes. Stir in the lemon juice and season to taste with salt and pepper. Stir in the chopped cilantro and serve immediately.

222 lao chicken & green beans

PREPARATION TIME: *15 minutes*   **COOKING TIME:** *25 minutes*

3 tbsp peanut oil

1½ lb skinless, boneless chicken thighs,
   cut into bite-sized pieces

6 Asian red shallots, chopped

4 garlic cloves, chopped

3-inch piece fresh ginger,
   peeled and grated

2 hot red chilies, seeded
   and chopped

2 handfuls of fine green beans,
   trimmed and sliced

12 cremini mushrooms,
   halved or quartered if large

1 tbsp fish sauce

2 cups coconut milk

juice of 1 lime

salt

handful of cilantro leaves,
   roughly chopped

1   Heat a large wok until hot. Add 2 tablespoons of the oil, then add the chicken and stir-fry it
    until lightly browned, 3–4 minutes. Transfer to a plate lined with paper towels and keep warm.

2   Put the shallots into the wok and stir-fry for 2 minutes. Add the garlic, ginger, and chilies and
    stir-fry for 1 more minute. Remove the shallot mixture from the wok and set on one side.

3   Add more oil to the wok, if necessary, then toss in the beans and mushrooms and stir-fry for
    3 minutes. Return the chicken and shallot mixture to the wok and stir in the fish sauce and
    coconut milk. Bring to a boil, then reduce the heat to low and simmer until the chicken is
    tender, 12–15 minutes.

4   Stir in the lime juice, season to taste with salt, and serve,
    sprinkled with the chopped cilantro.

223 burmese chicken with lime

PREPARATION TIME: *20 minutes* **COOKING TIME:** *25 minutes*

1 tsp dried shrimp paste
⅔ cup hot water
1 tbsp vegetable oil
1 tbsp toasted sesame oil
2 onions, minced
8–10 skinless, boneless chicken thighs,
    cut into 1-inch cubes
2 cloves garlic, chopped
2-inch piece fresh ginger,
    peeled and grated
1 mildly hot, long, red chili, minced

1 tsp turmeric
2 tsp ground coriander
3 whole cloves
3 kaffir lime leaves
1½ cups canned
    crushed tomatoes
juice of 2 limes
handful of cilantro leaves,
    roughly chopped
salt and freshly ground black pepper

1 Wrap the shrimp paste in foil, then place under a hot broiler for 1 minute. Turn and cook for
  another minute. Remove the shrimp paste from the foil and dissolve it in the hot water. Set
  on one side.
2 Heat a wok until hot. Add the oils, then toss in the onions and stir-fry them for 2 minutes. Add
  the chicken and stir-fry until it is lightly browned, 3–4 minutes.
3 Toss in the garlic, ginger, and chili and stir-fry for 30 seconds, then stir in the turmeric, ground
  coriander, cloves, and lime leaves and cook for a few more seconds.
4 Pour in the shrimp paste mixture and tomatoes and bring to a boil. Reduce the heat slightly
  and simmer until the sauce has reduced and thickened, about 15 minutes.
5 Stir in the lime juice and chopped cilantro, and season to taste with salt and pepper. Cook for
  a few more minutes, then serve hot.

224 balinese chicken

PREPARATION TIME: *20 minutes* **COOKING TIME:** *20 minutes*

4 tbsp vegetable oil
1¼ lb skinless, boneless chicken breast,
    cut into 1-inch cubes
2 onions, minced
4 cloves garlic, chopped
2 stalks lemongrass, crushed
6 small, hot red chilies, seeded
    and minced
2 tsp ground coriander

1 tsp turmeric
1 cup coconut milk
⅔ cup water
1 tbsp fish sauce
6 tbsp crunchy peanut butter
1 tbsp palm sugar or light brown sugar
juice of 1 lime
handful of cilantro leaves, roughly
    chopped

1 Heat a wok until hot. Add the oil, then add half of the chicken and stir-fry it until lightly
  browned, 3–4 minutes. Remove from the wok using a slotted spoon, drain on paper towels, and
  set on one side. Repeat with the remaining chicken.
2 Pour all but 2 tablespoons of the oil out of the wok. Add the onions and stir-fry for 3 minutes,
  then add the garlic, lemongrass, chilies, and ground spices and stir-fry for 1 more minute.
3 Pour in the coconut milk, stir, and bring to a boil. Reduce the heat and simmer for 5 minutes.
  Add the water and fish sauce and stir in the peanut butter and sugar.
4 Return the chicken to the wok and cook over low heat until the chicken is heated through and
  the sauce thickened, 3–5 minutes longer. Stir in the lime juice and serve with the chopped
  cilantro sprinkled over the top.

231 malay chicken curry

PREPARATION TIME: *20 minutes* **COOKING TIME:** *55 minutes*

2 tbsp peanut oil

2 onions, grated

8 chicken thighs

2-inch piece fresh ginger, peeled
  and grated

4 large cloves garlic, crushed

2 stalks lemongrass, peeled and bruised

1 tbsp ground cumin

1 tbsp ground coriander

2 tsp ground turmeric

2 cinnamon sticks

4 whole cloves

6 cardamom pods, split

1 tsp hot chili powder

1 hot Thai chili, chopped

3 tbsp water

1¼ cups coconut milk

1 cup vegetable stock

juice of 1 lime

salt

2 large handfuls of cilantro leaves,
  roughly chopped

1 Heat a large wok until hot. Add the oil, then toss in the onions and stir-fry them for 3 minutes. Add the chicken thighs and stir-fry until golden all over, about 5 minutes. Remove the chicken from the wok with a slotted spoon and set on one side.

2 Add the ginger, garlic, lemongrass, cumin, ground coriander, turmeric, cinnamon sticks, cloves, cardamom pods, chili powder, and Thai chili to the wok and stir-fry for 2 minutes. Pour in the water and stir-fry for 2 minutes longer.

3 Return the chicken to the wok along with the coconut milk and stock. Bring to a boil. Reduce the heat and simmer, covered, for 30 minutes, stirring occasionally. Uncover and simmer until the chicken is cooked through and the liquid has reduced and thickened, about 10 minutes.

4 Stir in the lime juice, season to taste with salt, and serve, sprinkled with the cilantro.

232 wok-smoked squab chicken

PREPARATION TIME: *25 minutes, plus 1 hour marinating time* **COOKING TIME:** *45–60 minutes*

2 tsp Szechuan peppercorns

1 tsp salt

2 tbsp light brown sugar

2 tbsp dark soy sauce

1 squab chicken

sunflower oil for brushing

SMOKING MIXTURE:

2 large handfuls of long-grain white rice

1 large handful of black tea leaves

2 tbsp brown sugar

1 star anise, broken into bits

1 Toast the Szechuan peppercorns in a dry wok, then grind using a mortar and pestle. Mix the ground pepper with the salt, sugar, and soy sauce in a small bowl and set on one side.

2 Place the chicken, breast side down, on a board. Using poultry shears, cut the bird down one side of the backbone, then cut down the other side of the backbone to remove it. Open out the bird, turn it over, and flatten by pressing along the breastbone with the flat of your hand. Secure the chicken in the flat position by inserting two skewers, crossing each other, diagonally through it.

3 Put the chicken in a shallow dish and spoon the Szechuan pepper mixture over, rubbing it in well. Let marinate for at least 1 hour.

4 Line the inside of the wok and lid with foil to protect them. Mix together the smoking mixture ingredients and put in the bottom of the wok. Lightly oil a rack and place it over the smoking mixture, making sure it is not touching.

5 Heat the wok and, when the mixture starts to smoke, put the chicken on the rack. Cover with a lid, making sure it is a tight fit – and open a window.

6 Reduce the heat to low (but high enough to make sure the mixture is still smoking) and smoke the chicken until it is cooked through and there is no trace of pinkness, 45–60 minutes. Let rest for 5 minutes, then remove the chicken from the wok and serve warm or cold with a vegetable dish or side salad.

233 filipino turkey in peanut sauce

PREPARATION TIME: *20 minutes* **COOKING TIME:** *20 minutes*

1 cup fresh shelled peanuts
2 tbsp peanut oil
1½ lb skinless, boneless turkey breast or
    thigh, cut into large bite-sized pieces
5 shallots, minced
3 cloves garlic, chopped
1 mildly hot, long, red chili, seeded
    and chopped

1 tsp hot chili powder
2 tsp paprika
1 tsp turmeric
3 cups chicken stock
2 tsp tamarind paste
3 kaffir lime leaves
1 tsp palm sugar or light brown sugar
salt and freshly ground black pepper

1   Heat a large wok, add the peanuts, and roast for a few minutes, turning, until lightly browned.
Remove from the wok and let cool slightly, then grind to a fine powder in a food processor
or blender. Set on one side.

2   Heat the oil in the hot wok. Add half the turkey and stir-fry until lightly browned, 3–4 minutes.
Remove from the wok using a slotted spoon, drain on paper towels, and set on one side.
Repeat with the remaining turkey.

3   Add the shallots and stir-fry for 2 minutes, then add the garlic, chili, chili powder, paprika,
and turmeric and stir-fry for 1 more minute. Pour in the stock, then stir in the tamarind, lime
leaves, and sugar. Bring to a boil. Reduce the heat and simmer for 3 minutes.

4   Stir in the ground peanuts and season to taste with salt and pepper. Simmer for 6 minutes. Stir
in the turkey and simmer, stirring occasionally, until heated through and tender, 3–4 minutes
longer. Serve hot.

234 golden chicken with garlic & cilantro

PREPARATION TIME: *15 minutes, plus 30 minutes marinating time* **COOKING TIME:** *10 minutes*

3 tbsp Shaoxing wine or medium sherry
3 tbsp light soy sauce
1 tbsp cornstarch
1¼ lb skinless, boneless chicken breast,
   cut into large bite-sized pieces
3 tbsp sunflower oil
4 cloves garlic, chopped
2-inch piece fresh ginger, peeled
   and grated

1 large, green bell pepper, sliced
5 scallions, sliced
⅔ cup chicken stock
2 tbsp oyster sauce
salt and freshly ground black pepper
handful of cilantro leaves,
   roughly chopped

1   Mix together the wine, soy sauce, and cornstarch in a bowl. Add the pieces of chicken and turn to coat them all over. Let marinate for 30 minutes, stirring occasionally. Drain, reserving the marinade.

2   Heat a wok until hot. Add the oil, then add half of the chicken and stir-fry it until lightly browned, 3–4 minutes. Remove the chicken from the wok using a slotted spoon, drain on paper towels, and set on one side. Repeat with the remaining chicken.

3   Toss the garlic, ginger, green pepper, and scallions into the wok and stir-fry for 1 minute. Stir in the reserved marinade, stock, and oyster sauce, then return the chicken to the wok. Stir-fry until the sauce has reduced and the chicken is cooked through. Season to taste with salt and pepper, then sprinkle with the chopped cilantro and serve.

235 duck green curry

PREPARATION TIME: *15 minutes* **COOKING TIME:** *30 minutes*

2 tbsp sunflower oil
2 large duck breast halves, about
   9 oz each, skinned and
   cut into bite-sized pieces
1 medium eggplant, cut into cubes
1 recipe quantity Thai Green Curry Paste
   (see page 15)
1¾ cups coconut milk

⅔ cup chicken stock
2 tsp fish sauce
12 cherry tomatoes, halved
juice of 1 lime
salt and freshly ground black pepper
handful of Thai basil leaves,
   roughly chopped

1   Heat a large wok until hot. Add the oil, then add the duck and stir-fry it until golden, about 3 minutes. Remove from the pan using a slotted spoon, drain on paper towels, and set aside.

2   Add the eggplant and stir-fry until lightly browned, about 6 minutes. Remove from the wok and set on one side.

3   Put the curry paste into the wok and cook for 1 minute, stirring. Stir in the coconut milk, then add the stock and fish sauce. Return the duck to the wok and bring to a boil. Reduce the heat and simmer for 10 minutes.

4   Add the tomatoes and eggplant and cook until the sauce has thickened, 5–8 minutes. Stir in the lime juice, season to taste with salt and pepper, and serve with the basil sprinkled over the top.

236 szechuan chicken

PREPARATION TIME: *20 minutes, plus 30 minutes marinating time*   **COOKING TIME:** *10 minutes*

1 medium egg white
1 tbsp dark soy sauce
1 tbsp cornstarch
1¼ lb skinless, boneless chicken
   breast, cut into ¾-inch cubes
3 tbsp sunflower oil
2 cloves garlic, crushed
2 mildly hot, long, red chilies, seeded
   and diced
1 large, red bell pepper, seeded
   and cut into pieces

2 tbsp rice wine or dry sherry
1 tsp toasted sesame oil
handful of cilantro leaves

SAUCE:
2 tbsp light soy sauce
1 tsp sugar
2 tsp rice vinegar
1 tsp Szechuan peppercorns
2 tbsp water
1 tsp cornstarch

1 Mix together the egg white, soy sauce, and cornstarch in a shallow dish. Add the chicken and stir to coat with the marinade. Let marinate for 30 minutes, turning the chicken occasionally. Mix together all the ingredients for the sauce in a bowl and set on one side.

2 Heat a wok until hot. Add 2 tablespoons of the sunflower oil, then add half the chicken and marinade and stir-fry until lightly browned, 3–4 minutes. Remove from the wok using a slotted spoon and set on one side. Repeat with the remaining chicken and marinade.

3 Heat the remaining sunflower oil in the wok. Toss in the garlic, chilies, and red pepper and stir-fry for 30 seconds. Pour in the wine. Return the cooked chicken to the wok and stir well, then add the sauce mixture and stir fry over high heat for 1 minute to heat through.

4 Stir in the sesame oil and serve immediately, sprinkled with the cilantro leaves.

237 vietnamese chicken balls
with nuac cham

PREPARATION TIME: *25 minutes, plus 30 minutes chilling time*   **COOKING TIME:** *15 minutes*

1 lb ground chicken
6 scallions, chopped
4 cloves garlic, chopped
2 handfuls of cilantro leaves,
   roughly chopped
2 large stalks lemongrass, peeled
   and minced
2 hot red chilies, chopped
2-inch piece fresh ginger, peeled
   and grated

salt and freshly ground pepper
3 tbsp vegetable oil
1 carrot, cut into ribbons with a
   potato peeler
½ English cucumber, cut into ribbons
   with a potato peeler
handful of Thai basil leaves,
   roughly chopped
1 recipe quantity Nuac Cham
   (see page 149)

1 Put the chicken, scallions, garlic, cilantro, lemongrass, chilies, and ginger in a food processor or blender and process to form a coarse paste.

2 Spoon the mixture into a bowl and season well with salt and pepper. Shape the mixture into 24 walnut-sized balls and place on a plate. Cover with plastic wrap and chill for 30 minutes.

3 Heat the oil in a wok. Add half the chicken balls and fry, turning occasionally, until golden, about 5 minutes. Remove from the wok with a slotted spoon and keep warm. Repeat with the remaining chicken balls.

4 Serve the chicken balls surrounded by the carrot and cucumber ribbons and with the basil sprinkled over the top. Offer a bowl of nuac cham for dipping.

238 ginger chicken with peppers

PREPARATION TIME: *15 minutes*   **COOKING TIME:** *15 minutes*

3 tbsp peanut oil
1¼ lb skinless, boneless chicken thighs,
    cut into bite-sized pieces
4 tomatoes, peeled, seeded, and diced
2 cloves garlic, chopped
2-inch piece fresh ginger, peeled
    and grated

3 tbsp water
salt and freshly ground black pepper
2 tsp toasted sesame oil
1 yellow bell pepper, sliced
1 red bell pepper, sliced
juice of 1 lemon

1   Heat a wok until hot. Add 2 tablespoons of the peanut oil, then add half the chicken and
    stir-fry until lightly browned, about 4 minutes. Remove from the wok, drain on paper towels,
    and set on one side. Repeat with the remaining chicken.
2   Add the tomatoes, garlic, and ginger to the wok and stir-fry for 1 minute. Return the chicken
    to the wok and pour in the water. Stir-fry over medium heat until the liquid is reduced and the
    chicken is cooked through. Season to taste with salt and pepper, then remove from the wok and
    keep warm.
3   Wipe the wok clean, then heat the remaining peanut oil and sesame oil in it. Add the peppers
    and stir-fry for 2 minutes. Pour in the lemon juice.
4   Divide the peppers among four warm serving plates, top with the warm chicken, and serve.

239 chinese braised duck with carrots

PREPARATION TIME: *15 minutes*   **COOKING TIME:** *35 minutes*

3 tbsp sunflower oil
2 duck breast halves, about
    8 oz each
2 onions, sliced
2 large carrots, sliced diagonally
3 star anise
1 tsp Chinese five-spice

2-inch piece fresh ginger, peeled
    and finely sliced
2 cups water
4 tbsp dark soy sauce
5 tbsp Chinese rice wine or dry sherry
2 tsp sugar
salt and freshly ground black pepper

1   Heat 2 tablespoons of the oil in a large wok. Add the duck breasts and sear until golden,
    2–3 minutes on each side. Remove from the wok using a slotted spatula, drain on paper towels,
    and set on one side.
2   Add the onions to the wok and stir-fry over medium heat for about 4 minutes, then add the
    carrots, star anise, five-spice, and ginger. Stir-fry for 1 more minute.
3   Pour in the water, soy sauce, wine, and sugar and add the seared duck breasts. Bring to a
    boil. Reduce the heat, cover, and simmer for 15 minutes. Season to taste with salt and pepper.
4   Remove the duck breasts. Heat the remaining oil in another wok or frying pan and fry the duck,
    skin side down, over high heat until the skin is crisp, 2–3 minutes. Remove the duck from the
    pan and let rest for 5 minutes.
5   Slice the duck and arrange on a serving plate. Spoon the carrots and sauce over the top
    and serve immediately.

240 red-cooked chicken

PREPARATION TIME: *10 minutes, plus 5 minutes infusing time*   **COOKING TIME:** *25–45 minutes*

1 cup dark soy sauce
6 tbsp Chinese rice wine or dry sherry
4 star anise
1-inch piece fresh ginger,
    peeled and thinly sliced
4 whole cloves

2 cinnamon sticks
grated zest of ½ lemon or orange
juice of 1 lemon or orange
1 tsp sugar
4 skinless, boneless chicken breasts,
    about 6 oz each

1   Put the soy sauce, wine, star anise, ginger, cloves, cinnamon, lemon or orange zest and juice,
    and sugar in a large wok and bring to a boil. Remove from the heat and set aside for 5 minutes
    to let the flavors infuse.
2   Add the chicken breasts to the wok and spoon the liquid over them, making sure the chicken is
    covered. Bring to a boil, then reduce the heat and simmer, covered, for 15–20 minutes, turning
    the chicken halfway through the cooking time and occasionally spooning the sauce over.
3   Serve each chicken breast with a little of the sauce. The remaining sauce can be chilled or
    frozen for later use. It makes a good base stock for other poultry and meat dishes.

241 chinese crispy duck

PREPARATION TIME: *15 minutes, plus 2 hours marinating time* COOKING TIME: *1 hour*

1 tsp Chinese five-spice
3-inch piece fresh ginger,
   peeled and grated
2 tbsp dark soy sauce
1 tbsp Chinese rice wine or dry sherry
2 tbsp honey
1 tbsp vegetable oil,
   plus extra for deep-frying

4 duck breast halves, about
   6 oz each
salt
4 tbsp Chinese plum sauce
8–10 Chinese pancakes, warmed
4–6 scallions, shredded
½ English cucumber, peeled and
   cut into thin sticks

1   Mix together the five-spice, ginger, soy sauce, wine, honey, and 1 tablespoon of the oil to make a paste. Rub the mixture over the top of each duck breast and let marinate in the refrigerator for at least 2 hours.

2   Place the duck breasts in a large bamboo steamer lined with parchment paper. Cover and steam over a large wok of simmering water until cooked through, about 25 minutes. Remove the duck from the steamer and set aside to cool.

3   Half-fill the wok with oil and heat until it is hot enough to brown a cube of day-old bread in about 30 seconds. Add two of the steamed duck breasts and deep-fry until the skin turns golden and crisp, 3–5 minutes. Remove from the wok, drain on paper towels, and set on one side. Repeat with the remaining two duck breasts.

4   Let the duck rest for 5 minutes, then shred the meat, using two forks, or cut into thin slices. Spread a little of the plum sauce on one side of each warm pancake and place a few pieces of duck, scallion, and cucumber on top, then roll up and serve.

242 stir-fried kaffir lime chicken

PREPARATION TIME: *15 minutes* COOKING TIME: *13 minutes*

1 tbsp fish sauce
1 tsp palm sugar or light brown sugar
2 tbsp light soy sauce
juice of 1 lime
4 tbsp sunflower oil
1¼ lb skinless, boneless chicken breast,
   cut into strips

1 large eggplant, cut into small
   bite-sized pieces
4 cloves garlic, chopped
1 mildly hot, long, red chili, seeded and
   thinly sliced into rounds
4 kaffir lime leaves, shredded
salt
handful of purple basil leaves

1   Mix together the fish sauce, sugar, soy sauce, and lime juice in a small bowl and set on one side.

2   Heat a wok until hot. Add half of the oil, then add the chicken and stir-fry it until golden and cooked through, 3–4 minutes. Remove from the wok using a slotted spoon, drain on paper towels, and set on one side.

3   Heat the remaining oil in the wok. Toss in the eggplant and stir-fry until golden and tender, 5–6 minutes. Remove from the wok, drain on paper towels, and set on one side.

4   Add the garlic, chili, and lime leaves to the wok and stir-fry for 30 seconds, then return the chicken and eggplant to the wok, followed by the fish sauce mixture. Cook over medium heat, stirring, until the sauce has reduced and thickened. Season to taste with salt and serve topped with the basil leaves.

243 vietnamese-style chicken with lemon

PREPARATION TIME: *20 minutes* **COOKING TIME:** *20 minutes*

4 large handfuls of baby spinach leaves,
   shredded
4 skinless, boneless chicken breast
   halves, about 6 oz each
1-inch piece fresh ginger, peeled
   and cut into thin strips
3 stalks lemongrass, peeled
   and minced
2 large handfuls of mint leaves, chopped
2 large handfuls of basil leaves,
   chopped, plus extra for garnish
4 tsp sunflower oil

2 tbsp light soy sauce
salt and freshly ground black pepper

NUAC CHAM:
1 clove garlic, chopped
1 small, hot red chili, seeded
   and chopped
1 tbsp sugar
juice of 1 lime
2 tbsp rice wine or rice vinegar
2 tbsp fish sauce
3 tbsp water

1 Divide the spinach leaves among 4 pieces of parchment paper, each large enough to wrap loosely around a chicken breast. Top each pile of spinach with a chicken breast, then sprinkle with the ginger, lemongrass, mint, and basil. Spoon the oil and soy sauce over. Season to taste with salt and pepper. Fold up the paper around the chicken to make four loose packets.

2 Place the chicken packets in a large bamboo steamer. Cover and steam over a wok of simmering water until the chicken is cooked, 15–20 minutes.

3 While the chicken is steaming, put all the ingredients for the nuac cham in a blender or food processor and process until well combined.

4 Remove the packets from the steamer and place on four warm serving plates. Open each packet, spoon in the nuac cham, and serve.

244 teriyaki-style chicken with scallion

PREPARATION TIME: *15 minutes, plus 1 hour marinating time* **COOKING TIME:** *11 minutes*

5 tbsp light soy sauce
2 tbsp sake
4 tbsp mirin
2 tsp sugar
1½ lb skinless, boneless chicken breast,
   cut into thin strips
2 tbsp sunflower oil

1 tsp toasted sesame oil
2 cloves garlic, chopped
1-inch piece fresh ginger, peeled
   and grated
large handful of snow peas, trimmed
4 scallions, sliced diagonally
1 tbsp sesame seeds, toasted

1 Mix together the soy sauce, sake, mirin, and sugar in a shallow bowl. Add the chicken and stir well until it is coated with the marinade. Let marinate for 1 hour. Lift the chicken out of the marinade with a slotted spoon and set on one side.

2 Pour the marinade into a small saucepan and simmer gently, stirring occasionally, until reduced and syrupy, then set on one side

3 Heat the oils in a wok. Add half the chicken and stir-fry until lightly browned, 3–4 minutes. Remove the chicken from the wok using a slotted spoon and keep warm. Repeat with the remaining chicken.

4 Add the garlic, ginger, snow peas, and scallions to the wok and stir-fry for 1 minute. Return the chicken to the wok and heat through gently, then stir in the reduced marinade. Toss well until the chicken is coated with the glossy liquid, then serve, sprinkled with the sesame seeds.

245 chicken & cashew stir-fry

PREPARATION TIME: *15 minutes, plus 30 minutes marinating time* **COOKING TIME:** *8 minutes*

1 egg white, lightly beaten
4 tbsp Chinese rice wine or dry sherry
1 tbsp light soy sauce
4 tbsp water
1 tbsp cornstarch
1½ lb skinless, boneless chicken
   breast, cut into large
   bite-sized pieces
2 tbsp sunflower oil

4 scallions, sliced diagonally
2 cloves garlic, chopped
2-inch piece fresh ginger,
   peeled and minced
2 large handfuls of snow peas,
   trimmed
handful of unsalted
   cashew nuts, toasted

1 Mix together the egg white, half the wine, the soy sauce, water, and cornstarch in a bowl. Add the chicken and stir to coat. Let marinate for 30 minutes. Drain, reserving the marinade.
2 Heat a wok until hot. Add the oil, then toss in the scallions, garlic, ginger, and snow peas and stir-fry for 30 seconds. Add the chicken and stir-fry it for 3–4 minutes.
3 Pour in the remaining wine and the reserved marinade and stir well. Cook over medium heat until the sauce is reduced and thickened and the chicken is cooked through. Serve sprinkled with the toasted cashew nuts.

246 sunshine chicken stir-fry

PREPARATION TIME: *15 minutes, plus 30 minutes marinating time* **COOKING TIME:** *5 minutes*

4 tbsp Chinese rice wine or dry sherry
2-inch piece fresh ginger, peeled
   and grated
2 cloves garlic, crushed
1 lb skinless, boneless chicken breast,
   cut into strips
2 tbsp sunflower oil

1 red bell pepper, sliced
1 yellow bell pepper, sliced
½ tsp dried chili flakes
grated zest of ½ lemon
juice of 1 lemon
2 tbsp light soy sauce

1 Mix together the wine, ginger, and garlic in a shallow dish. Add the chicken and stir well to coat with the marinade. Let marinate for 30 minutes.
2 Heat a wok until hot. Add the oil, then toss in the red and yellow peppers and the chili flakes. Stir-fry for 1 minute.
3 Add the chicken and the marinade and stir-fry for 3 minutes. Add the lemon zest and juice and the soy sauce and stir-fry for 1 minute longer, then serve.

247 indonesian chicken stir-fry

PREPARATION TIME: *15 minutes* **COOKING TIME:** *13 minutes*

1 tbsp sunflower oil
1 lb skinless, boneless chicken thighs,
   cut into 1-inch cubes
3 cloves garlic, chopped
½–1 tsp dried chili flakes
2 tsp ground coriander
1 tsp turmeric

4 tbsp sambal oelek
   (Indonesian chilli sauce)
2 tbsp rice vinegar
2 handfuls of cilantro leaves,
   roughly chopped

1 Heat a wok until hot. Add the oil, then add half of the chicken and stir-fry it until golden, 3–4 minutes. Remove from the wok with a slotted spoon, drain on paper towels, and set on one side. Repeat with the remaining chicken.
2 Return the chicken to the wok, then add the garlic, chili flakes, ground coriander, and turmeric. Stir-fry for 30 seconds. Spoon in the sambal oelek and rice vinegar and cook for 3 minutes, adding a little water if the mixture becomes too dry. Serve sprinkled with the cilantro.

248 japanese-style duck

PREPARATION TIME: *10 minutes, plus 1 hour marinating* **COOKING TIME:** *10 minutes*

4 tbsp Japanese soy sauce
4 tbsp mirin
4 tbsp sake
2 tsp sugar
1-inch piece fresh ginger, peeled and cut
   into very thin strips

1½ lb skinless duck breasts, cut
   into ½-inch strips
2 tbsp sunflower oil
2 scallions, shredded

1   Mix together the soy sauce, mirin, sake, sugar, and ginger in a shallow dish. Add the duck
     strips and turn to coat them with the marinade. Let marinate for at least 1 hour. Drain,
     reserving the marinade.
2   Heat a wok until hot. Add the oil, then add half of the duck and stir-fry it for 3 minutes. Remove
     from the wok with a slotted spoon and set on one side. Add the remaining duck and stir-fry
     for 3 minutes.
3   Return the first batch of duck to the wok, add the reserved marinade, and stir-fry until the duck
     is coated in a glossy sauce. Arrange on a serving plate, scatter the scallions over, and serve.

CHAPTER 6

FISH
& SHELLFISH

All kinds of fish and shellfish can be cooked successfully in a wok. Thick fillets of fish with a firm texture are particularly suited to stir-frying, and whole fish or fillets can be steamed in minutes on a rack placed over a wok of simmering water. To keep the fish really moist and help retain nutrients, it is often steamed wrapped in a packet with a selection of aromatic herbs, slivers of ginger or garlic, or dried spices, plus a splash of Chinese wine, mirin, or soy sauce, to add extra interest and flavor.

A wok can also be used to smoke fish (or meat), giving it a deliciously subtle tang. Any firm fillet of fish can be substituted in the Tea-Smoked Salmon recipe on page 167. In fact, most of the recipes in this chapter can be made using a different type of fish or shellfish from that stated. There are just two things to remember: First, buy the freshest fish or seafood you can find. Second, timing is of the essence—fish and shellfish take only minutes to cook.

The dishes selected for this chapter reflect the popularity of fish and shellfish right across Asia. They range from the creamy coconut curries of southern India to the lemongrass-infused, steamed preparations of Vietnam and the vibrant shrimp and scallop stir-fries of China.

249 coconut fish curry

PREPARATION TIME: *20 minutes* **COOKING TIME:** *17 minutes*

1½ tbsp vegetable oil

2 tsp cumin seeds

1 large onion, grated

2 hot green chilies, minced

2 large cloves garlic, grated

1-inch piece fresh ginger, peeled
   and grated

2 tsp ground turmeric

2 tsp ground coriander

2 tsp garam masala

1¾ cups coconut milk

1½ cups canned crushed tomatoes

1¼ lb skinless haddock or cod fillets,
   cut into 1-inch pieces

juice of ½ lemon

salt

handful of cilantro leaves,
   roughly chopped

1   Heat the oil in a wok, stir in the cumin seeds, and fry until they begin to darken and sizzle. Add the onion and stir-fry until it begins to brown, about 4 minutes. Add the chilies, garlic, ginger, turmeric, ground coriander, and garam masala, and stir-fry for 30 seconds.

2   Pour in the coconut milk and crushed tomatoes and bring to a boil. Reduce the heat and simmer over low heat for 5 minutes.

3   Add the fish and cook, stirring occasionally and taking care not to break up the fish, until the sauce has thickened and the fish is cooked, about 5 minutes.

4   Stir in the lemon juice and season to taste with salt. Spoon into bowls, sprinkle with the chopped cilantro, and serve.

250 trout rolls with cilantro

PREPARATION TIME: *20 minutes* **COOKING TIME:** *14 minutes*

1½ tbsp sunflower oil

4 scallions, thinly sliced

3 cloves garlic, minced

2-inch piece fresh ginger,
   peeled and grated

1 stalk lemongrass, peeled
   and minced

2 handfuls of cilantro leaves, chopped

grated zest and juice of 2 limes

8 trout fillets, skinned

salt and freshly ground
   black pepper

4 large lettuce leaves

lime wedges for serving

1   Heat a wok until hot. Add the oil, then toss in the scallions, garlic, ginger, and lemongrass and stir-fry them for 1 minute. Remove the onion mixture from the wok, place in a bowl, and mix in the cilantro and lime zest and juice.

2   Season the fish fillets to taste with salt and pepper and spoon the onion mixture along the middle of each fillet. Carefully roll up the fillets, from the thinnest end, and secure each with one or two wooden toothpicks.

3   Place the lettuce leaves in the bottom of a large bamboo steamer and place the fish rolls on top. Cover and steam over a wok of simmering water for about 6 minutes.

4   Arrange the lettuce leaves on four warm serving plates and top each one with two fish rolls. Serve with lime wedges.

251 golden fish with soy & ginger

PREPARATION TIME: *15 minutes, plus 30 minutes marinating time*   **COOKING TIME:** *15 minutes*

2 tbsp cornstarch

½ tsp salt

4 tbsp Chinese cooking wine or dry sherry

1 lb thick white fish fillets, such as cod, halibut, monkfish, or haddock, cut into 1-inch pieces

3 tbsp all-purpose flour

1 egg white, lightly beaten

½ cup vegetable oil

2 tbsp light soy sauce

1 tsp sugar

1-inch piece fresh ginger, peeled and finely grated

⅔ cup water

2 scallions, cut into strips

1   Mix together 1 tablespoon of the cornstarch, the salt, and the wine in a shallow dish. Add the fish and turn to coat it with the mixture, then let marinate for 30 minutes.

2   Mix together the remaining cornstarch and the flour on a plate. Dip the fish pieces into the egg white, then in the flour. Heat the oil in a wok until a cube of day-old bread will turn golden in 30 seconds. Fry the fish in 2–3 batches until golden. Drain on paper towels and keep warm.

3   Pour off all but 2 tablespoons of the oil from the wok, then add the soy sauce, sugar, ginger, and water. Cook until the liquid has reduced slightly. Return the fish to the wok and heat for a few minutes until the sauce has thickened. Serve garnished with the scallion strips.

252 soy-glazed sesame mackerel

PREPARATION TIME: *10 minutes, plus 30 minutes marinating time* **COOKING TIME:** *26 minutes*

2 cloves garlic, crushed
grated zest and juice of 1 lime
1 tbsp vegetable oil
2 tsp toasted sesame oil
3 tbsp mirin or dry sherry

3 tbsp light soy sauce
4 whole fresh mackerel, head and tail
   removed and gutted
salt and freshly ground black pepper
toasted sesame seeds for garnish

1. Mix together the garlic, lime zest and juice, oils, mirin, and soy sauce to make a marinade.
2. Using a sharp knife, make 3 slashes on each side of the fish. Place the fish in a large, shallow dish and pour the marinade over, rubbing it into the cuts. Cover and let marinate in the refrigerator for 30 minutes.
3. Place the mackerel in a large bamboo steamer lined with parchment paper, reserving any remaining marinade. Season well with salt and pepper, then cover and steam over a wok of simmering water until the fish is cooked, 10–12 minutes.
4. Remove the fish from the steamer and place on warm serving plates. Pour any juices in the baking paper over the fish. Keep warm.
5. Pour away the water in the wok. Add the reserved marinade to the wok and simmer until reduced. Pour this sauce over the fish, sprinkle with the sesame seeds, and serve.

253 burmese fish balls with lime

PREPARATION TIME: *20 minutes* **COOKING TIME:** *15 minutes*

1 slice white bread
12 oz white fish fillets, such as
   cod or haddock,
   roughly chopped
1 onion, roughly chopped
½ tsp salt
1 clove garlic, crushed

2-inch piece fresh ginger,
   peeled and grated
2 handfuls of cilantro leaves,
   chopped, plus extra for garnish
juice of 1 lime
1 recipe quantity lime sauce
   (see Burmese Chicken with Lime, p139)

1. Soak the bread in hot water; squeeze dry and break up into small pieces. Put the fish and onion in a food processor and process until ground. Scoop the mixture into a bowl, then mix with the remaining ingredients, including the soaked bread. Form into 20 walnut-sized balls, squeezing each to remove any excess water. Set on one side.
2. Make the lime sauce following the recipe for Burmese Chicken with Lime, omitting the chicken in Step 2 and adding the fish balls after the sauce has reached boiling point in Step 4.
3. Spoon the sauce over the balls, cover, and cook over medium heat for 12–15 minutes, removing the lid for the last 3 minutes. Serve sprinkled with chopped cilantro.

254 black bean & chili haddock

PREPARATION TIME: *10 minutes, plus 1 hour marinating time* **COOKING TIME:** *7 minutes*

6 tbsp black bean sauce
2 tbsp sweet chili sauce
1-inch piece fresh ginger, peeled
   and grated

salt and freshly ground black pepper
4 thick haddock or cod fillets, about
   6 oz each
1 mildly hot, red chili, sliced

1. Mix together the black bean and sweet chili sauces. Stir in the ginger and season with salt and pepper to taste. Spoon the mixture over the fish and let marinate in the refrigerator for 1 hour.
2. Place the fish in a large bamboo steamer lined with parchment paper. Sprinkle the chili over the fish, then cover and steam over a wok of simmering water for about 7 minutes.
3. Use a slotted spatula to transfer the fish to warm serving plates. Spoon the cooking juices from the paper over the fish and serve immediately.

255 sweet & sour fish

PREPARATION TIME: *15 minutes* **COOKING TIME:** *12 minutes*

1 lb firm white fish fillets, such
   as cod or haddock, cut into
   1-inch pieces
2 tbsp cornstarch
3 tbsp sunflower oil
1 large carrot, cut into thin strips
2 stalks celery, sliced

3 tbsp tomato paste
3 tbsp light soy sauce
3 tbsp rice vinegar or
   white wine vinegar
5 tbsp pineapple juice
4 tbsp water
salt and freshly ground black pepper

1 Dip the fish in the cornstarch and turn until lightly coated. Heat a wok until hot. Add the oil, then add half of the fish and fry it until golden on all sides, about 3 minutes. Remove using a slotted spatula and set on one side. Repeat with the remaining fish.

2 Put the carrot and celery in the wok and stir-fry for 2 minutes. Add the tomato paste, soy sauce, vinegar, pineapple juice, and water and stir-fry for 2 minutes. Add the cooked fish, cover, and heat through. Add extra water if the sauce appears too dry. Season to taste with salt and pepper and serve.

256 cilantro cod with garlic

PREPARATION TIME: *20 minutes* **COOKING TIME:** *7 minutes*

2 tbsp sunflower oil
3 cloves garlic, chopped
2 leeks, thinly sliced
1 mildly hot, long, red chili, seeded and
   thinly sliced
2 carrots, cut into long, thick strips
2 zucchini, sliced

4 thick cod fillets, about 6 oz each,
   cut into 1-inch cubes
2 large handfuls of cilantro leaves, chopped
1 tbsp light soy sauce
5–8 tbsp water
large handful of beansprouts
salt and freshly ground black pepper

1 Heat a wok until hot. Add the oil, then toss in the garlic, leeks, chili, carrots, and zucchini and stir-fry for 2 minutes. Remove the vegetables from the wok using a slotted spoon and set on one side.

2 Add the fish to the wok and sear for 1 minute, without moving it, then turn it over and cook for 1 more minute. Return the vegetables to the wok along with 4 tablespoons of the cilantro.

3 Pour in the soy sauce and water and stir gently, then cover. Cook for 1–2 minutes. Stir in the beansprouts, season to taste with salt and pepper, and serve, sprinkled with the remaining chopped cilantro.

257 aromatic stuffed trout

PREPARATION TIME: *15 minutes* **COOKING TIME:** *25 minutes*

4 lemongrass stalks, peeled
   and minced
2 cloves garlic, thinly sliced
2 kaffir lime leaves, shredded
2-inch piece fresh ginger,
   peeled and cut into matchsticks
grated zest and juice of 2 limes

2 large handfuls of cilantro leaves,
   chopped
2 large handfuls of Thai basil leaves,
   chopped
4 whole trout, head and tail removed
   and gutted
salt and freshly ground black pepper

1 Mix together the lemongrass, garlic, lime leaves, ginger, lime zest, and half the chopped cilantro and basil. Open out each trout slightly and stuff some of this filling mixture into the cavity. Pour the lime juice over each fish and season well with salt and pepper.

2 Place the fish in a large bamboo steamer lined with parchment paper. Cover and steam over a wok of simmering water until cooked, about 12 minutes. Transfer the fish to four warm serving plates, sprinkle the remaining cilantro and basil over, and serve.

258 asian salmon packets with basil

PREPARATION TIME: *15 minutes* **COOKING TIME:** *12 minutes*

1 tbsp sunflower oil
1 tbsp toasted sesame oil
1-inch piece fresh ginger, peeled
   and cut into thin strips
2 large cloves garlic, minced
2 tbsp light soy sauce

juice of 2 limes
4 thick salmon fillets, about
   5 oz each
3 scallions, cut into fine strips
10 large basil leaves, torn
salt and freshly ground black pepper

1   Heat the oils in a wok, add the ginger and garlic, and stir-fry for a few seconds. Stir in the soy sauce and lime juice.

2   Place each fish fillet on a piece of parchment paper large enough to wrap around it and make a packet. Spoon the ginger and garlic sauce over the fish. Sprinkle with the scallions and two-thirds of the basil and season to taste with salt and pepper. Fold up the paper around the fish to make loose packets, sealing well.

3   Place the packets in a large bamboo steamer. Cover and steam over a wok of simmering water until the fish is cooked, 8–10 minutes.

4   Remove the fish from the steamer and place on four warm serving plates. Open each packet, sprinkle with the remaining basil, and serve.

259 sweet chili & honey tuna

PREPARATION TIME: *10 minutes, plus 30 minutes marinating time* **COOKING TIME:** *10 minutes*

4 thick tuna steaks,
   about 5 oz each
salt and freshly ground black pepper
2 tbsp sunflower oil

MARINADE:
1 tsp Szechuan peppercorns,
   toasted and crushed

3 tbsp light soy sauce
1 tbsp toasted sesame oil
1-inch piece fresh ginger,
   peeled and grated
1 large clove garlic, thinly sliced
2 tbsp honey
3 tbsp Chinese cooking wine
   or dry sherry

1   Mix together the ingredients for the marinade in a shallow dish. Season the tuna steaks to taste with salt and pepper, place in the marinade and turn until well coated, then let marinate for 30 minutes to 1 hour.

2   Heat the sunflower oil in a wok. Remove the tuna from the marinade using a slotted spatula and place in the wok. Sear for 1–2 minutes on each side, depending on the thickness of the steaks—they should remain pink in the center.

3   Transfer the tuna to a warm serving platter and keep warm. Pour off any excess oil in the wok and add the marinade. Boil until slightly reduced, then pour over the tuna and serve.

260 steamed fish in herb sauce

PREPARATION TIME: *10 minutes* COOKING TIME: *12 minutes*

4 whole flatfish, such as sole
  or flounder, cleaned and trimmed
salt and freshly ground black pepper

HERB SAUCE:
4 tbsp butter
2 shallots, minced
4 tbsp Chinese rice wine
  or dry sherry

2 tsp light soy sauce
⅔ cup fish or vegetable stock
large handful of Thai basil leaves,
  minced
large handful of cilantro leaves,
  minced
handful of chives, minced

1 First make the sauce. Heat 1 tablespoon of the butter in a pan over medium heat. Add the shallots and fry for 2 minutes. Pour in the rice wine and cook until reduced, then add the soy sauce and stock. Increase the heat and cook until the stock has reduced by half. Stir in the rest of the butter, 1 tablespoon at a time, then stir in the herbs. Set on one side and keep warm.
2 Place the fish, in a single layer, in a large bamboo steamer lined with parchment paper (you may need to cook the fish in two batches). Sprinkle with salt and pepper to taste. Cover and steam over a wok of simmering water for about 5 minutes.
3 Serve the fish immediately with the warm sauce spooned over.

261 monkfish with ginger & scallions

PREPARATION TIME: *15 minutes* COOKING TIME: *9 minutes*

2 tbsp cornstarch
1 lb monkfish fillet, skinned
  and cut into 1-inch cubes
1 tbsp sunflower oil
1 tbsp toasted sesame oil
2-inch piece fresh ginger,
  peeled and grated
2 large cloves garlic,
  minced

4 scallions, white and green parts
  separated and sliced diagonally
2 tbsp Chinese cooking wine
  or dry sherry
2 tbsp light soy sauce
6 tbsp water
salt and freshly ground black pepper
handful of cilantro leaves,
  roughly chopped

1 Put the cornstarch on a plate, add the monkfish, and turn until lightly coated all over. Heat the oils in a wok and add half of the monkfish. Fry until golden on all sides, about 3 minutes. Carefully remove the fish using a slotted spatula and keep warm. Repeat with the remaining fish, adding more oil to the wok, if necessary.
2 Add the ginger, garlic, and white part of the scallions to the hot oil and stir-fry for a few seconds. Pour in the wine and soy sauce, followed by the water. Stir, then return the fish to the wok. Cover and simmer until the fish is cooked through, 2–3 minutes.
3 Season to taste with salt and pepper and serve, sprinkled with the green part of the scallions and the chopped cilantro.

262 vietnamese steamed fish

PREPARATION TIME: *15 minutes* **COOKING TIME:** *20 minutes*

4 large handfuls of baby spinach
  leaves, washed
4 thick white fish fillets,
  such as cod or haddock,
  about 6 oz each
2 stalks lemongrass, peeled
  and chopped
2 handfuls of mint leaves, chopped

1-inch piece fresh ginger,
  peeled and cut into thin strips
2 handfuls of basil leaves, chopped,
  plus extra for garnish
4 tsp olive oil
4 tsp light soy sauce
salt and freshly ground black pepper

1   Cut out 4 pieces of parchment paper, each large enough to wrap around a fish fillet and make
    a packet. Divide the spinach leaves equally among the pieces of parchment, then place a piece
    of fish on top of the spinach. Mix together the lemongrass, mint, ginger, and chopped basil, and
    sprinkle equal amounts over each fish fillet. Spoon the oil and soy sauce over and season to
    taste with salt and pepper. Fold up the parchment around each piece of fish to make a loose
    packet, sealing well.
2   Place the fish packets in a single layer in a large bamboo steamer, cover, and steam over a wok
    of simmering water until the fish is cooked, 8–10 minutes.
3   Remove the fish packets from the steamer and place on four warm plates. Open each packet
    and serve with extra basil sprinkled over.

263 sesame fish strips with japanese dipping sauce

PREPARATION TIME: *20 minutes* **COOKING TIME:** *12 minutes*

scant 1 cup all-purpose flour
⅛ tsp salt
1 tbsp sunflower oil
2 tbsp mirin or dry sherry
½ cup water
2 egg whites
4 sole or flounder fillets
peanut oil for deep-frying
3 tbsp sesame seeds

DIPPING SAUCE:
4 tbsp mirin or dry sherry
1 tbsp rice vinegar
2 cloves garlic, crushed
1 mildly hot, long, red chili, seeded
  and minced
1 tsp sugar
juice of 2 limes
handful of cilantro leaves, chopped

1   First make the dipping sauce by mixing together all the ingredients in a small bowl.
2   Sift the flour and salt into a mixing bowl. Gradually beat in the oil, mirin, and water. Beat
    the eggs whites until they form stiff peaks, then fold them into the flour mixture to form a
    coating batter.
3   Rinse and pat dry the fish fillets. Cut each fillet into about 8 strips. Pour oil into a wok until
    it is one-third full, then heat until the oil is hot enough to brown a cube of day-old bread in
    about 30 seconds.
4   Dip each piece of fish into the batter, then into the sesame seeds and fry, in 3–4 batches, until
    crisp and golden, 2–3 minutes per batch. Drain on paper towels. Keep warm while frying the
    remaining fish. Serve with the dipping sauce.

264 spice battered fish sticks
with sweet chili mayo

PREPARATION TIME: *20 minutes* **COOKING TIME:** *15 minutes*

4 sole fillets, about 6 oz each
scant 1 cup all-purpose flour
½ tsp paprika
⅛ tsp salt
1 tbsp vegetable oil, plus extra
  for deep-frying
⅔ cup water
2 egg whites

SWEET CHILI MAYO:
4 tbsp mayonnaise
2 tbsp sweet chili sauce
1 tsp grated fresh ginger
1 mildly hot, red chili, minced

1   Mix together all the ingredients for the sweet chili mayo in a small bowl and set on one side.
    Rinse the sole fillets and pat dry. Cut each fillet into about 8 strips.
2   Sift the flour, paprika, and salt into a mixing bowl. Gradually beat in 1 tablespoon of the oil and
    the water. Beat the eggs whites until they form stiff peaks, then fold them into the flour
    mixture, to form a coating batter.
3   Pour oil into a wok until it is one-third full, then heat the oil until it is hot enough to brown a
    cube of day-old bread in about 30 seconds. Divide the fish into 3 or 4 batches. Cook each batch
    by dipping the pieces of fish into the batter, then frying in the hot oil until crisp and golden,
    2–3 minutes. Drain on paper towels and keep warm until all the fish is cooked. Serve the fish
    sticks immediately with the sweet chili mayo for dipping.

265 monkfish & zucchini kadahi

PREPARATION TIME: *20 minutes* **COOKING TIME:** *15 minutes*

2 tbsp peanut oil

4 hot green chilies, cut down
   one side and seeded

1 lb monkfish or other firm
   white fish fillet,
   skinned and cut into
   bite-sized pieces

all-purpose flour for dusting

1 large onion, thinly sliced

2 zucchini, thinly sliced

8 curry leaves

1 tsp yellow mustard seeds

2 cloves garlic, minced

1-inch piece fresh ginger,
   peeled and chopped

1 tsp chili powder

1 cup fish or vegetable stock

2 tbsp lemon juice

2 handfuls of cilantro leaves,
   roughly chopped

salt

1   Heat the oil in a wok until hot. Add the chilies and stir-fry for 1 minute, then remove from the
    wok and discard. Lightly dust the fish pieces with the flour.

2   Add the floured fish to the wok and gently stir-fry for about 2 minutes over medium heat,
    then remove using a slotted spoon. Set on one side and keep warm.

3   Add the onion and zucchini to the wok and stir-fry for 3 minutes, then add the curry leaves and
    mustard seeds and cook for 1 more minute. Add the garlic, ginger, and chili powder and stir-fry
    for 1 minute longer.

4   Pour in the stock and lemon juice, stir, and cook over medium heat until slightly reduced, then
    add the fish and half of the cilantro. Season to taste with salt, cover, and cook over low heat
    for 5 minutes. Serve sprinkled with the remaining cilantro.

266 braised fish with black beans

PREPARATION TIME: *15 minutes* **COOKING TIME:** *15 minutes*

4 tbsp salted black beans

2 tbsp sunflower oil

1 tbsp toasted sesame oil

10 large broccoli florets,
   cut into small florets
   and stems sliced

1 red bell pepper, thinly sliced

2-inch piece fresh ginger,
   peeled and cut into thin strips

4 scallions, sliced diagonally

3 tbsp Chinese cooking wine
   or dry sherry

3 tbsp light soy sauce

¾ cup water

4 salmon fillets, about 5 oz each

1 onion, chopped and
   fried until crisp and golden

1   Soak the beans in hot water for 10 minutes to remove the excess salt. Drain and leave
    on one side.

2   Heat a wok until hot. Add the oils, then toss in the broccoli and stir-fry it for 2 minutes. Add the
    red pepper, ginger, and scallions and stir-fry for 2 more minutes.

3   Pour in the wine, soy sauce, and water and stir, then place the salmon fillets on top of the
    vegetables and spoon some of the liquid over them.

4   Cover the wok and simmer gently until the fish is cooked, 8–10 minutes. Add the drained beans
    to the wok 3 minutes before the end of the cooking time. Serve sprinkled with the crisp onion.

267 sole & asparagus rolls

PREPARATION TIME: *20 minutes* **COOKING TIME:** *8 minutes*

4 sole or flounder fillets, about 6 oz each,
   skinned
1 tbsp toasted sesame oil
1 tbsp light soy sauce
salt and freshly ground black pepper
12 thin asparagus spears, trimmed
12 thin strips of red bell pepper
handful of cilantro leaves,
   roughly chopped

SAUCE:
1 clove garlic, chopped
4 tbsp water
1 tbsp light soy sauce
4 tbsp yellow bean sauce
2 tbsp Chinese cooking wine
   or dry sherry

1 Cut each fish fillet into 4 long strips. Mix together the sesame oil and soy sauce, then drizzle over the fish. Sprinkle with salt and pepper to taste. Place an asparagus spear and strip of red pepper across each strip and roll up the fish. Secure with a wooden toothpick.

2 Place the fish rolls in a large bamboo steamer lined with parchment paper. Cover and steam the fish over a wok of simmering water for 3–4 minutes.

3 Meanwhile, make the sauce: Put all the ingredients in a small saucepan and simmer until thickened, about 3 minutes.

4 Arrange the cooked fish rolls on a serving platter, pour the sauce over them, garnish with the chopped cilantro, and serve.

268 japanese sea bass with stir-fried asparagus

PREPARATION TIME: *20 minutes, plus 30 minutes marinating time* **COOKING TIME:** *16 minutes*

juice of 2 limes
2 tsp rice wine vinegar
8 sea bass fillets
salt and freshly ground black pepper
1 tbsp sunflower oil
1 tbsp toasted sesame oil
12 asparagus spears, trimmed
   and sliced diagonally
2 cloves garlic, minced

1 mildly hot, long, red chili, seeded
   and cut into strips
1 carrot, finely shredded
2-inch piece English cucumber,
   seeded and shredded
2 tbsp mirin or dry sherry
2 tbsp light soy sauce
2 scallions, shredded

1 Mix together the juice of 1 lime and the rice wine vinegar. Put the fish fillets in a large, shallow dish and pour the lime juice mixture over them. Season to taste with salt and pepper, then let marinate for 30 minutes.

2 Place the fish in a large bamboo steamer lined with parchment paper. Cover and steam over a wok of simmering water until the fish is cooked, about 5 minutes. Remove the fish from the steamer and place on a plate. Add any juices and cover the fish to keep warm.

3 Pour away the water in the wok and dry it. Heat the oils in the wok, add the asparagus, and stir-fry for 2 minutes. Add the garlic, chili, carrot, and cucumber and stir-fry for 2 more minutes.

4 Add the mirin and soy sauce, stir, and heat through, adding a little water if the vegetables start to dry out. Place two fish fillets on each serving plate. Top with the vegetables and any juices, sprinkle with the scallions, and serve.

269 lime & chili swordfish with herb oil

PREPARATION TIME: *20 minutes, plus 30 minutes marinating time* **COOKING TIME:** *20 minutes*

4 swordfish steaks,
   about 6 oz each
large handful of mint leaves,
   roughly chopped
large handful of Thai basil leaves,
   roughly chopped
large handful of cilantro leaves,
   roughly chopped
3 tbsp olive oil
salt and freshly ground black pepper

MARINADE:
1 tbsp olive oil
grated zest and juice of 2 limes
1 mildly hot, long, red chili, seeded
   and thinly sliced
1-inch piece fresh ginger,
   peeled and grated

1   Mix together the ingredients for the marinade in a shallow dish and add the swordfish steaks,
    turning until well coated. Let marinate for 30 minutes.
2   Make the herb oil: Put the mint, basil, and cilantro in a blender with the olive oil and process
    until smooth. Season to taste with salt and pepper.
3   Take the swordfish out of the marinade and put each steak onto a piece of parchment paper
    large enough to wrap around it and make a packet. Spoon the marinade over the fish. Fold up
    the paper around each piece of fish to make a loose packet, sealing well.
4   Place the fish packets in a bamboo steamer. Cover and steam over a wok of simmering water
    until the fish is cooked, 8–10 minutes.
5   Remove the fish from the packets and transfer to warm serving plates. Pour any juices in the
    baking paper over the fish, then spoon on the prepared herb oil and serve.

270 red snapper with orange & chili glaze

PREPARATION TIME: *15 minutes* **COOKING TIME:** *22 minutes*

3-lb whole red snapper,
    scaled, gutted, and head
    and tail removed
2 tsp olive oil
finely grated zest
    of 1 orange

salt and freshly ground black pepper
6 tbsp fresh orange juice
3 tbsp sweet chili sauce
2 handfuls of cilantro leaves,
    roughly chopped

1   Rinse the fish and dry with paper towels. Make three slashes down each side. Mix together the oil, orange zest, and salt and pepper to taste, and rub this mixture onto each side of the fish, working it into the slashes.

2   Place the fish in a large bamboo steamer lined with parchment paper. Cover and steam over a wok of simmering water until the fish is cooked, about 20 minutes.

3   Remove the fish from the steamer and place on a plate. Pour any juices in the baking paper over the fish and cover to keep warm.

4   Pour the water from the wok and dry it. Mix together the orange juice, sweet chili sauce, and salt and pepper to taste in the wok. Simmer briefly until reduced and thickened.

5   Divide the fish among four warm serving plates, pour the sauce over, sprinkle with the chopped cilantro, and serve.

271 wok-seared salmon
with sesame-soy marinade

PREPARATION TIME: *15 minutes, plus 1 hour marinating time* **COOKING TIME:** *8 minutes*

4 salmon fillets, about 5 oz each
1-inch piece fresh ginger, peeled
    and minced
1 tbsp toasted sesame oil
3 tbsp light soy sauce

1 tbsp honey
juice of 1 lime
1–2 tbsp sunflower oil
2 large handfuls of snow peas, trimmed
2 scallions, sliced diagonally

1   Cut the salmon on the diagonal into ¾-inch-thick slices. Mix together the ginger, sesame oil, soy sauce, honey, and lime juice in a shallow dish to make a marinade. Place the salmon in the marinade and let marinate for about 1 hour.

2   Heat the sunflower oil in a wok, add the snow peas, and stir-fry for 1 minute, then remove using a slotted spoon and set on one side.

3   Remove the salmon from the marinade. Add half to the wok and sear over medium heat for 1 minute without moving. Turn over and sear the other side. Remove from the wok and keep warm. Repeat with the remaining salmon, adding extra oil to the wok, if necessary.

4   Return the first batch of salmon to the wok along with the snow peas and pour in the marinade. Increase the heat slightly and cook for a few seconds until the marinade has reduced and thickened. Serve sprinkled with the scallions.

272 indonesian fish balls with crisp basil

PREPARATION TIME: *20 minutes, plus 30 minutes chilling* **COOKING TIME:** *14 minutes*

10 oz white fish fillets, such as cod
  or haddock, skinned
10 oz raw shrimp, peeled
1 large onion, quartered
1-inch piece fresh ginger,
  peeled and finely grated
3 cloves garlic, minced
2 tsp fish sauce
1 tsp sambal oelek (Indonesian
  chili sauce) or 1 mildly hot,
  long, red chili, seeded
  and minced

1 tbsp kecap manis
  (Indonesian soy sauce)
grated zest of 1 lime
handful of cilantro leaves, chopped
½ tsp turmeric
2 handfuls of fresh bread crumbs
large pinch of ground cinnamon
salt and freshly ground black pepper
1 medium egg, lightly beaten
vegetable oil for deep-frying
handful of basil leaves

1 Put the fish, shrimp, and onion in a food processor and process to form a coarse paste. Transfer to a bowl and mix in the ginger, garlic, fish sauce, sambal oelek, kecap manis, lime zest, cilantro, turmeric, bread crumbs, cinnamon, and salt and pepper to taste. Mix in the egg, then cover and refrigerate the mixture for 30 minutes.

2 Shape the fish mixture into 20 walnut-sized balls. Heat enough oil in a wok to deep-fry the balls until it is hot enough to brown a cube of day-old bread in about 35 seconds. Add the basil leaves and fry for a few seconds until crisp, then remove and let drain on paper towels.

3 Divide the fish balls into 3 or 4 batches. Fry each batch until golden and cooked through, 3–4 minutes, then remove and drain on paper towels. Keep warm until all the fish balls have been deep-fried

4 Serve the fish balls hot, garnished with the crisp basil leaves, either on their own or with a dipping sauce, such as Nuac Cham (see page149).

273 mackerel with lime & mango

PREPARATION TIME: *20 minutes* **COOKING TIME:** *15 minutes*

2 tbsp olive oil
4 shallots, minced
2 cloves garlic, chopped
2 hot green chilies, seeded
  and finely sliced
2 kaffir lime leaves, finely sliced
2 tsp fish sauce
1 tsp sugar

juice of 1 lime
4 mackerel, gutted and head
  and tail removed
1 small mango, peeled and
  cut into small dice
salt
handful of cilantro leaves
  for garnish

1 Heat a wok until hot. Add the oil, then toss in the shallots and stir-fry them for 1 minute. Add the garlic, chilies, and lime leaves and stir-fry for 1 more minute. Pour in the fish sauce and sugar and stir until the sugar has dissolved. Remove from the heat and stir in the lime juice. Set aside while you steam the mackerel.

2 Place the mackerel in a large bamboo steamer lined with parchment paper. Cover and steam over a wok of simmering water for about 6 minutes. While the fish is steaming, stir the mango into the shallot mixture and season well with salt.

3 Place the cooked mackerel on warm serving plates and spoon the mango salsa over them. Sprinkle with the chopped cilantro and serve.

274   tea-smoked salmon

PREPARATION TIME: *15 minutes, plus 1 hour marinating time*   **COOKING TIME:** *32 minutes*

2 tsp Szechuan peppercorns, toasted
   and crushed
½ tsp Chinese five-spice
1 tsp salt
1 tbsp light brown sugar
4 salmon fillets, about 5 oz each
sunflower oil for greasing

SMOKING MIXTURE:
2 large handfuls of long-grain
   white rice
large handful of black tea leaves
2 tbsp light brown sugar

1   Mix the Szechuan pepper, five-spice, salt, and sugar together. Put the salmon fillets in a
   shallow dish and spoon the spice and sugar mixture over them, pressing it into the fish. Let
   marinate for at least 1 hour, or preferably overnight.
2   Line the inside of the wok and lid with foil to protect them. Mix the smoking mixture
   ingredients together and put into the wok. Lightly oil a rack and place it over the smoking
   mixture, making sure it is not touching.
3   Heat the wok and, when the mixture starts to smoke, put the salmon on the rack and cover with
   a tightly fitting lid.
4   Reduce the heat as low as possible, making sure that the mixture in the wok is still smoking,
   and smoke the fish for 30 minutes. Keep the kitchen well ventilated. Remove from the heat and
   let stand for 5 minutes. Remove the fish from the wok and serve.

275 japanese-style salmon

PREPARATION TIME: *20 minutes* **COOKING TIME:** *9 minutes*

2 tbsp all-purpose flour
2 tsp wasabi powder or
   English mustard powder
1 lb salmon fillet, skinned
   and cut into 1½-inch pieces
2–3 tbsp sunflower oil
2 cloves garlic, chopped
4 tbsp light soy sauce

½ cup mirin or dry sherry
4 tbsp fresh apple juice
4 cups shredded fresh spinach
½ cup water
2 scallions, sliced diagonally
1 tbsp sesame seeds, toasted

1   Mix together the flour and wasabi powder on a plate. Dip the salmon pieces into the flour until lightly coated all over.

2   Heat a wok until hot. Add the oil, then add half of the salmon and sear it, without moving, for 1 minute. Turn and sear the other side for 1 minute. Remove from the wok and keep warm. Repeat with the remaining salmon.

3   Add the garlic, soy sauce, mirin, apple juice, spinach, and water to the wok and stir-fry until the spinach has wilted, about 2 minutes. Return the fish to the wok and stir to coat with the sauce, then cook for 1–2 minutes. Serve with the scallions and sesame seeds sprinkled on top.

276 asian fish packets

PREPARATION TIME: *20 minutes* **COOKING TIME:** *16 minutes*

4 thick white fish fillets, about 6 oz each
2 cloves garlic, thinly sliced
½-inch piece fresh ginger,
   peeled and cut into matchsticks
4 baby leeks, cut into thin strips
1 carrot, cut into thin strips
1 red bell pepper, cut into thin strips

2 lemongrass stalks, peeled and minced
juice of 2 limes
2 tbsp light soy sauce
1 tbsp toasted sesame oil
salt and freshly ground black pepper
handful of cilantro leaves,
   roughly chopped

1   Place each fish fillet on a sheet of parchment paper that is large enough to wrap around the fish and make a packet. Arrange the garlic, ginger, leeks, carrot, red pepper, and lemongrass on top of each piece of fish. Mix together the lime juice, soy sauce, and sesame oil, and spoon the mixture over the fish. Season well with salt and pepper, then fold the paper over the fish to make a loose packet, sealing well.

2   Place the fish packets in a large bamboo steamer. Cover and steam over a wok of simmering water for about 8 minutes. Open the packets, sprinkle with the chopped cilantro, and serve.

277 sea bass with citrus marinade

PREPARATION TIME: *15 minutes, plus 30 minutes marinating time* **COOKING TIME:** *10 minutes*

juice of 2 oranges
1-inch piece fresh ginger, peeled
   and minced
2 cloves garlic, crushed

1 tbsp sunflower oil
salt and freshly ground black pepper
8 sea bass fillets
2 scallions, shredded

1   Mix together the orange juice, ginger, garlic, oil, and salt and pepper to taste. Spoon the mixture over the sea bass. Let marinate for 30 minutes.

2   Place the fish in a large bamboo steamer lined with parchment paper. Cover and steam over a wok of simmering water until the fish is cooked, about 5 minutes.

3   Remove the fish from the steamer and place on warm serving plates. Pour any juices from the baking paper over the fish, scatter on the scallions, and serve.

278 spiced marinated tuna

PREPARATION TIME: *10 minutes, plus 30 minutes marinating time*   **COOKING TIME:** *5 minutes*

3 tbsp sunflower oil	salt and freshly ground black pepper
1 tsp ground coriander	4 tuna steaks, about 5 oz each, cut
1 tsp ground cumin	into slices on the diagonal
juice of 1 lemon	handful of cilantro leaves

1   Mix together 1 tablespoon of the oil, the ground spices, lemon juice, and salt and pepper to taste in a shallow dish. Add the slices of tuna and turn until they are well coated. Let marinate for 30 minutes.

2   Heat the remaining oil in a wok. Take the tuna out of the marinade using a slotted spatula and place in the wok. Sear for about 1 minute on each side, depending on the thickness of the fish; it should still be pink in the center.

3   Pour in the marinade and heat through. Serve immediately, garnished with cilantro leaves.

279 stir-fried fish with choy sum

PREPARATION TIME: *15 minutes*   **COOKING TIME:** *8 minutes*

2 tbsp sunflower oil	2 tbsp light soy sauce
2 scallions, sliced diagonally	2 tbsp oyster sauce
2 cloves garlic, minced	1 lb firm white fish fillets,
1-inch piece fresh ginger, peeled	such as cod or haddock,
and finely grated	cut into 1-inch pieces
8 oz choy sum (Chinese flowering	2 tsp cornstarch
cabbage), leaves and stems separated	3 tablespoons water
and cut into thick diagonal slices	

1   Heat a wok until hot. Add the oil, then toss in the scallions, garlic, ginger, and choy sum and stir-fry them for 1 minute. Stir in the soy sauce and oyster sauce.

2   Add the fish, cover, and cook over medium heat, gently stirring occasionally, until the fish is just cooked, 3–4 minutes.

3   Mix the cornstarch with the water and stir into the wok. Bring the sauce to a boil and simmer until slightly thickened. Serve immediately.

280 monkfish with mushrooms

PREPARATION TIME: *5 minutes, plus 30 minutes marinating time*   **COOKING TIME:** *12 minutes*

2 cloves garlic, crushed	1 lb monkfish fillet, skinned
1 tsp turmeric	and cut into ¾-inch cubes
1 tsp ground cumin	3 tbsp peanut oil
1 tsp ground coriander	2 cups sliced cremini mushrooms
1 tsp chili powder	salt
juice of 1 large lemon	handful of cilantro leaves, roughly chopped

1   Mix together the garlic, turmeric, cumin, coriander, chili powder, and lemon juice. Add the monkfish and turn until the fish is coated with the spice mixture. Let marinate for 30 minutes.

2   Heat a wok until hot. Add the oil, then toss in the mushrooms and stir-fry them for 2 minutes. Remove from the wok and set on one side. Put the fish in the wok, reserving the marinade, and stir-fry for 5–7 minutes, taking care not to break it up. Remove from the wok and keep warm.

3   Return the mushrooms to the wok and add the reserved spice marinade along with a little water if the stir-fry appears too dry.

4   Return the fish to the wok, season to taste with salt, and stir to coat the fish well with the spices. Sprinkle with the chopped cilantro before serving.

281 lobster with fragrant butter

PREPARATION TIME: *15 minutes* **COOKING TIME:** *6 minutes*

4 tbsp butter

1 tbsp olive oil

5 scallions, sliced on the diagonal

2 stalks lemongrass, peeled
   and minced

2 kaffir lime leaves, finely shredded

6 tbsp Chinese cooking wine
   or dry sherry

1 tbsp light soy sauce

¾ cup fish or vegetable stock

2 cooked lobsters,
   halved lengthwise
   and claws cracked

handful of basil leaves

4 lime wedges for serving

1   Heat 1 tablespoon of the butter and the oil in a wok over medium-low heat. Add the scallions,
    lemongrass, and lime leaves and stir-fry them for 2 minutes. Pour in the wine and simmer until
    reduced by about half, then add the soy sauce and stock.

2   Increase the heat and cook until the liquid has reduced by half. Stir in the remaining butter,
    1 tablespoon at a time.

3   Arrange the cold lobster on a serving platter. Spoon the warm butter sauce over the halves and
    sprinkle with the basil leaves. Serve immediately, with the wedges of lime.

282 clams with garlic & chili

PREPARATION TIME: *20 minutes, plus 15 minutes soaking time* **COOKING TIME:** *7 minutes*

3½ lb small hardshell clams
2 tbsp peanut oil
4 cloves garlic, minced
1-inch piece fresh ginger,
   peeled and minced
2 mildly hot, long, red chilies, seeded
   and minced

6 tbsp Chinese cooking wine
   or dry sherry
6 tbsp water
2 tbsp light soy sauce
handful of cilantro leaves,
   roughly chopped

1   Scrub and rinse the clams well under cold running water. Discard any clams that have broken shells or those that remain open when tapped. Leave the clams immersed in cold salted water until ready to use.

2   Heat the oil in a large wok. Reduce the heat slightly and add the garlic, ginger, and chili and stir-fry for a few seconds.

3   Increase the heat, add the wine, water, and soy sauce, and bring to a boil. Reduce the heat to medium, tip in the clams, and cover the wok. Cook, shaking the wok and tossing the clams regularly, for a few minutes until the shells open. Discard any clams that remain closed.

4   Divide the clams among four shallow serving bowls. Pour the sauce over them, sprinkle with the chopped cilantro, and serve.

283 thai-style mussels

PREPARATION TIME: *20 minutes* **COOKING TIME:** *12 minutes*

4½ lb mussels
2 tbsp peanut oil
2 Asian red shallots or
   4 small shallots, chopped
2 lemongrass stalks, peeled and minced
3 large cloves garlic, chopped
1 mildly hot, long, red chili, seeded
   and sliced

4 kaffir lime leaves
4 tbsp Chinese cooking wine
   or dry sherry
1 cup fish stock
4 tbsp Thai tom yam paste
juice of 1 lime
handful of cilantro leaves, minced, plus
   sprigs for garnish

1   Scrub and rinse the mussels well under cold running water, removing the beards. Discard any mussels with broken shells or those that remain open when tapped.

2   Heat a wok until hot. Add the oil, then toss in the shallots and stir-fry them for 2 minutes. Add the lemongrass, garlic, chili, and lime leaves, and stir-fry for 30 seconds.

3   Pour in the wine and fish stock and, when the liquid is boiling, stir in the tom yam paste. Lower the heat and simmer until the sauce has reduced slightly, about 2 minutes.

4   Toss in the mussels, cover, and simmer over medium heat, shaking the wok occasionally, until the mussels have opened, about 5 minutes. Discard any that do not open. Stir in the lime juice and minced cilantro. Serve immediately, garnished with cilantro sprigs.

284 malaysian-style seafood pot

PREPARATION TIME: *20 minutes* **COOKING TIME:** *15 minutes*

1 onion, chopped
3 cloves garlic, chopped
2-inch piece fresh ginger,
   peeled and chopped
2 tsp coriander seeds
2 lemongrass stalks,
   peeled and minced
2 tbsp peanut oil
2 mildly hot, long, red chilies,
   seeded and finely sliced
2 tsp turmeric

1¾ cups coconut milk
juice of 1½ limes
2 tsp fish sauce
2 large handfuls of cilantro leaves,
   roughly chopped
12 oz skinless white fish fillets,
   cut into large, bite-sized pieces
10 oz raw mixed shellfish,
   such as large shrimp,
   mussels, and squid rings
salt

1   Blend the onion, garlic, ginger, coriander seeds, lemongrass, oil, chilies, and turmeric with 1 tablespoon of water in a food processor or blender to make a coarse paste.

2   Put the paste in a large wok and cook over medium heat for 4 minutes, stirring constantly. Add the coconut milk, lime juice, fish sauce, and chopped cilantro and bring to a boil, then reduce the heat and simmer for 3 minutes.

3   Add the white fish and cook for about 5 minutes, stirring occasionally and taking care not to break up the fish. Stir in the shellfish and simmer until hot and cooked, 2–3 minutes longer. Season to taste with salt and serve.

285 chinese spiced shrimp

PREPARATION TIME: *15 minutes, plus 30 minutes marinating time* **COOKING TIME:** *7 minutes*

1 tbsp Szechuan pepper,
   toasted and crushed
1 tsp chili powder
2 tbsp peanut oil
1 lb raw large shrimp, peeled
salt
1 tbsp toasted sesame oil
1 red bell pepper, sliced lengthwise

4 small heads bok choy, sliced
3 handfuls of beansprouts
2 tbsp light soy sauce
1-inch piece fresh ginger,
   peeled and finely grated
juice of 1 lime
2 large handfuls of cilantro leaves,
   roughly chopped

1   Mix together the Szechuan pepper, chili powder, and oil in a bowl. Add the shrimp and season with salt, then stir well until the shrimp are coated with the spice mixture. Let marinate for 30 minutes.

2   Heat a wok over high heat. Add the shrimp and marinade and fry, tossing and turning, until the shrimp are pink, about 3 minutes. Remove from the wok and keep warm.

3   Pour the sesame oil into the wok and add the red pepper and bok choy. Stir-fry for 2 minutes, then add the beansprouts, soy sauce, ginger, and lime juice and stir-fry for 1 more minute.

4   Divide the stir-fry among four serving bowls, top with the shrimp, and sprinkle with the chopped cilantro, then serve.

286 goan-style coconut mussels

PREPARATION TIME: *20 minutes* **COOKING TIME:** *10 minutes*

4½ lb mussels
2 tbsp peanut oil
2 onions, minced
1-inch piece fresh ginger,
   peeled and minced
3 cloves garlic, minced
2 mildly hot, long, red chilies,
   seeded and finely sliced
½ tsp fenugreek seeds

4 cardamom pods, split
½ tsp cumin seeds
1 tsp turmeric
1 cup coconut milk
½ cup water
2 tbsp lime juice
salt and freshly ground black pepper
handful of cilantro leaves,
   roughly chopped

1 Scrub and rinse the mussels well under cold running water. Discard any mussels with broken shells or those that remain open when tapped.

2 Heat a wok until hot. Add the oil, then toss in the onions and stir-fry for 2 minutes. Add the ginger and garlic and stir-fry for 2 more minutes. Add the chilies, fenugreek, cardamom, and cumin seeds and stir-fry for 1 minute longer. Mix in the turmeric.

3 Pour in the coconut milk and water and bring to a boil. Add the mussels and lime juice, reduce the heat, cover, and cook over medium heat until the mussels have opened, about 5 minutes. Discard any mussels that do not open. Season to taste with salt and pepper.

4 Spoon the mussels into four large serving bowls, pour the sauce over them, garnish with the chopped cilantro, and serve immediately.

287 thai seafood green curry

PREPARATION TIME: *20 minutes* **COOKING TIME:** *12 minutes*

all-purpose flour for dusting
10 oz firm white fish fillets, cut into
   large, bite-size chunks
3 tbsp peanut oil
2 Asian red shallots
2 heaped tbsp Thai Green Curry Paste
   (see page 15)
1¼ cups coconut milk
⅔ cup water

1 tbsp fish sauce
10 oz cooked mixed seafood
5 oz baby spinach leaves
   (about 1½ cups)
juice of 1 lime
2 handfuls of cilantro leaves,
   roughly chopped
2 handfuls of basil leaves, torn
salt

1 Put a little flour onto a flat plate. Add the fish chunks and turn them in the flour until lightly dusted. Heat the oil in a wok, add the fish, and fry for 2 minutes, turning it once and taking care not to break it up. Remove from the wok using a slotted spatula and set on one side.

2 Pour all but 1 tablespoon of the oil out of the wok. Add the shallots and stir-fry for 2 minutes, then stir in the curry paste and cook for 1 more minute. Pour in the coconut milk, water, and fish sauce and stir well, then cook for 3 minutes. Add the seafood, cooked fish chunks, and spinach and cook until the fish and seafood are heated through, about 2 minutes.

3 Stir in the lime juice and half the cilantro and basil. Season to taste with salt, sprinkle with the remaining herbs, and serve.

288 sri lankan shrimp in coconut sauce

PREPARATION TIME: *20 minutes* COOKING TIME: *18 minutes*

2 tbsp peanut oil

1 onion, chopped

2 tsp cumin seeds

4 cloves garlic, chopped

1-inch piece fresh ginger,
    peeled and minced

10 curry leaves

4 cardamom pods, split

1 cinnamon stick

2 hot green chilies, sliced

2 tsp chili powder

1 tsp turmeric

3 tomatoes, chopped

1 cup water

1 lb raw tiger shrimp,
    peeled and deveined

1¾ cups coconut milk

salt and freshly ground black pepper

1 Heat a large wok until hot. Add the oil, then toss in the onion and cumin seeds and stir-fry them for 3 minutes. Add the garlic, ginger, curry leaves, cardamom, cinnamon stick, and green chilies and stir-fry for 1 more minute.

2 Add the chili powder, turmeric, tomatoes, and water. Stir, then bring to a boil. Lower the heat and let simmer for 5 minutes.

3 Add the shrimp and cook over medium heat until pink, about 2 minutes. Stir in the coconut milk, season to taste with salt and pepper, and bring to a boil. Stir well, adding some extra water if the sauce becomes a little too thick and dry. Serve immediately.

289 thai scallops on stir-fried vegetables

PREPARATION TIME: *15 minutes, plus 30 minutes marinating time* COOKING TIME: *12 minutes*

2 tbsp Thai Red Curry Paste (see page 15)

1 tsp fish sauce

1 tsp palm sugar or light brown sugar

juice of ½ lime

6 tbsp coconut milk

16 sea scallops, rinsed and patted dry

2 tbsp sunflower oil

2 kaffir lime leaves, shredded

8 baby zucchini, sliced lengthwise

8 ears baby corn, sliced in half lengthwise

1 red bell pepper, cut into thin strips

2 handfuls of beansprouts

6 tablespoons water

salt

1 Mix together the curry paste, fish sauce, sugar, lime juice, and coconut milk in a shallow dish. Add the scallops, spoon the curry paste mixture over them, and let marinate for 30 minutes.

2 Heat half of the oil in a large wok. Divide the scallops into 4 batches. Using a slotted spoon, lift one batch out of the marinade, place in the wok, and sear over medium heat, without moving, for 1 minute on each side. Remove from the wok and keep warm. Repeat with the remaining three batches of scallops.

3 Add the remaining oil to the hot wok, then add the lime leaves, zucchini, and corn and stir-fry for 1 minute. Toss in the red pepper and beansprouts and cook for 30 seconds longer, then pour in the water and remaining marinade. Season to taste with salt. Simmer until the liquid is slightly reduced.

4 Lift the vegetables out of the wok with a slotted spoon and divide among four warm serving plates. Place the warm scallops on top and spoon the hot sauce over them. Serve immediately.

290 clams in red curry sauce

PREPARATION TIME: *20 minutes, plus 15 minutes soaking time* COOKING TIME: *15 minutes*

3½ lb small hardshell clams

1 cup water

1 cup coconut milk

1 recipe quantity Thai Red Curry Paste
   (see page 15)

2 tsp fish sauce

1 tsp palm sugar or
   light brown sugar

3 kaffir lime leaves

juice of 1 lime

small basil leaves for garnish

1   Scrub and rinse the clams well under cold running water. Discard any with broken shells or
    those that remain open when tapped. Place the clams in a wok, add the water, and cook over
    high heat, shaking the wok regularly, until the clams open. Lift out the clams with a slotted
    spoon, discarding any that remain closed, and set on one side. Strain the cooking liquid through
    a fine strainer and reserve.
2   Pour the coconut milk into the wok and heat gently until almost boiling. Stir in the curry paste
    and cook, stirring, over low heat for 3 minutes. Add the reserved clam cooking liquid, fish
    sauce, sugar, and lime leaves and cook over low heat for 7 minutes, stirring frequently.
3   Pour in the lime juice, then toss in the clams and gently warm through. Serve immediately,
    garnished with the basil leaves.

291 red-spiced squid

PREPARATION TIME: *20 minutes*   **COOKING TIME:** *6 minutes*

1¾ lb small squid, cleaned and tentacles
   separated
1 recipe quantity Thai Red Curry Paste
   (see page 15)
2 egg whites, lightly beaten

all-purpose flour for dusting
vegetable oil for frying
handful of cilantro leaves,
   roughly chopped
2 limes, cut into wedges

1   Rinse the squid and pat dry using paper towels. Cut along both sides of each squid pouch and open out flat. Using the tip of a sharp knife, lightly score a diamond pattern across the surface of each flattened squid. Leave the tentacles whole.
2   Beat together the curry paste and egg whites in a bowl. Pour some flour onto a plate.
3   Fill a wok one-third full of oil and heat until it is hot enough to brown a cube of day-old bread in 30 seconds. Dip the squid pieces into the curry paste mixture, then into the flour until they are lightly dusted. Deep-fry the squid, 2–3 pieces at a time, until crisp and golden brown, about 1 minute. Remove using a slotted spoon and drain on paper towels.
4   Serve hot, sprinkled with the chopped cilantro and accompanied by the lime wedges.

292 stir-fried scallops in oyster sauce

PREPARATION TIME: *10 minutes*   **COOKING TIME:** *5 minutes*

2 tbsp sunflower oil
16 sea scallops, rinsed
   and patted dry
2 zucchini, sliced
1 clove garlic, chopped

2 tbsp soy sauce
3 tbsp oyster sauce
⅔ cup water
handful of cilantro leaves,
   roughly chopped

1   Heat the oil in a large wok, add the scallops, and sear until golden, about 1 minute on each side. Remove from the wok with a slotted spatula and keep warm.
2   Add the zucchini and garlic to the wok and stir-fry for 1 minute. Pour the soy sauce, oyster sauce, and water into the wok, and simmer until the liquid has reduced and thickened.
3   Arrange the scallops on warmed serving plates, spoon the zucchini and sauce over them, garnish with the chopped cilantro, and serve.

293 masala tiger shrimp

PREPARATION TIME: *20 minutes*   **COOKING TIME:** *12 minutes*

2 tbsp peanut oil
1 onion, minced
1 tbsp cumin seeds
1 tsp fenugreek seeds
1 tbsp coriander seeds, ground
3 cardamom pods, split
2 small, hot red chilies, seeded
   and sliced

2 cloves garlic, chopped
1 cup canned crushed tomatoes
⅔ cup water
salt
1 lb raw tiger shrimp, peeled
   and deveined

1   Heat a wok until hot. Add the oil, then toss in the onion and stir-fry it for 2 minutes. Add the cumin, fenugreek, coriander, and cardamom pods and stir-fry for 1 more minute. Stir in the chilies and garlic and stir-fry for 30 seconds.
2   Pour in the crushed tomatoes and water. Bring to a boil, then lower the heat and simmer until the sauce has reduced and thickened, about 5 minutes.
3   Season to taste with salt, then stir in the shrimp and cook until they turn pink, 2–3 minutes. Serve immediately.

294 wok-fried seafood

PREPARATION TIME: *15 minutes* **COOKING TIME:** *5 minutes*

3 tbsp coconut cream
2 tbsp Thai Red Curry Paste
  (see page 15)
2 tbsp water
juice of 1 lime
2 tsp cornstarch
2 tbsp sunflower oil

8 small squid, cleaned, pouches cut into
  rings and tentacles separated
10 oz raw tiger shrimp, peeled
  and deveined
salt
handful of cilantro leaves,
  roughly chopped

1 Mix together the coconut cream, red curry paste, water, and lime juice. Stir in the cornstarch.
2 Heat the oil in a wok until hot. Add the squid and shrimp and stir-fry for 1 minute. Stir in the red
   curry paste mixture and stir-fry until the seafood is cooked, 1–2 minutes longer.
3 Season to taste with salt, sprinkle with the chopped cilantro, and serve.

295 japanese-style cockles with spinach

PREPARATION TIME: *20 minutes* **COOKING TIME:** *7 minutes*

3½ lb fresh cockles
3 tbsp mirin or dry sherry
1 tsp wasabi paste
3 tbsp Japanese soy sauce
2 tbsp sunflower oil

3 scallions, shredded
1 lb baby spinach leaves
salt
1 tbsp toasted sesame seeds
  for garnish

1 Scrub and rinse the cockles well under cold running water. Discard any cockles with broken
   shells or those that remain open when tapped.
2 Mix together the mirin, wasabi, and soy sauce and set on one side. Heat the oil in a large wok,
   add the scallions, and stir-fry for 30 seconds.
3 Pour in the mirin mixture, then add the cockles. Cover and cook until the cockle shells have
   opened, shaking the wok occasionally. Discard any that remain closed.
4 Add the spinach and stir-fry briefly until wilted. Season to taste with salt. Divide among warm
   serving bowls, sprinkle with the sesame seeds, and serve.

296 mussels with fragrant broth

PREPARATION TIME: *20 minutes* **COOKING TIME:** *5 minutes*

4½ lb mussels
1-inch piece fresh ginger,
  peeled and minced
2 cloves garlic, minced
2 mildly hot, long, red chilies, seeded
  and sliced
5 tbsp mirin or dry sherry
½ cup fish or chicken stock

juice of 1 lemon
juice of 1 lime
2 tsp fish sauce
4 scallions, sliced diagonally
3 handfuls of baby spinach leaves
handful of cilantro leaves,
  roughly chopped

1 Scrub and rinse the mussels well under cold running water. Discard any mussels with broken
   shells or those that remain open when tapped.
2 Put the mussels in a large wok and add all the remaining ingredients, apart from the scallions,
   spinach, and cilantro. Cover and bring to a boil, then reduce the heat and simmer gently for
   2 minutes, shaking the wok occasionally.
3 Stir in the scallions and spinach. Continue cooking, covered, until the mussels have opened,
   2–3 minutes longer. Discard any mussels that do not open. Spoon into large shallow serving
   bowls, sprinkle with the chopped cilantro, and serve.

297 shrimp & scallops in yellow bean sauce

PREPARATION TIME: *20 minutes* **COOKING TIME:** *7 minutes*

2 tbsp sunflower oil
1 tsp toasted sesame oil
8 sea scallops, cut into thirds
10 oz raw tiger shrimp, peeled
  and deveined
2 stalks celery, sliced
1 red bell pepper, cut into bite-sized pieces
1 carrot, cut into bite-sized pieces

2 scallions, sliced diagonally
2 cloves garlic, chopped
1-inch piece fresh ginger, chopped
2 tbsp Chinese cooking wine
  or dry sherry
1 tbsp light soy sauce
4 tbsp yellow bean sauce
salt and freshly ground black pepper

1   Heat the oils in a wok over high heat. Add the scallops and sear for 1 minute on each side, then remove using a slotted spatula and set on one side. Add the shrimp to the hot oil and stir-fry until they start to turn pink, about 2 minutes. Remove and set on one side.

2   Add the celery, red pepper, and carrot to the hot oil and stir-fry for 2 minutes, then add the scallions, garlic, and ginger and stir-fry for 30 seconds longer.

3   Reduce the heat slightly and stir in the wine, soy sauce, and yellow bean sauce. Season to taste with salt and pepper. Simmer briefly until the sauce has reduced and thickened, adding a little water if the mixture becomes too dry.

4   Return the shrimp and scallops to the wok and heat through. Serve immediately.

298 malay shrimp pot

PREPARATION TIME: *20 minutes* **COOKING TIME:** *17 minutes*

2 tbsp peanut oil
1 red bell pepper, diced
8 oz bok choy, stems thinly sliced
  and leaves chopped
2 large cloves garlic, chopped
1 tsp ground turmeric
1 tbsp garam masala
1½ tsp chili powder
4 tbsp smooth peanut butter

⅔ cup hot fish or vegetable stock
1¼ cups coconut milk
4 tsp light soy sauce
1 lb raw tiger shrimp, peeled
  and deveined
2 scallions, finely sliced
  diagonally
2 tsp toasted sesame seeds

1   Heat a large wok until hot. Add the oil, then toss in the red pepper, bok choy stems, and garlic and stir-fry them for 2 minutes. Add the turmeric, garam masala, chili powder, and bok choy leaves and stir-fry for 1 more minute.

2   Stir the peanut butter into the hot stock until it has dissolved, then add to the wok along with the coconut milk and soy sauce. Bring to a boil. Lower the heat and simmer until reduced and thickened, 8–10 minutes.

3   Add the shrimp and simmer until pink, about 3 minutes. Spoon into shallow serving bowls, sprinkle with the chopped scallions and sesame seeds, and serve.

299 singapore crab

PREPARATION TIME: *30 minutes* **COOKING TIME:** *6 minutes*

2 cooked small crabs
2 tbsp chili sauce
4 tbsp ketchup
1 tsp palm sugar or light brown sugar
2 tbsp light soy sauce
juice of 1 lime

⅔ cup water
2 tbsp peanut oil
3 cloves garlic, minced
1-inch piece fresh ginger,
    peeled and minced
1 hot red chili, seeded and minced

1   Scrub the crab shells. Detach the claws and crack them. Cut the crab bodies in half, or
    into quarters if large.
2   Mix together the chili sauce, ketchup, sugar, soy sauce, lime juice, and water.
3   Heat the oil in a wok, add the garlic, ginger, and chili, and stir-fry for a few seconds. Pour in
    the ketchup mixture, then add the crab to the wok and stir well.
4   Reduce the heat slightly, then simmer the crab until the sauce has reduced and thickened, 3–5
    minutes. Serve immediately.

300 szechuan squid

PREPARATION TIME: *25 minutes* **COOKING TIME:** *6 minutes*

1 tsp Szechuan peppercorns
½ tsp black peppercorns
½ tsp sea salt flakes
2 tbsp sunflower oil
1¾ lb small squid,
   cleaned and tentacles
   separated

2 large handfuls of snow peas,
   sliced diagonally in half
1 mildly hot, long, red chili, seeded
   and thinly sliced
3 scallions, thinly sliced diagonally
4 large handfuls of shredded napa
   cabbage, steamed, for serving

1   Heat a wok over medium heat and toast the peppercorns for a few seconds, shaking the wok constantly as they start to darken. Put them into a mortar, add the salt, and coarsely crush with a pestle.

2   Add the oil to the hot wok, then add half of the squid and stir-fry it for 1–2 minutes. Remove from the pan with a slotted spoon and keep warm. Repeat with the remaining squid.

3   Return all of the squid to the wok and add the crushed pepper and salt mixture, the snow peas, chili, and scallions and stir-fry for 1 more minute.

4   Serve the squid on a bed of steamed, shredded napa cabbage.

301 seafood jungle curry

PREPARATION TIME: *15 minutes* **COOKING TIME:** *9 minutes*

2 tbsp peanut oil
2 large handfuls of snow peas, sliced in
   half diagonally
1 clove garlic, chopped
1 recipe quantity Jungle Curry Paste
   (see page 14)
1½ cups fish stock
2 tsp fish sauce

juice of 1 lime
1 cup canned bamboo shoots,
   rinsed and drained
8 oz cooked, peeled large shrimp
2¼ lb cooked mussels in their shells
handful of Thai basil leaves,
   roughly chopped

1 Heat a wok until hot. Add the oil, then toss in the snow peas and garlic and stir-fry them for 30 seconds. Add the curry paste and stir-fry for 2 minutes longer.
2 Pour in the stock, fish sauce, and lime juice. Bring to a boil, then reduce the heat and simmer for 3 minutes.
3 Add the bamboo shoots, shrimp, and mussels and cook until heated through, about 2 minutes. Spoon into large, shallow serving bowls, sprinkle with the basil, and serve.

302 chinese crab & asparagus stir-fry

PREPARATION TIME: *15 minutes, plus 15 minutes marinating time* **COOKING TIME:** *5 minutes*

1 tbsp light soy sauce
1 tsp sugar
10 oz crab meat, canned or fresh
1 tbsp cornstarch
3 tbsp Chinese cooking wine or dry sherry
4 tbsp water
3 tbsp sunflower oil

1 cup asparagus cut into
   1-inch lengths
1-inch piece fresh ginger, peeled
   and minced
4 scallions, sliced on the diagonal
handful of cilantro leaves for garnish

1 Mix together the soy sauce and sugar. Put the crab meat in a bowl with the cornstarch, wine, and water. Stir, then set aside for 15 minutes.
2 Heat the oil in a wok and stir-fry the asparagus for 2 minutes, then add the ginger and scallions and cook for 30 seconds longer.
3 Reduce the heat slightly. Stir in the crab meat along with the soy sauce marinade and heat through, adding more water if too dry. Sprinkle with the cilantro leaves and serve.

303 quick shrimp & spinach curry

PREPARATION TIME: *15 minutes* **COOKING TIME:** *8 minutes*

2 tbsp ghee or peanut oil
1 large onion, thinly sliced
2 cloves garlic, chopped
2 hot green chilies, finely sliced
2 tsp ground turmeric
2 tsp ground coriander
2 tbsp dried shredded coconut

1 lb raw tiger shrimp, peeled
8 oz fresh spinach leaves
⅔ cup coconut milk
½ cup water
salt
large handful of cilantro leaves,
   roughly chopped

1 Heat the ghee or oil in a wok. Add the onion and stir-fry for 3 minutes. Add the garlic and chilies and cook for 1 more minute. Add the turmeric, coriander, and coconut and stir until they are well combined.
2 Add the shrimp, spinach, coconut milk, and water and simmer until the sauce has reduced and the shrimp are pink, about 3 minutes. Season to taste with salt, sprinkle with the chopped cilantro, and serve.

304 stir-fried tiger shrimp
with mustard seeds
PREPARATION TIME: *15 minutes* **COOKING TIME:** *4 minutes*

2 tbsp peanut oil
1 tsp black mustard seeds
2 large cloves garlic, minced
15 curry leaves

1 lb raw tiger shrimp, peeled
½ tsp chili powder
3 tbsp lemon juice
2 tsp sugar

1 Heat the oil in a wok, add the mustard seeds, and fry until they start to pop. Stir in the garlic and curry leaves, then add the shrimp. Stir-fry until the shrimp start to turn pink, about 2 minutes. Mix in the chili powder, lemon juice, and sugar. Stir well, then serve immediately.

305 mussels in spiced tomato broth
PREPARATION TIME: *20 minutes* **COOKING TIME:** *14 minutes*

4½ lb mussels
1 tbsp sunflower oil
1 large onion, minced
3 cloves garlic, crushed
2 tsp cumin seeds
2 tsp coriander seeds
½ tsp dried chili flakes

1½ cups dry white wine
½ cup canned crushed tomatoes
1 tbsp lemon juice
salt and freshly ground black pepper
handful of cilantro leaves,
    roughly chopped

1 Scrub and rinse the mussels well under cold running water. Discard any mussels with broken shells or those that remain open when tapped.
2 Heat the oil in a large wok, then add the onion and stir-fry for 3 minutes. Add the garlic, cumin, coriander, and chili flakes and stir-fry for 1 more minute.
3 Increase the heat, pour in the wine, and boil until reduced, about 2 minutes. Reduce the heat, add the tomatoes, and simmer until reduced by one-third.
4 Toss in the mussels, cover the wok, and cook, shaking the wok occasionally, until the mussels have opened, about 5 minutes. Discard any mussels that remain closed.
5 Stir in the lemon juice and season to taste with salt and pepper. Spoon into large bowls and pour the juices over. Serve immediately, garnished with the chopped cilantro.

306 shrimp & egg fu yung
PREPARATION TIME: *10 minutes* **COOKING TIME:** *7 minutes*

8 eggs, lightly beaten
2 tbsp water
2 tbsp soy sauce
3 tbsp sunflower oil
2 tsp butter
1 large onion, minced

1 clove garlic, minced
1 hot red chili, seeded and sliced
8 oz cooked, peeled small shrimp
2 handfuls of beansprouts
handful of cilantro leaves
    for garnish

1 Mix together the eggs, water, and soy sauce in a bowl and set on one side.
2 Heat the oil and butter in a wok. Add the onion and stir-fry for 3 minutes. Add the garlic and chili and stir-fry for 2 minutes longer. Pour in the egg mixture and stir constantly with a spatula until the eggs just begin to scramble.
3 Toss in the shrimp and beansprouts and stir until the shrimp are heated through and the eggs are lightly scrambled. Scatter the cilantro leaves over the top and serve immediately.

307 shrimp & snow pea stir-fry

PREPARATION TIME: *15 minutes* COOKING TIME: *5 minutes*

2 tbsp sunflower oil
2 large cloves garlic, chopped
5 oz snow peas
1-inch piece fresh ginger,
    peeled and grated
½ cup Chinese cooking wine or dry sherry

½ cup fish stock or water
1 lb raw tiger shrimp, peeled
2 tbsp light soy sauce
2 large handfuls of beansprouts
2 tsp toasted sesame oil
salt and freshly ground black pepper

1 Heat a wok until hot. Add the oil, then toss in the garlic and snow peas and stir-fry them for 1 minute. Add the ginger, wine, stock, shrimp, and soy sauce and stir-fry until the shrimp turn pink, about 2 minutes.
2 Add the beansprouts, sesame oil, and salt and pepper to taste, then stir-fry for a few more seconds to heat through. Serve immediately.

308 steamed scallops and asparagus with sweet ginger dip

PREPARATION TIME: *10 minutes* COOKING TIME: *17 minutes*

16 asparagus spears, trimmed
16 sea scallops, rinsed and patted dry

SWEET GINGER DIP:
1 mildly hot, long, red chili, seeded
    and thinly sliced

1-inch piece fresh ginger,
    peeled and grated
2 tbsp mirin or dry sherry
4 tbsp vegetable stock or water
2 tbsp sweet chili sauce

1 Mix together all the ingredients for the sweet ginger dip in a small bowl and set on one side.
2 Place the asparagus in a large bamboo steamer lined with parchment paper. Cover and steam over a wok of simmering water for about 3 minutes. Remove from the steamer and keep warm.
3 Put the scallops into the bamboo steamer, cover, and steam until opaque, about 6 minutes. You may have to do this in two batches, keeping the first batch warm while cooking the second.
4 Arrange the asparagus and scallops on warm serving plates, spoon on the ginger dip, and serve.

309 garlic & lemon squid

PREPARATION TIME: *20 minutes* COOKING TIME: *5 minutes*

1¾ lb medium squid, cleaned and
    tentacles separated
4 tbsp sunflower oil
4 cloves garlic, chopped
2 hot, red Thai chilies, seeded
    and finely sliced

grated zest of 1 lemon
juice of 2 lemons
3 tbsp water
salt and freshly ground black pepper
2 handfuls of cilantro leaves,
    roughly chopped

1 Slice each squid pouch into three pieces. Rinse and pat dry on paper towels.
2 Heat a wok until hot. Add the oil, then add half of the squid and stir-fry it for 1–2 minutes. Remove with a slotted spoon, drain on paper towels, and set on one side. Add the remaining squid to the wok and stir-fry for 1 minute. Add the garlic, chilies, and lemon zest and stir-fry for 30 seconds longer. Return the first batch of squid to the wok.
3 Pour in the lemon juice and water, and season to taste with salt and pepper. Stir-fry for a few seconds to heat through. Serve immediately, sprinkled with the chopped cilantro.

CHAPTER 7
VEGETARIAN DISHES

Since stir-fried vegetables are cooked in a matter of minutes, they retain much of their vitamin and mineral content, making it possible to prepare meat-free meals in a wok that are as packed with nutrients as they are appealing to the senses. Asian countries also offer up a treasure trove of vegetarian culinary delights that are not only quick to prepare but are also highly colorful, rich in flavor, and varied in texture, with a deliciously light, fresh quality.

When stir-frying vegetables in a wok, it is important to remember a few rules. Always cut them up into uniform-sized pieces, so that they cook evenly. Add denser vegetables, such as carrots and green beans, to the wok first, as they require a longer cooking time than, say, zucchini or beansprouts. And do bear in mind the shape of the vegetable. Cutting long vegetables on the diagonal makes them look more appealing than chunks or slices and creates a bigger surface area, speeding up cooking time.

In addition, a wok can also be used in the same way as the Indian kadahi (a wok-shaped pan with round handles on either side) to create fabulously fragrant curries, such as vegetable kormas and dahls, as well as Thai green and red curries and Malaysian coconut curries.

310 half-moon eggplant with chili & garlic

PREPARATION TIME: *10 minutes, plus 30 minutes standing time* **COOKING TIME:** *15–22 minutes*

2 medium eggplants, sliced into rounds
    and then halved
salt and freshly ground black pepper
4 tbsp sunflower oil
4 cloves garlic, chopped

2 hot, red Thai chilies,
    seeded and minced
juice of 1 lemon
handful of basil leaves, torn

1   Put the eggplant pieces on a plate and sprinkle generously with salt. Cover and let drain for
30 minutes. Rinse well, then pat dry with paper towels.

2   Heat a wok until hot. Add the oil, then toss in half of the eggplant and stir-fry it until lightly
browned and tender, about 7 minutes. Remove from the wok with a slotted spoon and set on
one side. Add the remaining eggplant and stir-fry for 7 minutes.

3   Return the first batch of eggplant to the wok, then toss in the garlic and chilies and stir-fry for
30 seconds. Stir in the lemon juice, season to taste with salt and pepper, and serve, sprinkled
with the torn basil leaves.

311 asian mushrooms in hoisin sauce

PREPARATION TIME: *15 minutes* **COOKING TIME:** *6 minutes*

4 tbsp hoisin sauce
4 tbsp water
1 tsp cornstarch
3 tbsp sunflower oil
2 cloves garlic, chopped
2-inch piece fresh ginger,
    peeled and minced
1 large, green bell pepper, cut into
    bite-sized pieces

4 oz shiitake mushrooms, halved
4 oz cremini mushrooms, halved
4 oz oyster mushrooms,
    halved if large
4 oz enoki mushrooms
3 tbsp Shaoxing wine or
    Scotch whisky
1 tsp toasted sesame oil

1   Mix together the hoisin sauce, water, and cornstarch in a small bowl and set on one side.

2   Heat a wok until hot. Add the sunflower oil, then toss in the garlic and ginger and stir-fry them
for 30 seconds. Add the green pepper and stir-fry for 1 more minute.

3   Add the shiitake and cremini mushrooms and stir-fry for 2 minutes, then add the oyster and
enoki mushrooms and stir-fry until all the mushrooms are tender, about 1 minute longer.

4   Pour in the wine and stir until reduced, then add the hoisin sauce mixture. Cook over medium
heat until the mushrooms are glazed, about 1 minute, adding more water if the mixture
becomes too dry. Stir in the sesame oil and serve immediately.

312 sweet & sour vegetables

PREPARATION TIME: *10 minutes* **COOKING TIME:** *5 minutes*

4 tbsp vegetable stock
1 tbsp Chinese rice vinegar
1 tbsp sugar
2 tbsp light soy sauce
2 tbsp peanut oil
2 onions, sliced
12 ears baby corn

2 large handfuls of snow peas, trimmed
2 cups thickly sliced
    shiitake mushrooms
2 cloves garlic, chopped
2 small heads bok choy, sliced
    lengthwise
2 handfuls of beansprouts

1   Mix together the stock, rice vinegar, sugar, and soy sauce in a small bowl and set on one side.

2   Heat a wok until hot. Add the oil, then toss in the onions and stir-fry them for 2 minutes. Add
the baby corn, snow peas, mushrooms, garlic, and bok choy and stir-fry for 1 more minute.

3   Stir in the stock mixture and cook for 1 minute. Toss in the beansprouts and serve immediately.

313 spring vegetable stir-fry

PREPARATION TIME: *15 minutes* **COOKING TIME:** *6 minutes*

1 tbsp sunflower oil
10 oz broccoli, cut into small florets and
   stems sliced
4 scallions, sliced on the diagonal
1 large, yellow bell pepper, sliced
4 small heads choy sum (Chinese
   flowering cabbage), sliced
2 handfuls of shelled fresh green peas

2 cloves garlic, chopped
2-inch piece fresh ginger, peeled
   and minced
2 tbsp Chinese cooking wine or
   dry sherry
4 tbsp fresh apple juice
2 tbsp light soy sauce
1 tsp toasted sesame oil

1   Heat a wok until hot. Add the sunflower oil, then toss in the broccoli florets and stems and stir-fry for 2 minutes. Add the scallions and yellow pepper and fry, tossing the vegetables constantly, for 2 minutes longer.

2   Toss in the choy sum, peas, garlic, and ginger and stir-fry for 1 minute. Pour in the wine, apple juice, and soy sauce and cook for 1–2 minutes longer, adding a little water if the stir-fry becomes too dry. Stir in the sesame oil and serve.

314 chinese vegetable pancakes

PREPARATION TIME: *15 minutes* **COOKING TIME:** *7 minutes*

2 tbsp hoisin sauce
2 tbsp water
2 tbsp light soy sauce
1 tbsp sunflower oil
1 large onion, sliced
2 carrots, sliced into thin sticks
1 red bell pepper, thinly sliced
6 baby zucchini, sliced into thin sticks

2 cloves garlic, chopped
1-inch piece fresh ginger, peeled
   and minced
2 large handfuls of beansprouts
1 tsp toasted sesame oil
8–12 Chinese pancakes, warmed
2 scallions, shredded, for garnish

1   Mix together the hoisin sauce, water, and soy sauce in a small bowl and set on one side.

2   Heat a wok until hot. Add the oil, then toss in the onion and stir-fry it for 2 minutes. Toss in the carrots and stir-fry for 1 minute. Add the red pepper and zucchini and cook for 2 minutes.

3   Add the garlic, ginger, and beansprouts. Stir, then pour in the hoisin sauce mixture and sesame oil, and cook for 1 more minute.

4   Divide the vegetables among the warm pancakes. Fold the pancakes in half to enclose the vegetables, sprinkle with the shredded scallions, and serve.

315 stir-fried vegetables in yellow bean sauce

PREPARATION TIME: *10 minutes* **COOKING TIME:** *5 minutes*

2 tbsp peanut oil
1 large onion, sliced
16 ears baby corn
3 handfuls of fine green beans, trimmed
   and sliced diagonally
2 handfuls of snow peas, trimmed
2 zucchini, sliced
2 hot green chilies, seeded and chopped

2 cloves garlic, chopped
1-inch piece fresh ginger, peeled
   and chopped
handful of sprouted mixed beans
5 tbsp yellow bean sauce
2 tbsp light soy sauce
3 tbsp water

1   Heat a wok until hot. Add the oil, then toss in the onion and stir-fry it for 2 minutes. Add the corn, beans, snow peas, zucchini, chilies, garlic, and ginger and stir-fry for 2 more minutes.

2   Add the sprouted beans, then pour in the yellow bean sauce, soy sauce, and water. Cook for 1 minute longer, then serve.

316 cauliflower & potato kadahi

PREPARATION TIME: *15 minutes* **COOKING TIME:** *25 minutes*

2 tbsp peanut oil

4 hot green chilies, cut down one side
and seeded

1 large onion, thinly sliced

8 large cauliflower florets, cut into small
florets and stems sliced

8 curry leaves

1 tsp black mustard seeds, crushed

1 tsp cumin seeds

3 cloves garlic, minced

2-inch piece fresh ginger, peeled
and minced

1 tsp chili powder

2 large potatoes, peeled, cooked, and
cut into bite-sized pieces

1 cup vegetable stock

juice of 1 lemon

handful of cilantro leaves,
roughly chopped

salt

1 Heat a wok until hot. Add the oil, then toss in the chilies and stir-fry them for 1 minute. Remove
the chilies from the wok and discard.

2 Put the onion into the wok and stir-fry for 2 minutes. Add the cauliflower and cook for 2 more
minutes. Stir in the curry leaves, mustard seeds, and cumin seeds and cook for 1 minute longer.
Add the garlic, ginger, and chili powder and stir-fry for 1 minute.

3 Add the potatoes and pour in the stock and lemon juice. Stir-fry over medium heat until the
liquid is reduced. Stir in half of the chopped cilantro and season to taste with salt. Cover and
cook over low heat for 5 minutes. Serve sprinkled with the remaining chopped cilantro.

317 stir-fried tofu with scallions and sesame seeds

PREPARATION TIME: *15 minutes, plus 30 minutes marinating time* **COOKING TIME:** *8 minutes*

4 tbsp hoisin sauce

1 tsp toasted sesame oil

2 tbsp dark soy sauce

12 oz firm tofu, sliced into bars

2 tbsp sunflower oil

2 handfuls of fine green beans, trimmed
and halved

4 large leaves napa cabbage,
shredded

2-inch piece fresh ginger, peeled and
cut into fine strips

3 scallions, chopped

3 tbsp water

1 tbsp sesame seeds, toasted

1 Mix together the hoisin sauce, sesame oil, and soy sauce in a shallow dish. Add the tofu and
turn to coat it with the marinade. Let marinate for 30 minutes, occasionally spooning the
marinade over the tofu. Drain, reserving the marinade.

2 Heat a wok until hot. Add half of the oil, then toss in the green beans and stir-fry them for
1 minute. Toss in the napa cabbage, ginger, and scallions and stir-fry for 1 more minute.
Remove from the wok and set on one side.

3 Pour in the rest of the oil, add half the tofu, and fry for 5 minutes, turning once. Remove from
the wok with a slotted spoon, drain on paper towels, and set on one side. Put the remaining
tofu in the wok and fry for 5 minutes, turning once. Return the first batch of tofu to the wok.

4 Stir in the water and reserved marinade, then add the reserved vegetables. Heat through. Serve
sprinkled with the toasted sesame seeds.

318 sri lankan egg curry

PREPARATION TIME: *15 minutes* **COOKING TIME:** *15 minutes*

2 tbsp peanut oil

1 large onion, chopped

2 tsp cumin seeds

4 cloves garlic, chopped

1-inch piece fresh ginger,
   peeled and chopped

10 curry leaves

4 cardamom pods, split

2 hot green chilies, sliced

2 tsp chili powder

1 tsp turmeric

3 medium tomatoes, peeled,
   seeded, and chopped

5 large handfuls of spinach leaves,
   tough stems removed

1 cup water

1¼ cups coconut milk

salt and freshly ground black pepper

6 extra large eggs, hard-cooked
   and halved

large handful of cilantro leaves,
   roughly chopped

1   Heat the oil in a wok. Add the onion and cumin seeds and stir-fry for 3 minutes. Add the garlic, ginger, curry leaves, cardamom pods, and green chilies and stir-fry for 1 minute.

2   Add the chili powder, turmeric, tomatoes, spinach, water, and coconut milk. Season to taste with salt and pepper and bring to a boil. Stir, then reduce the heat and simmer until thickened and reduced, about 10 minutes. Serve topped with the hard-cooked eggs and sprinkled with the chopped cilantro.

319 braised chinese vegetables with tofu
PREPARATION TIME: *15 minutes* **COOKING TIME:** *20 minutes*

1 tbsp light soy sauce
1 tsp sugar
1 tsp cornstarch
3 tbsp water
9 oz firm tofu, cut into
   ½-inch cubes
3 tbsp sunflower oil
1 large onion, sliced
1 carrot, sliced diagonally

2 handfuls of snow peas, trimmed
12 ears baby corn
2 cups thickly sliced oyster
   mushrooms
1-inch piece fresh ginger, peeled
   and thinly sliced
½ cup halved canned water chestnuts,
   drained and rinsed
1 tsp toasted sesame oil

1   Mix together the soy sauce, sugar, cornstarch, and water in a small bowl and set on one side.
2   Bring a saucepan of lightly salted water to a boil, add the tofu, and cook until the cubes firm up slightly, about 2 minutes. Remove using a slotted spoon and drain on paper towels.
3   Heat a wok until hot. Add the sunflower oil, then add half of the tofu and stir-fry it until golden, about 4 minutes. Remove using a slotted spoon, drain on paper towels, and set on one side. Repeat with the remaining tofu.
4   Put the onion into the wok and stir-fry for 2 minutes, then add the carrot and stir-fry for 1 more minute. Toss in the snow peas, baby corn, oyster mushrooms, ginger, and water chestnuts and stir-fry for 1–2 minutes longer.
5   Stir in the soy sauce mixture, then return the tofu to the wok. Cover, reduce the heat, and braise for 2 minutes. Pour in the sesame oil and cook over low heat, stirring, until the sauce has thickened, then serve.

320 tempeh with broccoli & ginger
PREPARATION TIME: *15 minutes* **COOKING TIME:** *12 minutes*

2 tbsp light soy sauce
1 tbsp cornstarch
3 tbsp Chinese cooking wine or dry sherry
⅔ cup vegetable stock
3 tbsp sunflower oil
9 oz tempeh, cut into bite-sized cubes
1 large onion, sliced
12 stems gai lan (Chinese kale),
   stems sliced

1 large, red bell pepper, sliced
3 cloves garlic, chopped
2-inch piece fresh ginger, peeled
   and minced
freshly ground black pepper
large handful of unsalted cashew
   nuts, toasted

1   Mix together the soy sauce, cornstarch, wine, and stock in a small bowl and set on one side.
2   Heat a wok until hot. Add the oil, then add half of the tempeh and stir-fry it until lightly browned, 3–4 minutes. Remove from the wok with a slotted spatula, drain on paper towels, and keep warm. Repeat with the remaining tempeh.
3   Toss the onion into the wok and stir-fry for 2 minutes. Add the gai lan, red pepper, garlic, and ginger and stir-fry for 2 minutes longer, then pour in the soy sauce mixture. Stir well.
4   Return the tempeh to the wok. Cook until the liquid has reduced and thickened. Season to taste with pepper and serve, with the cashew nuts sprinkled over the top.

321 thai red butternut squash curry

PREPARATION TIME: *15 minutes* **COOKING TIME:** *20 minutes*

2 tbsp peanut oil

3 Asian red shallots, chopped

3 cloves garlic, chopped

2-inch piece fresh ginger,
   peeled and minced

1 medium-sized butternut squash,
   peeled, seeded, and cubed

2 kaffir lime leaves

½ tsp turmeric

1 recipe quantity Thai Red Curry Paste
   (see page 15)

1¾ cups coconut milk

1 cup vegetable stock

juice of 1 lime

salt and freshly ground black pepper

handful of cilantro leaves

handful of beansprouts

1 large onion, chopped and
   fried until crisp and golden

1   Heat a wok until hot. Add the oil, then toss in the shallots and stir-fry them for 1 minute. Add
    the garlic, ginger, squash, and lime leaves and stir-fry for 4 minutes longer.
2   Stir in the turmeric and curry paste, then pour in the coconut milk and stock and bring to a boil.
    Reduce the heat and simmer, covered, for 10 minutes.
3   Stir in the lime juice and season to taste with salt and pepper. Cook until the liquid has reduced
    and thickened, about 2 minutes. Serve hot, topped with the cilantro leaves, beansprouts,
    and crisp-fried onion.

322 japanese vegetable mista

PREPARATION TIME: *15 minutes* **COOKING TIME:** *25 minutes*

¾ oz dried arame seaweed

3 tbsp mirin

1 tsp yellow miso paste

2 tbsp Japanese soy sauce

½ cup water

2 tbsp sunflower oil

3 carrots, sliced diagonally

9 oz asparagus spears, stalks sliced

3 zucchini, sliced diagonally

7 oz sugarsnap peas

3 cups sliced shiitake mushrooms

½ tsp dried chili flakes

salt

1   Rinse the arame in a strainer under cold running water, then place in a bowl, cover with cold water, and let soak until doubled in volume, about 5 minutes. Drain and place in a saucepan. Cover with cold water and bring to a boil, then reduce the heat and simmer until tender, about 20 minutes. Drain and set on one side.

2   Meanwhile, mix together the mirin, miso paste, soy sauce, and water in a small bowl and set on one side.

3   Heat a wok until hot. Add the oil, then toss in the carrots and stir-fry them for 2 minutes. Add the asparagus and zucchini and stir-fry for 1 more minute. Add the arame, sugarsnap peas, and mushrooms and stir-fry for 1 minute longer.

4   Pour in the mirin mixture and add the chili flakes. Cook until the liquid has reduced slightly, about 2 minutes. Season with salt to taste and serve.

323 indian cauliflower with tomato

PREPARATION TIME: *20 minutes* **COOKING TIME:** *40 minutes*

1 large onion, quartered

3 cloves garlic, chopped

1-inch piece fresh ginger, peeled
   and sliced

1 tsp coriander seeds

1 tsp cumin seeds

½ tsp fenugreek seeds

4 tbsp peanut oil

1 tsp turmeric

9 curry leaves

1 mildly hot, long, red chili, seeded and
   thinly sliced into rounds

4 medium tomatoes, peeled, seeded,
   and chopped

1 medium-sized head cauliflower,
   cut into small florets

⅔ cup water

juice of ½ lemon

salt

handful of cilantro leaves,
   roughly chopped

1   Put the onion, garlic, and ginger into a food processor and process to a smooth paste. Grind the coriander, cumin, and fenugreek seeds to a powder using a mortar and pestle.

2   Heat the oil in a wok. Add the ground spices, turmeric, curry leaves, and chili and stir-fry for 30 seconds. Add the onion paste and stir-fry for 5 minutes.

3   Stir in the tomatoes and cauliflower. Pour in the water, then reduce the heat to very low, cover, and cook, stirring occasionally, until the cauliflower is tender, about 30 minutes. Add a little extra water if the mixture becomes very dry.

4   Stir in the lemon juice, season to taste with salt, and serve with the chopped cilantro sprinkled over the top.

324 malay-style coconut vegetables

PREPARATION TIME: *15 minutes* **COOKING TIME:** *10 minutes*

4 tbsp smooth peanut butter
⅔ cup hot vegetable stock
2 tbsp peanut oil
1½ cups sliced cremini mushroooms
2 carrots, cut lengthwise, then sliced
2 yellow bell peppers, diced
3 small heads bok choy, stems thinly
  sliced and leaves chopped
2 large cloves garlic, chopped

1 tsp ground turmeric
1 tbsp garam masala
1½ tsp chili powder
1¾ cups coconut milk
2 tbsp soy sauce
2 scallions, finely sliced on
  the diagonal
2 tsp sesame seeds, toasted

1 Put the peanut butter into a small bowl, pour on the hot stock, and stir until the peanut butter has dissolved. Set on one side.

2 Heat a large wok until hot. Add the oil, then toss in the mushrooms, carrots, yellow peppers, bok choy stems, and garlic and stir-fry for 3 minutes. Add the turmeric, garam masala, chili powder, and bok choy leaves and stir-fry for 1 more minute.

3 Add the peanut butter mixture to the wok along with the coconut milk and soy sauce. Cook until the sauce has reduced and thickened, about 5 minutes.

4 Spoon into warm, shallow serving bowls, sprinkle with the scallions and sesame seeds, and serve immediately.

325 malaysian soy tofu

PREPARATION TIME: *10 minutes, plus 30 minutes marinating time* **COOKING TIME:** *10 minutes*

4 tbsp kecap manis
  (Indonesian soy sauce)
1 tsp Chinese five-spice
13 oz firm tofu, cubed
3 tbsp peanut oil
3 cloves garlic, chopped
1 stick cinnamon

4 whole cloves
2-inch piece fresh ginger,
  peeled and minced
½ cup water
4 eggs, hard-cooked and halved

1 Mix together the kecap manis and Chinese five-spice in a shallow dish. Add the tofu and turn to coat it with the marinade. Let marinate for at least 30 minutes, turning occasionally. Drain, reserving the marinade

2 Heat half of the oil in a wok. Add half the tofu and fry for 2–3 minutes, without moving it, then carefully turn over and fry on the other side, until it is lightly browned all over. Remove from the wok using a slotted spatula, drain on paper towels, and keep warm. Add the remaining oil to the wok and fry the remaining tofu. Remove from the wok, drain on paper towels, and set on one side with the first batch.

3 Reduce the heat slightly and add the garlic, cinnamon, cloves, and ginger to the wok. Stir-fry for 30 seconds. Pour in the water and the marinade and stir, then return the tofu to the wok. Turn it carefully until it is heated through and the liquid has reduced.

4 Remove the cinnamon stick and cloves. Lift the tofu out of the sauce using a slotted spoon and arrange on a warm serving platter with the hard-cooked egg. Pour the sauce over and serve.

326 tempeh satay stir-fry

PREPARATION TIME: *15 minutes*   COOKING TIME: *18 minutes*

2 tbsp crunchy peanut butter

2 tbsp soy sauce

2 tsp fish sauce

6 tbsp hot water

½ cup creamed coconut

1 tbsp palm sugar or light
   brown sugar

2 tbsp sunflower oil

10 oz tempeh, thinly sliced

2 large handfuls of snow peas

1 large, red bell pepper, sliced

2 mildly hot, long, red chilies, seeded
   and thinly sliced into rounds

1-inch piece fresh ginger,
   peeled and minced

2 cloves garlic, minced

2 scallions, sliced

salt

handful of cilantro leaves,
   roughly chopped

1   Mix together the peanut butter, soy sauce, fish sauce, water, creamed coconut, and sugar in a small bowl and set on one side.

2   Heat the oil in a wok. Add half the tempeh and fry until lightly browned, 2–3 minutes on each side. Remove from the wok with a slotted spatula, drain on paper towels, and keep warm. Repeat with the remaining tempeh.

3   Put the snow peas, red pepper, and chilies into the wok and stir-fry for 1 minute. Add the ginger, garlic, and scallions and stir-fry for 30 seconds longer.

4   Add the peanut butter mixture and season to taste with salt. Stir-fry until the sauce has reduced and thickened, 1–2 minutes. Add more water if the sauce appears too dry.

5   Arrange the tempeh on a warm serving platter, spoon the hot sauce over, and sprinkle with the chopped cilantro. Serve immediately.

327 eggplant & shiitake
in ginger tomato sauce

PREPARATION TIME: *15 minutes, plus 30 minutes salting time*   COOKING TIME: *25 minutes*

2 medium eggplants, cut into rounds,
   then cut into bite-sized pieces

salt and freshly ground black pepper

4 tbsp sunflower oil

1 large onion, sliced

2½ cups sliced shiitake mushrooms

3-inch piece fresh ginger, peeled
   and minced

3 large cloves garlic, chopped

4 tbsp Chinese cooking wine or dry sherry

6 large tomatoes, peeled, seeded,
   and chopped

⅔ cup vegetable stock

2 tbsp light soy sauce

handful of cilantro leaves,
   roughly chopped

1   Spread the eggplant pieces on a plate and sprinkle generously with salt, then let drain for 30 minutes. Rinse, then pat dry with paper towels.

2   Heat a wok until hot. Add the oil, then add the eggplant and stir-fry for 5 minutes. Toss in the onion, mushrooms, ginger, and garlic and stir-fry for 3 minutes longer.

3   Pour in the wine and stir for 30 seconds, then add the tomatoes, stock, and soy sauce. Reduce the heat, cover, and braise for 10 minutes. If the sauce is still very thin and runny, cook uncovered until reduced. Season to taste with salt and pepper and serve, sprinkled with the chopped cilantro.

328 vietnamese lemongrass vegetables

PREPARATION TIME: *10 minutes* **COOKING TIME:** *10 minutes*

1 tbsp vegetarian fish sauce

1 tbsp rice wine or dry sherry

1 tbsp light soy sauce

2–3 tbsp water

1 tsp palm sugar or light brown sugar

1 tbsp peanut oil

1 onion, thinly sliced

2 large cloves garlic, chopped

1 hot red chili, seeded and chopped

2 stalks lemongrass, peeled and
minced

3 carrots, sliced diagonally

2 cups sliced cremini mushrooms

2 zucchini, sliced

2 small heads bok choy, sliced

salt and freshly ground black pepper

1 Mix together the fish sauce, rice wine, soy sauce, water, and sugar in a small bowl and set
on one side.

2 Heat a wok until hot. Add the oil, then toss in the onion, garlic, chili, and lemongrass and
stir-fry them for 1 minute. Add the carrots and stir-fry for 2 minutes, then add the mushrooms,
zucchini, and bok choy and stir-fry for 2 more minutes.

3 Pour in the fish sauce mixture and stir-fry for 2 minutes, then season to taste with salt and
pepper and serve.

329 braised mixed mushrooms

PREPARATION TIME: *15 minutes, plus 20 minutes soaking time* **COOKING TIME:** *8 minutes*

½ oz dried Chinese black mushrooms
3 tbsp sunflower oil
2 large cloves garlic, chopped
1 mildly hot, long, red chili, thinly sliced
1 lb mixed fresh Asian mushrooms,
   thickly sliced
4 oz cremini mushrooms,
   halved if large

4 tbsp Shaoxing wine or Scotch whisky
2 tbsp light soy sauce
1 tsp sugar
3 tbsp water
2 scallions, minced
large handful of cilantro leaves,
   roughly chopped

1 Put the dried mushrooms in a small bowl, pour on boiling water to cover, and let soak for 20 minutes. Drain, reserving the soaking liquid. Strain the liquid and set on one side. Cut off the black mushroom stems and halve the caps.

2 Heat a wok until hot. Add the oil, then toss in the garlic and chili and stir-fry for 30 seconds. Add all the mushrooms and stir-fry for about 3 minutes.

3 Pour in the reserved mushroom soaking liquid, wine, soy sauce, sugar, and water and cook until the liquid has reduced. Serve sprinkled with the chopped scallions and cilantro.

330 sag paneer

PREPARATION TIME: *10 minutes* **COOKING TIME:** *15 minutes*

1 tbsp peanut oil
2 tbsp soft butter
10-oz block paneer
2 onions, chopped
2 cloves garlic, chopped
1 tbsp cumin seeds

1 tsp turmeric
1 lb spinach leaves,
   tough stems removed
4 tbsp water
salt and freshly ground
   black pepper

1 Put the oil and butter in a wok and heat until the butter has melted. Add the paneer and cook until golden on one side, then turn over and cook the second side until golden. Remove from the pan and drain on paper towels. Cut into cubes and set on one side.

2 Add the onions to the wok and stir-fry for 2 minutes. Add the garlic, cumin seeds, and turmeric and cook for 1 more minute, stirring constantly.

3 Toss in the spinach and water and stir-fry for 2 minutes. Season to taste with salt and pepper, then place the cubes of paneer on top of the spinach. Cook until the paneer melts slightly, about 2 minutes, then stir it in and serve.

331 squash & spinach szechuan stir-fry

PREPARATION TIME: *15 minutes* **COOKING TIME:** *6 minutes*

1 medium-sized butternut squash, peeled,
   seeded, and cubed
1 tsp Szechuan pepper, crushed
2 tbsp light soy sauce
1 tbsp Shaoxing wine or Scotch whisky

4 tbsp water
1 tbsp sunflower oil
3 cloves garlic, chopped
5 large handfuls of spinach leaves,
   tough stems removed

1 Plunge the cubes of butternut squash into a pan of boiling water for 2 minutes, then drain, refresh under cold running water, and set on one side. Toss the Szechuan pepper into a dry wok and roast over high heat for about 1 minute, then remove from the wok and set on one side. Mix together the soy sauce, wine and water in a small bowl and set on one side.

2 Reheat the wok until hot. Add the oil, then toss in the squash and stir-fry it for 2 minutes. Add the garlic, Szechuan pepper, and spinach and stir-fry for 1 more minute.

3 Pour in the soy sauce mixture and cook until the liquid has reduced slightly, then serve.

332 spiced chickpeas & spinach

PREPARATION TIME: *10 minutes* **COOKING TIME:** *5 minutes*

2 tbsp peanut oil

2 tsp cumin seeds

2 tsp coriander seeds, crushed

1 mildly hot, long, red chili, seeded
and minced

14 oz canned chickpeas, drained
and rinsed

2 large cloves garlic, chopped

1 lb spinach leaves, tough
stems removed

juice of 1 lemon

salt and freshly ground black pepper

handful of cilantro leaves

1 Heat the oil in a wok. Add the cumin and coriander seeds and fry for a few seconds. Add the chili and chickpeas and stir-fry for 2 minutes, then add the garlic and spinach and cook for 2 minutes longer.

2 Stir in the lemon juice, season to taste with salt and pepper, and serve sprinkled with the cilantro leaves.

333 indonesian vegetable stir-fry with peanuts

PREPARATION TIME: *20 minutes* **COOKING TIME:** *6 minutes*

2 tbsp peanut oil

2 onions, chopped

2 carrots, diced

2 handfuls of fine green beans, trimmed
and halved

2½ cups shredded white cabbage

2 stalks celery, sliced

3 cloves garlic, chopped

2 tsp ground coriander

1 tsp turmeric

1 tsp ground ginger

1 tsp sambal oelek (Indonesian chili sauce)

3 tbsp kecap manis (Indonesian soy sauce)

2 tbsp rice vinegar

handful of unsalted peanuts, roasted
and crushed

handful of cilantro leaves,
roughly chopped

1 Heat a wok until hot. Add the oil, then toss in the onions and stir-fry them for 2 minutes. Add the carrots and green beans and stir-fry for 1 more minute. Add the cabbage and celery and cook for 1 minute, tossing the vegetables constantly.

2 Add the garlic, ground coriander, turmeric, and ground ginger and stir-fry for 30 seconds. Stir in the sambal oelek, kecap manis, and rice vinegar, along with a little water if the mixture appears too dry.

3 Stir well, then serve immediately, sprinkled with the peanuts and chopped cilantro.

334 steamed indonesian tofu with cilantro

PREPARATION TIME: *10 minutes, plus 30 minutes marinating time* **COOKING TIME:** *5 minutes*

4 tbsp kecap manis
(Indonesian soy sauce)

1 tbsp toasted sesame oil

13 oz firm tofu, cut into bars

2-inch piece fresh ginger,
peeled and cut into thin strips

2 scallions, shredded

2 handfuls of cilantro leaves,
roughly chopped

2 handfuls of basil leaves, torn

1 Mix together the kecap manis and sesame oil in a shallow dish. Add the tofu and spoon the marinade over the tofu until well coated. Let marinate for at least 30 minutes. Drain, reserving the marinade.

2 Place the tofu in a large bamboo steamer lined with parchment paper. Sprinkle with the ginger, cover, and steam over a wok of simmering water for 5 minutes.

3 Carefully remove the tofu and ginger from the steamer and arrange on a warm serving plate. Spoon the reserved marinade over the tofu, sprinkle with the scallions, chopped cilantro, and basil leaves, and serve.

335 japanese nori egg roll

PREPARATION TIME: *15 minutes* **COOKING TIME:** *20 minutes*

1 tbsp mirin
1 tbsp Japanese soy sauce
1 tsp brown miso paste
3 tbsp sunflower oil
8 oz broccoli raab, stems
  sliced and florets left whole
1 carrot, cut into thin sticks

1-inch piece fresh ginger, peeled
  and grated
2 large cloves garlic, crushed
6 scallions, sliced on the diagonal
2 zucchini, cut into thin sticks
6 extra large eggs, lightly beaten
salt and freshly ground black pepper
1½ tbsp nori flakes

1   Mix together the mirin, soy sauce, and miso paste in a small bowl and set on one side.
2   Heat a wok until hot. Add 2 tablespoons of the oil, then toss in the broccoli and carrot and
    stir-fry them for 2 minutes. Add the ginger, garlic, scallions, and zucchini and stir-fry until
    tender, 1–2 minutes. Stir in the mirin mixture and cook for 1 more minute. Remove from the
    wok and keep warm.
3   Season the beaten eggs to taste with salt and pepper and stir in the nori flakes. Heat a little
    of the remaining oil in the wok or a large frying pan and add one-quarter of the beaten egg
    mixture. Swirl it around so that it covers the bottom of the pan and forms a thin omelet. Cook
    until set, then turn onto a plate and keep warm. Use the remaining egg mixture to make three
    more omelets, adding more oil to the pan when necessary.
4   Spoon one-quarter of the vegetable stir-fry down the middle of each omelet, roll up loosely,
    and serve.

336 thai-style steamed vegetables
PREPARATION TIME: *15 minutes* COOKING TIME: *15 minutes*

2 tsp vegetarian fish sauce
2 tbsp light soy sauce, plus
    extra for serving
½ tsp sugar
1 stalk lemongrass, peeled and
    minced
2-inch piece fresh ginger, peeled
    and cut into thin strips
9 oz broccoli raab, stems sliced
    and florets left whole

2 handfuls of green beans, trimmed
    and halved across
2 carrots, cut into thick sticks
4 small heads bok choy, halved lengthwise
12 cremini mushrooms, halved
    or quartered if large
12 ears baby corn
2 tsp toasted sesame oil
1 mildly hot, long, red chili, seeded and
    cut into thin strips

1   Mix together the fish sauce, soy sauce, sugar, lemongrass, and ginger in a small bowl and
    set on one side.
2   Toss together the broccoli, green beans, and carrots and place in a large bamboo steamer
    lined with parchment paper. Spoon half of the fish sauce mixture over the vegetables, cover,
    and steam over a wok of simmering water until the vegetables are tender, 6–8 minutes.
    Carefully remove the vegetables from the steamer and keep warm.
3   Re-line the steamer, then place the bok choy, mushrooms, and baby corn in it and spoon the
    remaining fish sauce mixture over them. Cover and steam over a wok of simmering water until
    the vegetables are tender, 5–8 minutes.
4   Carefully remove the vegetables from the steamer and arrange with the first batch of steamed
    vegetables on a warm serving platter, pouring any juices remaining in the steamer over them,
    along with the chopped lemongrass and ginger strips. Sprinkle with the sesame oil and the
    chili strips and serve.

337 okra kadahi
PREPARATION TIME: *15 minutes* COOKING TIME: *35 minutes*

12 oz okra, stems removed
2 tbsp peanut oil
1 large onion, thinly sliced
2 hot green chilies, seeded
    and minced
8 curry leaves
1 tsp mustard seeds, slightly crushed
1 tsp cumin seeds
½ tsp fenugreek seeds, slightly crushed
3 cloves garlic, minced

2-inch piece fresh ginger,
    peeled and minced
½ tsp chili powder
1 large, green bell pepper, chopped
14 oz canned crushed tomatoes
1 cup vegetable stock
juice of 1 lemon
salt
handful of cilantro leaves,
    roughly chopped

1   Prick each okra two or three times, then toss into a pan of boiling water and cook for 8 minutes.
    Drain, refresh under cold running water, and set on one side.
2   Heat a wok until hot. Add the oil, then toss in the onion and stir-fry it for 4 minutes. Add the
    chilies, curry leaves, and mustard, cumin, and fenugreek seeds and cook for 1 more minute. Add
    the garlic, ginger, chili powder, green pepper, and okra and stir-fry for 1 minute longer.
3   Stir in the crushed tomatoes and stock, cover, and cook over medium heat for 15–20 minutes,
    stirring occasionally. Add more water if the curry becomes very dry. Stir in the lemon juice,
    season to taste with salt, and serve, sprinkled with the chopped cilantro.

338 vegetable tempura with dip

PREPARATION TIME: *20 minutes* **COOKING TIME:** *20 minutes*

1½ lb mixed vegetables, such as bell
    peppers, peeled cooked potatoes,
    onions, broccoli and cauliflower
    florets, ears baby corn,
    and mushrooms
scant 1 cup all-purpose flour
½ tsp paprika
⅛ tsp salt
1 tbsp sunflower oil,
    plus extra for deep-frying
⅔ cup water
2 egg whites

DIP:
6 tbsp rice vinegar
3 tbsp sugar
1 tbsp dark soy sauce
1 hot, red Thai chili, seeded
    and minced
juice of 1 lime
handful of cilantro leaves,
    minced

1 Make the dipping sauce by simmering the rice vinegar, sugar, and soy sauce in a small saucepan until becoming syrupy. Remove from the heat, pour into a bowl, and let cool. When cool, stir in the chili, lime juice, and cilantro and set on one side.

2 Prepare the vegetables: Cut bell peppers, potatoes, and onions into thick slices, and broccoli and cauliflower into medium-sized florets. Leave baby corn and mushrooms whole.

3 Sift the flour, paprika, and salt into a mixing bowl. Gradually beat in the 1 tablespoon of sunflower oil and the water. Beat the egg whites until they form stiff peaks, then fold them into the batter.

4 Pour sunflower oil into a large wok until it is one-third full. Heat the oil until it will brown a cube of day-old bread in about 30 seconds. Divide the vegetables into 3 or 4 batches. Take the first batch and dip each piece of vegetable into the prepared batter, then carefully place in the oil and fry until crisp and golden, 2–3 minutes. Remove from the wok with a slotted spoon, drain on paper towels, and keep warm while frying the remaining batches of vegetables.

5 As soon as the last batch is cooked, serve the vegetable tempura with the bowl of dipping sauce.

339 tofu & vegetables in black bean sauce

PREPARATION TIME: *15 minutes, plus 1 hour marinating time* **COOKING TIME:** *25 minutes*

1 tbsp honey
2 tbsp dark soy sauce
1 clove garlic, chopped
1 tsp toasted sesame oil
6 tbsp black bean sauce
13 oz firm tofu, cut into cubes
1 tbsp sunflower oil, plus extra for
    greasing

8 large broccoli florets, cut into small
    florets and stems sliced
1 large, red bell pepper, sliced
3 small heads bok choy, sliced
4 tbsp water
salt and freshly ground black pepper
2 scallions, thinly sliced
2 tsp sesame seeds, toasted

1 Mix together the honey, soy sauce, garlic, sesame oil, and black bean sauce in a shallow dish. Add the tofu and turn to coat with the marinade, then let marinate for at least 1 hour. Drain, reserving the marinade.

2 Preheat the oven to 350°F. Arrange the tofu on a lightly oiled baking sheet and roast in the oven, turning once, until golden and crisp, 20–25 minutes.

3 Meanwhile, heat a wok until hot. Add the oil, then toss in the broccoli and stir-fry it for 1 minute. Add the bell pepper and bok choy, then pour in the reserved marinade and the water and cook until the vegetables are tender and the liquid has reduced. Season with salt and pepper.

4 Arrange the vegetables on a warm serving platter. Top with the roasted tofu, scatter the scallions and sesame seeds all over, and serve.

340 vietnamese pancakes with vegetables

PREPARATION TIME: *20 minutes, plus 30 minutes standing time* **COOKING TIME:** *25 minutes*

1 tbsp peanut oil, plus extra for
   cooking pancakes
4 oz dried rice vermicelli
4 red Asian shallots, sliced
2 carrots, cut into thin sticks
3 cloves garlic, chopped
1 large, red bell pepper, sliced
2 cups sliced shiitake mushrooms
2 tbsp light soy sauce
1 tbsp fish sauce
4 tbsp sweet chili sauce

PANCAKES:
1¼ cups all-purpose flour
1 tsp baking powder
1 tsp sugar
½ tsp turmeric
¾ cup coconut milk
1½ cups water
½ tsp salt

1   Put all the ingredients for the pancakes into a blender or food processor and process to make a smooth batter. Set aside for at least 30 minutes.

2   Heat enough oil to lightly coat the bottom of a large frying pan. Pour in enough batter to make a thin, crêpe-like pancake, swirl it around the pan, and cook for 2 minutes. Carefully turn it over and cook the other side for 2 minutes. Remove from the pan and keep warm. Use the remaining batter to make 7 more pancakes. Keep them warm while preparing the filling.

3   Cook the noodles following the package directions. Drain, refresh under cold running water, and set on one side.

4   Heat a wok until hot. Add the 1 tablespoon of oil, then toss in the shallots and stir-fry them for 1 minute. Add the carrots and cook for 1 more minute, then add the garlic, red pepper, and mushrooms and stir-fry for 1 minute longer.

5   Stir in the soy sauce and fish sauce, then toss in the noodles and heat through. Divide the vegetables and noodles among the pancakes and fold each one over to enclose the filling. Drizzle some sweet chili sauce over the pancakes and serve.

341 asian vegetable-stuffed omelet

PREPARATION TIME: *15 minutes, plus 10 minutes soaking time* **COOKING TIME:** *20 minutes*

3 tbsp black beans
4 tbsp sunflower oil
8 oz gai lan (Chinese kale), stems sliced
1-inch piece fresh ginger, peeled
   and grated
2 large cloves garlic, crushed
2 hot red chilies, seeded and
   thinly sliced

6 scallions, sliced on the diagonal
4 cups shredded napa cabbage
3 large handfuls of beansprouts
2 large handfuls of cilantro leaves,
   roughly chopped
6 extra large eggs, lightly beaten
salt and freshly ground black pepper

1   Put the black beans in a bowl, pour in enough boiling water to cover, and let soak for 10 minutes. Drain and set on one side.

2   Heat a wok until hot. Add 1 tablespoon of the oil, then add the gai lan and stir-fry it for 2 minutes. Toss in the ginger, garlic, half of the chilies, the scallions, napa cabbage, and black beans. Stir-fry for 1 more minute. Add the beansprouts, then stir in half the chopped cilantro. Heat through, then remove from the heat and keep warm.

3   Season the beaten eggs to taste with salt and pepper. Heat a little of the remaining oil in a large frying pan and add one-quarter of the beaten egg. Swirl the egg until it covers the bottom of the pan and forms a thin omelet. Cook until just set, then turn onto a plate and keep warm. Repeat with the remaining egg mixture to make three more omelets, adding extra oil to the pan when necessary.

4   Spoon one-quarter of the vegetable stir-fry down the middle of each omelet and roll up loosely. Cut each roll in half crosswise on the diagonal so the filling is visible. Sprinkle with the remaining chopped cilantro and chili, and serve.

342 chickpea & sweet potato curry

PREPARATION TIME: *20 minutes*   **COOKING TIME:** *30 minutes*

2 onions, quartered

5 cloves garlic

2-inch piece fresh ginger, peeled
 and sliced

2 tbsp peanut oil

2 mildly hot, long, red chilies, seeded
 and minced

2 tsp ground cumin

2 tsp ground coriander

1 tsp turmeric

4 cardamom pods, split

1 large sweet potato, peeled and cut into
 bite-sized pieces

2 cups sliced cremini mushrooms

1¼ cups vegetable stock

1⅓ cups canned crushed tomatoes

14 oz canned chickpeas,
 drained and rinsed

salt

1 Put the onions, garlic, and ginger in a food processor or blender and process to form a coarse paste. Heat the oil in a wok. Add the paste and fry for 2 minutes, stirring constantly. Add the chilies, ground cumin, ground coriander, turmeric, and cardamom pods and cook for 1 more minute.

2 Add the sweet potato and mushrooms and stir-fry for 1 minute. Pour in the stock and tomatoes. Bring the mixture to a boil, then reduce the heat and simmer, covered, for 15 minutes.

3 Stir in the chickpeas and cook for 10 minutes longer, covering the wok if the curry becomes too dry. Season with salt and serve.

343 tamarind tofu with bok choy

PREPARATION TIME: *15 minutes*   **COOKING TIME:** *30 minutes*

½ cup vegetable stock

1 tsp tamarind paste

1–2 tsp sugar

2 tbsp light soy sauce

3 tbsp sunflower oil

12 oz firm tofu, sliced into bars

1 large onion, sliced

3 small heads bok choy, sliced

1 large, red bell pepper, sliced

2-inch piece fresh ginger,
 peeled and minced

2 cloves garlic, chopped

salt and freshly ground black pepper

handful of cilantro leaves,
 roughly chopped

1 Mix together the stock, tarmarind paste, sugar, and soy sauce in a small bowl and set on one side.

2 Heat the oil in a wok. Add half the tofu and fry, turning occasionally, until golden, 4–5 minutes. Drain on paper towels and set on one side. Repeat with the remaining tofu.

3 Pour off all but 1 tablespoon of the oil from the wok, add the onion, and stir-fry for 2 minutes. Add the bok choy, red pepper, ginger, and garlic and stir-fry for 1 more minute.

4 Pour the tamarind mixture into the wok and cook until reduced and thickened, about 2 minutes. Season to taste with salt and pepper and add more sugar, if necessary. Carefully stir in the tofu, heat through, and serve, sprinkled with the chopped cilantro.

344 thai asparagus rolls

PREPARATION TIME: *15 minutes* **COOKING TIME:** *20 minutes*

12 asparagus spears, trimmed
1 tbsp toasted sesame oil
2 tbsp peanut oil
2 Asian red shallots, finely chopped
3 scallions, minced
1 mildly hot, long, red chili, seeded and minced
6 extra large eggs, lightly beaten

salt and freshly ground black pepper
large handful of cilantro leaves, minced

FOR GARNISH:
2 scallions, shredded
1 hot red chili, seeded and cut into fine strips
handful of cilantro leaves

1. Mix the asparagus spears with the sesame oil in a bowl until well coated all over. Heat a wok until hot. Toss in the asparagus and stir-fry until tender, 2–3 minutes. Remove from the wok and keep warm.
2. Add half of the peanut oil to the wok, then add the shallots and the minced scallions and chili and stir-fry for 1 minute. Remove from the wok and keep warm.
3. Season the beaten eggs to taste with salt and pepper, then stir in the minced cilantro. Add a little more oil to the wok or large frying pan, then pour in one-quarter of the egg mixture and swirl it around to make a large, thin omelet. Cook until set, then slide the omelet onto a plate and keep warm. Repeat with the remaining egg mixture to make three more omelets, adding more oil when necessary.
4. Spoon one-quarter of the shallot mixture down the center of each omelet, then arrange 3 asparagus spears on top. Roll up the omelets and cut each roll into ½-inch lengths.
5. Divide among four serving plates and sprinkle the shredded scallions, chili strips, and cilantro leaves over the top. Serve immediately.

345 stir-fried lemongrass tofu

PREPARATION TIME: *10 minutes, plus 2 hours marinating time* COOKING TIME: *20 minutes*

1 tbsp toasted sesame oil
3 stalks lemongrass, peeled and
  minced
2 hot green chilies, seeded and thinly
  sliced into rounds
2 large cloves garlic, thinly sliced
13 oz firm tofu, cut into cubes
2 tbsp sunflower oil

1 large, red bell pepper, diced
juice of 2 limes
8 oz spinach, tough stems removed
salt
2 scallions, thinly sliced on
  the diagonal
large handful of cilantro leaves,
  roughly chopped

1 Mix together the sesame oil, lemongrass, chilies, and garlic in a shallow dish. Add the tofu and turn to coat it with the marinade. Cover with plastic wrap and let marinate in the refrigerator for 2 hours. Drain, reserving the marinade

2 Heat the oil in a wok. Add half of the tofu and fry, turning once, until golden, about 5 minutes. Remove from the wok using a slotted spatula, drain on paper towels, and set on one side. Repeat with the remaining tofu.

3 Put the red pepper, reserved marinade, and lime juice into the wok and stir-fry for 2 minutes. Return the tofu to the wok along with the spinach and stir-fry until the spinach has wilted, 1–2 minutes. Season to taste with salt and serve hot, with the scallions and chopped cilantro sprinkled over the top.

346 indonesian stir-fry with egg

PREPARATION TIME: *15 minutes* COOKING TIME: *8 minutes*

3 tbsp peanut oil
4 Asian red shallots, sliced
2 cloves garlic, chopped
1 mildly hot, long, red chili, seeded
  and minced
2 leaves napa cabbaage, shredded
2 carrots, halved lengthwise,
  then thinly sliced
1 large, red bell pepper, thinly sliced

3 medium-sized tomatoes, peeled,
  seeded, and chopped
2 tbsp kecap manis (Indonesian soy sauce)
1 tbsp light soy sauce
4 extra large eggs
2 scallions, sliced on
  the diagonal
handful of cilantro leaves,
  roughly chopped

1 Heat a wok until hot. Add 2 tablespoons of oil, then toss in the shallots and stir-fry them for 1 minute. Add the garlic, chili, napa cabbage, carrots, and red pepper and stir-fry for 3 minutes.

2 Stir in the tomatoes, kecap manis, and light soy sauce and cook for 2 minutes. Cover, remove from the heat, and keep warm while cooking the eggs.

3 Heat the remaining oil in a large frying pan. Break the eggs into the pan and fry until the whites are set and the yolks are set or a bit runny, according to taste.

4 Divide the vegetable stir-fry among four warm serving plates and top each serving with a fried egg. Sprinkle with the scallions and chopped cilantro and serve immediately.

347 winter vegetable stir-fry with chili cashews

PREPARATION TIME: *15 minutes* **COOKING TIME:** *12 minutes*

2 tbsp sunflower oil

2 handfuls of unsalted cashew nuts

1 tsp chili bean paste

6 large cauliflower florets, cut into small florets and stems sliced

6 large broccoli florets, cut into small florets and stems sliced

2 carrots, sliced diagonally

2 turnips, peeled and thinly sliced

4 large leaves napa cabbage, shredded

2-inch piece fresh ginger, peeled and chopped

2 tbsp Shaoxing wine or Scotch whisky

2 tbsp light soy sauce

2 tbsp water

1 tsp toasted sesame oil

1   Heat 1 teaspoon of the sunflower oil in a wok, then toss in the cashew nuts and chili bean paste and stir-fry for 1 minute. Remove the cashews with a slotted spoon and set on one side

2   Wipe the wok, then pour in and heat the remaining sunflower oil. Add the cauliflower and broccoli and stir-fry for 2 minutes. Remove from the wok and set on one side. Put the carrots and turnips into the wok and stir-fry for 2 minutes.

3   Return the broccoli and cauliflower to the wok along with the napa cabbage and ginger. Stir-fry for 1 minute, then pour in the wine, soy sauce, water, and sesame oil. Cook for 1 more minute. Serve with the chili cashews sprinkled over the top.

348 thai eggplant curry

PREPARATION TIME: *15 minutes, plus 30 minutes salting time* **COOKING TIME:** *20 minutes*

1 large eggplant, sliced, then cut into bite-sized pieces

salt

3 tbsp sunflower oil

5 oz cremini mushrooms, halved or quartered if large

1 recipe quantity Thai Red Curry Paste (see page 15)

1¼ cups coconut milk

1 cup vegetable stock

2 tsp palm sugar or light brown sugar

1-inch piece galangal, peeled and minced

2 tbsp light soy sauce

8 oz spinach leaves, tough stems removed

handful of Thai basil leaves

1   Spread the eggplant on a plate and sprinkle generously with salt. Let drain for 30 minutes. Rinse well to remove the salt and bitter juices, then pat dry with paper towels.

2   Heat a wok until hot. Add the oil, then toss in the eggplant and stir-fry it until softened and lightly browned, about 6 minutes. Add the mushrooms and stir-fry for 2 minutes longer.

3   Stir in the curry paste, then add the coconut milk, stock, sugar, galangal, and soy sauce. Cover and cook over medium heat for 8 minutes.

4   Stir in the spinach and cook until the liquid has a sauce-like consistency, about 2 minutes. Season to taste with salt and serve wilth the basil sprinkled over the top.

349 mixed vegetable curry

PREPARATION TIME: *20 minutes* COOKING TIME: *30 minutes*

1 medium-sized butternut squash,
   peeled, seeded, and cut
   into bite-sized pieces
1 carrot, cut into bite-sized pieces
2 tbsp vegetable oil
2 tsp cumin seeds
4 cardamom pods, split
2 tsp mustard seeds
2 onions, minced
2 tsp ground coriander
2 tsp turmeric

2 tsp hot chili powder
2 bay leaves
3-inch piece fresh ginger, peeled
   and grated
4 garlic cloves, crushed
5 oz cremini mushrooms, halved
1⅓ cups canned crushed tomatoes
1¼ cups vegetable stock
1⅓ cups frozen peas
5 oz frozen spinach leaves
salt

1 Put the butternut squash and carrot into a bamboo steamer lined with parchment paper. Cover and steam over a large wok of simmering water until crisp-tender, 6–8 minutes. Remove the vegetables from the steamer and set on one side. Pour the water out of the wok and wipe dry.

2 Heat the oil in the wok. Add the cumin seeds, cardamom pods, and mustard seeds. When they begin to darken in color and sizzle, add the onions and fry, stirring frequently, until golden, about 4 minutes.

3 Add the ground coriander, turmeric, chili powder, bay leaves, ginger, garlic, and mushrooms and stir-fry for 2 minutes. Add the crushed tomatoes and vegetable stock and bring to a boil. Toss in the steamed squash and carrot, then reduce the heat and simmer, covered and stirring occasionally, until the vegetables are cooked, 10–15 minutes.

4 Stir in the peas and spinach and cook, uncovered, for 3 minutes longer. If the sauce looks too watery, continue simmering to reduce it. Season to taste with salt and serve.

350 vegetable korma

PREPARATION TIME: *20 minutes* COOKING TIME: *38 minutes*

4 medium-sized sweet potatoes, cubed
4 tbsp ground almonds
2 hot green chilies, seeded and chopped
2 cloves garlic, chopped
1-inch piece fresh ginger, peeled
   and chopped
2 tbsp water
4 cardamom pods, split
1 tsp coriander seeds
1 tsp cumin seeds
2 tbsp peanut oil
1 large onion, minced

3 whole cloves
1 cinnamon stick
1 tsp turmeric
2 large carrots, diced
12 cremini mushrooms, thickly sliced
1¼ cups vegetable stock
1⅓ cups frozen peas
5 oz spinach leaves, tough
   stems removed
½ cup light cream
juice of ½ lemon
handful of cilantro leaves, roughly chopped

1 Put the sweet potato into a bamboo steamer lined with parchment paper. Cover and steam over a wok of simmering water until just tender, about 5 minutes. Remove from the steamer and set on one side. Pour the water out of the wok and wipe dry.

2 Put the ground almonds, chilies, garlic, ginger, and water into a food processor or blender and process to form a coarse paste. Set on one side.

3 Heat the wok. Add the cardamom pods and the coriander and cumin seeds and toast for a few minutes, then remove from the wok and crush. Place in a small bowl and set on one side.

4 Add the oil to the wok, then toss in the onion and stir-fry for 2 minutes. Add the toasted, crushed spices, the almond paste, and the cloves, cinnamon, and turmeric. Stir-fry for 1 minute.

5 Toss in the carrots and mushrooms and stir-fry for 2 minutes longer. Add the stock and bring to a boil, then reduce the heat, cover, and simmer for 10 minutes.

6 Add the peas, spinach, and sweet potatoes and cook until they are tender, 3–4 minutes. Stir in the cream and lemon juice and heat gently. Serve sprinkled with the cilantro.

351 thai-style scrambled eggs with scallions

PREPARATION TIME: *5 minutes* **COOKING TIME:** *5 minutes*

8 extra large eggs, lightly beaten
3 tbsp peanut oil
salt and freshly ground black pepper
1 stalk lemongrass, peeled
   and minced

1-inch piece fresh ginger, peeled
   and minced
4 scallions, chopped
handful of cilantro leaves,
   roughly chopped

1   Beat the eggs with 2 tablespoons of the oil until well mixed. Season to taste with salt and pepper and set on one side.
2   Heat the remaining oil in a wok until medium-hot. Add the lemongrass, ginger, and scallions and stir-fry for 30 seconds.
3   Pour in the egg mixture and, using a wok scoop or spatula, keep turning until the eggs are softly scrambled. Serve immediately, sprinkled with the chopped cilantro.

352 masoor dahl with crisp onions

PREPARATION TIME: *10 minutes* **COOKING TIME:** *25 minutes*

1 heaped cup split red lentils, rinsed
2½ cups water
4 tbsp peanut oil
2 large onions, chopped
3 cloves garlic, minced
1-inch piece fresh ginger,
   peeled and minced

2 mildly hot, long, red chilies, seeded
   and chopped
1 tsp cumin seeds
1 tsp turmeric
3 tomatoes, peeled, seeded,
   and chopped
salt

1   Put the lentils in a saucepan, cover with the water and bring to a boil. Reduce the heat, half cover the pan, and simmer until the lentils are tender and the water has been absorbed, about 20 minutes. Beat the lentils with a wooden spoon until soft and mushy. Set on one side.
2   Heat half the oil in a wok and stir-fry half the onion until crisp and golden. Remove and set aside. Heat the rest of the oil in the wok, add the remaining onion, and stir-fry until softened. Add the garlic, ginger, chilies, cumin, and turmeric and stir-fry for 1 more minute.
3   Stir in the tomatoes and cooked lentils and heat through for a few minutes. Serve topped with the crisp-fried onion.

353 japanese vegetable packets
PREPARATION TIME: *15 minutes* COOKING TIME: *12 minutes*

4 tbsp Japanese soy sauce
2 tbsp sake
4 tbsp mirin
1 tsp sugar
1 lb asparagus, sliced diagonally
   into ½-inch pieces

4 carrots, cut into thin sticks
10 oz spinach leaves,
   tough stems removed
4 scallions, cut into strips
1 tbsp nori flakes for garnish

1 Mix together the soy sauce, sake, mirin, and sugar in a small bowl and set on one side.
2 Take two pieces of parchment paper, each large enough to wrap loosely around half the vegetables and make a packet. Divide the vegetables equally between the two pieces of paper, arranging them in the center. Spoon the soy sauce mixture over the vegetables, then carefully fold up the paper around the vegetables to make two large, loose packets, sealing well.
3 Place the packets in a large bamboo steamer. Cover and steam over a wok of simmering water until the vegetables are tender, 10–12 minutes. Remove the packets from the steamer and arrange the vegetables and any juices on a large, warm serving plate. Sprinkle with the nori flakes and serve.

354 chili-spiked tofu
PREPARATION TIME: *10 minutes* COOKING TIME: *17 minutes*

13 oz firm tofu
2-inch piece fresh ginger, peeled and
   sliced into thin strips
1 tsp sunflower oil
1 tsp chili bean sauce

3 tbsp kecap manis (Indonesian soy sauce)
2 tsp hoisin sauce
3 scallions, shredded
handful of cilantro leaves

1 Place the tofu and ginger in a bamboo steamer lined with parchment paper. Cover and steam over a wok of simmering water for 15 minutes. Remove the steamer from the wok, take out the tofu, and keep warm. Drain and dry the wok, discarding the ginger strips.
2 Put the oil, chili bean sauce, kecap manis, and hoisin sauce in the wok and heat gently.
3 Put the tofu on a warm serving plate, slice, and pour the warm sauce over it. Sprinkle with the scallions and cilantro leaves and serve.

355 sesame-fried stuffed tofu
PREPARATION TIME: *10 minutes, plus 1 hour marinating time* COOKING TIME: *8–16 minutes*

4 tbsp yellow bean sauce
1 tsp chili bean sauce
2 cloves garlic, grated
1-inch piece fresh ginger, peeled
   and grated
2 blocks firm tofu, 9 oz each, sliced
   in half horizontally

2 tbsp sunflower oil
1 tsp toasted sesame oil
1–2 tbsp soy sauce
1 hot green chili, seeded and sliced
   into thin rounds
2 tsp sesame seeds, toasted
handful of cilantro leaves

1 Mix together the yellow bean sauce, chili bean sauce, garlic, and ginger in a small bowl. Spread the mixture thickly over the top of two of the halves of tofu, then place the remaining tofu halves on top to make two tofu "sandwiches." Let marinate for 1 hour.
2 Heat the oils in a wok. Add one of the tofu "sandwiches" and fry until golden, about 4 minutes on each side. Carefully remove from the wok with a slotted spatula, drain on paper towels, and keep warm. Repeat with the remaining tofu "sandwich."
3 Place the tofu "sandwiches" on warm serving plates, sprinkle the soy sauce, chili, sesame seeds, and cilantro leaves over the top, and serve.

356 potato & vegetable massaman

PREPARATION TIME: *15 minutes* **COOKING TIME:** *15 minutes*

1 tbsp peanut oil
1 large onion, chopped
2 carrots, cut into bite-sized pieces
5 oz cremini mushrooms, halved
2 stalks lemongrass, crushed with the
   back of a knife
½ small head Savoy cabbage, shredded
5 oz sugarsnap peas

1 recipe quantity Massaman Curry Paste
   (see page 15)
1¾ cups coconut milk
1 cup vegetable stock
1 tsp tamarind paste
1 tsp palm sugar or light brown sugar
14 oz cooked new potatoes, halved or
   quartered if large
juice of 1 lime

1 Heat a wok until hot. Add the oil, then toss in the onion and stir-fry it for 2 minutes. Add the carrots and stir-fry for 2 more minutes. Toss in the mushrooms, lemongrass, cabbage, and sugarsnaps and stir-fry for 30 seconds longer.

2 Stir in the curry paste, then pour in the coconut milk, stock, tamarind paste, and sugar. Bring to a boil. Reduce the heat and simmer, covered, for 5 minutes

3 Stir in the potatoes and lime juice and simmer for 5 minutes longer, then serve.

357 chinese scrambled egg with red pepper

PREPARATION TIME: *5 minutes* **COOKING TIME:** *5 minutes*

8 extra large eggs, lightly beaten
2½ tbsp sunflower oil
salt and freshly ground black pepper

2 tsp toasted sesame oil
1 large red bell pepper, diced
4 scallions, finely sliced

1 Beat the eggs with 2 tablespoons of the sunflower oil until well mixed. Season to taste with salt and pepper and set on one side.

2 Heat a wok until medium-hot. Add the remaining sunflower oil and the sesame oil, then toss in the red pepper and scallions and stir fry them for 1 minute.

3 Pour in the egg mixture and, using a wok scoop or spatula, keep turning until the eggs are softly scrambled. Serve immediately.

358 eggplant & chickpea curry

PREPARATION TIME: *10 minutes, plus 30 minutes salting time* **COOKING TIME:** *20 minutes*

1 eggplant, sliced and
   cut into chunks
salt
3 tbsp peanut oil
1 large onion, chopped
5 oz cremini mushrooms,
   halved
2 stalks lemongrass, crushed
   with the back of a knife

1 recipe quantity Massaman Curry Paste
   (see page 15)
14 oz canned chickpeas,
   drained and rinsed
1¾ cups coconut milk
1 cup vegetable stock
1 tsp tamarind paste
1 tsp palm sugar or light brown sugar
juice of 1 lime

1 Spread the eggplant on a plate, sprinkle generously with salt, and let drain for 30 minutes. Rinse well to remove any salt and bitter juices and pat dry with paper towels.

2 Heat a wok until hot. Add the oil, then toss in the eggplant and stir-fry it until lightly browned and tender, about 6 minutes. Add the onion and stir-fry for 2 more minutes. Toss in the mushrooms and lemongrass and stir-fry for 30 seconds longer.

3 Stir in the curry paste and chickpeas, then pour in the coconut milk, stock, tamarind, and palm sugar. Bring to a boil. Reduce the heat, cover, and simmer for 10 minutes. Stir in the lime juice and serve.

359 teriyaki tofu & water spinach

PREPARATION TIME: *15 minutes, plus 1 hour marinating time* **COOKING TIME:** *15 minutes*

12 oz firm tofu, cut into cubes
2 tbsp sunflower oil
2-inch piece fresh ginger, peeled and
   cut into thin strips
5 leaves napa cabbage, thinly sliced
6 large handfuls of Chinese water
   spinach leaves, sliced
1 large, yellow bell pepper, sliced
1 mildly hot, long, red chili, seeded
   and sliced into rounds

MARINADE:
6 tbsp teriyaki sauce
1 tbsp toasted sesame oil
1 tbsp Japanese soy sauce
1 tbsp sugar

1   Mix together the ingredients for the marinade in a shallow dish. Add the tofu and turn to coat it with the marinade. Let marinate for at least 1 hour. Drain, reserving the marinade.

2   Heat half of the oil in a wok. Add half the tofu and fry, without moving, until lightly browned, 2–3 minutes, then carefully turn over and fry the other side until it is lightly browned. Remove from the wok using a slotted spatula, drain on paper towels, and keep warm. Add the remaining oil to the wok and fry the remaining tofu. Remove from the wok, drain on paper towels, and set on one side with the first batch.

3   Toss the ginger, napa cabbage, water spinach, yellow pepper, and chili into the wok and stir-fry for 2 minutes. Pour in the reserved marinade, then return the tofu to the wok. Stir-fry until the marinade has reduced slightly and thickened, then serve.

360 vegetable dahl

PREPARATION TIME: *20 minutes* **COOKING TIME:** *38 minutes*

2 tbsp peanut oil

2 onions, minced

2 carrots, diced

4 cloves garlic, chopped

1-inch piece fresh ginger,
   peeled and grated

2 tsp cumin seeds

2 tsp yellow mustard seeds

2 tsp turmeric

2 tsp chili powder

2 tsp garam masala

1 heaped cup split red lentils, rinsed

14 oz canned coconut milk

4 medium-sized tomatoes, peeled,
   seeded, and chopped

1¾ cups water

juice of 1 lime

handful of cilantro leaves,
   roughly chopped

salt and freshly ground black pepper

2 tbsp sliced almonds, toasted

1 Heat a large wok until hot. Add the oil, then toss in the onions and stir-fry them for 3 minutes. Add the carrots and stir-fry for 2 more minutes. Add the garlic, ginger, and cumin and mustard seeds and stir-fry for 1 minute longer. Stir in the turmeric, chili powder, and garam masala and stir-fry for a few seconds.

2 Add the lentils, coconut milk, tomatoes, and water. Bring to a boil, then reduce the heat and simmer, covered, for 20–25 minutes, stirring occasionally to prevent the lentils from sticking.

3 Stir in the lime juice and half the chopped cilantro. Season to taste with salt and pepper and cook for 5 minutes longer. Serve hot, sprinkled with the remaining chopped cilantro and the toasted almonds.

361 malay squash curry with crisp shallots

PREPARATION TIME: *20 minutes* **COOKING TIME:** *25 minutes*

2 tbsp peanut oil

2 onions, minced

1 medium-sized butternut squash, peeled,
   seeded, and cut into bite-sized pieces

2-inch piece fresh ginger, peeled
   and grated

4 large cloves garlic, crushed

2 stalks lemongrass, peeled and crushed

2 tsp ground cumin

2 tsp ground coriander

2 tsp turmeric

2 cinnamon sticks

4 whole cloves

6 cardamom pods, split

1 tsp hot chili powder

1 hot Thai chili, chopped

1¼ cups coconut milk

1 cup vegetable stock

juice of 1 lime

salt

2 large handfuls of cilantro leaves,
   roughly chopped

4 shallots, chopped and fried until
   crisp and golden

1 Heat a wok until hot. Add the oil, then toss in the onions and stir-fry them for 1 minute. Add the squash and stir-fry for 2 more minutes. Add the ginger, garlic, lemongrass, ground cumin and coriander, turmeric, cinnamon, cloves, cardamom pods, chili powder, and fresh chili and stir-fry for 2 minutes longer.

2 Stir in the coconut milk and stock. Bring to a boil, then reduce the heat and simmer, covered, for 15 minutes, stirring occasionally. Remove the lid and simmer until the squash is cooked through and the curry has reduced and thickened, about 5 minutes.

3 Stir in the lime juice and season to taste with salt. Serve sprinkled with the chopped cilantro and crisp-fried shallots.

362 thai green vegetable curry
PREPARATION TIME: *10 minutes* **COOKING TIME:** *18 minutes*

2 tbsp sunflower oil
1 recipe quantity Thai Green Curry Paste
   (see page 15)
1¾ cups coconut milk
1¼ cups vegetable stock
10 broccoli florets, cut into small florets
   and stems sliced

12 ears baby corn
2 red bell peppers, sliced
2 heaped cups shredded spinach
salt and freshly ground black pepper
handful of cilantro leaves,
   roughly chopped

1   Heat the oil in a large wok. Add the curry paste and stir-fry for 1 minute. Stir in the coconut milk and stock and bring to a boil. Reduce the heat and simmer until reduced, about 10 minutes.

2   Add the broccoli, corn, and red peppers and cook for 4 minutes, then add the spinach and cook until all the vegetables are just tender, about 2 more minutes.

3   Season to taste with salt and pepper and serve, sprinkled with the chopped cilantro.

363 japanese-style sesame vegetables
PREPARATION TIME: *10 minutes* **COOKING TIME:** *4 minutes*

3 tbsp mirin
1 tsp wasabi paste
3 tbsp Japanese soy sauce
2 tbsp sunflower oil
1 large, red bell pepper, sliced
2 zucchini, cut into batons
4 scallions, shredded

1-inch piece fresh ginger, peeled
   and minced
1 lb baby spinach leaves
salt
2 large handfuls of beansprouts
1 tsp toasted sesame oil
1 tbsp sesame seeds, toasted

1   Mix together the mirin, wasabi, and soy sauce in a small bowl and set on one side.

2   Heat a wok until hot. Add the oil, then toss in the red pepper and zucchini and stir-fry them for 1 minute. Add the scallions and ginger and stir-fry for 30 seconds longer.

3   Add the spinach and stir-fry until wilted. Season to taste with salt, then stir in the mirin mixture and cook until the liquid has reduced slightly, about 1 minute.

4   Stir in the beansprouts and sesame oil, adding a little water if the mixture is too dry. Serve sprinkled with the sesame seeds.

364 tofu jungle curry
PREPARATION TIME: *15 minutes* **COOKING TIME:** *20 minutes*

3 tbsp sunflower oil
12 oz tofu, cut into bars
5 oz snake beans or green beans, trimmed
   and sliced
5 oz cremini mushrooms, halved
1 clove garlic, chopped
1 recipe quantity Jungle Curry Paste
   (see page 14)

4 tbsp ground candlenuts or almonds
1 cup canned bamboo shoots,
   drained and rinsed
1½ cups vegetable stock
2 tsp vegetarian fish sauce
juice of 1 lime

1   Heat the oil in a wok. Add half the tofu and fry until lightly browned, 3–4 minutes on each side. Remove from the wok with a slotted spatula, drain on paper towels, and set on one side. Repeat with the remaining tofu.

2   Pour all but 1 tablespoon of the oil out of the wok. Add the beans and mushrooms and stir-fry for 2 minutes, then stir in the garlic and the curry paste.

3   Add the nuts, bamboo shoots, stock, fish sauce, and lime juice, stir, and bring to a boil. Reduce the heat and simmer for 5 minutes. Stir in the tofu, heat through, and serve.

365 mixed mushroom green curry

PREPARATION TIME: *15 minutes*   **COOKING TIME:** *20 minutes*

2 tbsp sunflower oil

1 recipe quantity Thai Green Curry Paste
  (see page 15)

1¼ cups coconut milk

1¼ cups vegetable stock

2 tsp vegetarian fish sauce

1 tsp palm sugar or light brown sugar

4 oz shiitake mushrooms, halved

4 oz cremini mushrooms, halved

1 large, red bell pepper, sliced

14 oz canned straw mushrooms, drained
  and rinsed

salt and freshly ground black pepper

handful of basil leaves, torn

1   Heat the oil in a large wok. Add the curry paste and stir-fry for 1 minute. Stir in the coconut milk
    and stock and bring to a boil. Stir in the fish sauce and sugar, then lower the heat and simmer
    until reduced, about 10 minutes.

2   Add the shiitake and cremini mushrooms and red pepper and cook for 5 minutes, then add the
    straw mushrooms and cook until all the vegetables are tender, about 2 minutes longer. Season
    to taste with salt and pepper and serve with the basil leaves sprinkled over the top.

Index

Author's acknowledgments

Many thanks to everyone at Duncan Baird who helped create this book, especially to Grace Cheetham for commissioning me and for her continued support and enthusiasm. Thanks, too, to Cecile Landau for her editing skills, as well as William Lingwood for the excellent photography and home economist, Marie-Ange LaPierre.